Wanted:
World Financial Stability

Edited by
Eduardo Fernández-Arias
and Ricardo Hausmann

Published by the Inter-American Development Bank
Distributed by The Johns Hopkins University Press

Washington, D.C.
2000

Acknowledgements

This book would not have been possible without the editing and coordination of Rita Funaro. Thanks also to Ronald Weber for his editorial support.

Cataloging-in-Publication data provided by the
Inter-American Development Bank
Felipe Herrera Library

Wanted: world financial stability / edited by Eduardo Fernández-Arias and Ricardo Hausmann.

p. cm.
"This volume examines ... issues ... discussed at two Inter-American Development Bank conferences: "Crisis and Contagion in Emerging Financial Markets: The New Policy Agenda" [and] "New Initiatives to Tackle International Financial Turmoil"—Preface.
Includes bibliographical references.
ISBN 1886938636

1. Economic stabilization–Congresses. 2. Financial crises–Congresses. 3. Financial institutions, International–Congresses. 4. Fiscal policy–Congresses. 5. Capital market–Congresses. 6. International economic integration–Congresses. 7. Foreign exchange rates–Congresses. I. Fernández-Arias, Eduardo. II. Hausmann, Ricardo. III. Inter-American Development Bank. IV. "Crisis and Contagion in Emerging Financial Markets: The New Policy Agenda" (1998 : Washington, DC). V. "New Initiatives to Tackle International Financial Turmoil" (1999 : Paris, France). 339.5 W37—dc21

Cover: Images © 1997 PhotoDisc, Inc.

Design/layout by CGM Communications
Distributed by The Johns Hopkins University Press
2715 North Charles Street
Baltimore, Maryland 21218-4319

Preface

Financial stability is hard to achieve, particularly in a world of open capital markets. Creating and maintaining an environment propitious to both growth and stability would be an enormous challenge in the best of times, but today's climate is most unsettling. The international community in general and Latin America in particular are struggling to repair, contain, and prevent damage from international financial turmoil.

The dimensions of this financial crisis have become truly global, affecting nearly every emerging market through contagion. Latin America was first engulfed in turmoil in 1994–1995 as the Tequila crisis developed in Mexico and later spilled over to Argentina. We learned a great deal at that time, and more has been learned in the aftermath of the Asian and Russian crises that have followed. Gradually, Latin America is learning to defend itself and manage difficult financial circumstances.

Still, many issues are unresolved. This new-style crisis—as Michel Camdessus, Managing Director of the International Monetary Fund (IMF), has called it—is forcing us to reflect on difficult and controversial subjects. This volume examines some of these issues as they were discussed at two Inter-American Development Bank (IDB) conferences. The first conference, "Crisis and Contagion in Emerging Financial Markets: The New Policy Agenda," was held at IDB headquarters in Washington, D.C., in October 1998 and coincided with the annual meeting of the IMF and the World Bank. The second conference, "New Initiatives to Tackle International Financial Turmoil," was held in Paris in March 1999 in conjunction with the IDB's annual meeting.

In the course of these two events we asked many questions. We began by reflecting on the origins of the crisis. What are the roots of this turmoil, how does it spread, and what should be done? This last question involves two levels of action: national and international.

First, what should individual countries do to insulate themselves from contagion and increase their capacity to navigate in these turbulent waters? We have argued for years that prevention is better than cure. The region has to prepare itself to deal with shocks from international quakes by putting in place broad macroeconomic structures, good institutions, and healthy financial and banking systems. We are considerably more knowledgeable now than we were a few years ago about measures to make these crises less likely and to contain damage once it occurs.

Exchange rate policy remains an area of vigorous debate. At the conferences, we heard arguments for and against both types of systems—flexible and fixed—as well as thoughts about other creative exchange rate arrangements. With integration acquiring crucial importance in the region, the monetary issue is bound to become part of that debate.

On the international level, what can be done? If this is a global crisis, then proposals for global solutions will be called for and suitable proposals must be developed. Proposed remedies in these two seminars range from calls for greater transparency to debate about capital flows and controls. There was also extensive discussion on the redesign of the international financial architecture.

The IDB, along with the other multilateral institutions, has a responsible role to play in this search for solutions—one we do not intend to shirk. Latin America has made a major effort in the past 10 to 15 years to put its house in order, assume greater responsibility in the area of macroeconomic policy, and implement sweeping structural changes. Now, however, all of this is threatened by financial contagion that spreads despite sound fundamentals. Emerging economies should have a voice in the international debate over how to deal with this phenomenon, which seems so intrinsically unfair. The markets—rattled by contagion—are very concerned despite the fact that we have been doing what has to be done on the macroeconomic front. This volume and the events it covers are intended to contribute to that search by airing the issues fully and involving emerging-economy policymakers in the design of answers. We are working closely with the IMF, the World Bank, and the private sector as an active partner in finding solutions because Latin America's future is tied to world financial stability.

Enrique V. Iglesias
President, Inter-American Development Bank

Contents

Introduction

Ricardo Hausmann

The old paradigm is dead. We once thought the market was a machine that measured a country's virtue. If a country behaved responsibly, the market rewarded it; if a country behaved irresponsibly, the market punished it. Markets were seen as the arm of God that maintained virtue in the world.

We have learned the painful lesson during the past decade that capital flows are very volatile. The question that bedevils us is, What is behind the financial turmoil that has wracked the world in recent years? What is this contagion that has infected almost every emerging market—virtuous or not—and brought the old paradigm to its knees? These were the types of questions that inspired the seminars upon which this book is based.

Part of the answer is found in the valuation of country risk. Spreads of the emerging market bond index show that the valuation of country risk over time is not only extremely unstable but is closely correlated in countries that have little or nothing to do with each other. For example there are very high correlations between Bulgaria and Brazil and between Mexico and Morocco. Russia is just the most conspicuous example of a distant, unrelated country impacting Latin America. Although there is a very close correlation between all countries, and the absolute valuations made by the market are extremely unstable, the relative valuations are very stable. This suggests that the problem is not one of policy changes in individual countries but of changes in market conditions. Hence, a new paradigm is born. Countries must not only be virtuous; they must be resilient to the vagaries of international capital markets.

This recognition of a market rather than a country-specific problem helps explain the global nature of this affliction. It also provides a strong justification for concern in developed and developing countries alike. And it acts as a magnet, continuously drawing our attention away from national responses and toward international efforts and innovations. After all, if this turmoil is so quick to permeate national borders, should we not be looking beyond these boundaries for solutions? In fact, is it even reasonable to expect a strictly national vision to be sufficient to steer countries safely through this treacherous financial fog? If what we want is world financial stability, should we not think in global rather than national terms?

In essence, this is the thread that binds together the papers, presentations, and comments of the distinguished roster of financial experts compiled in this book. When we looked for the roots of the crisis, our eyes continuously turned to the international arena. In the search for solutions, again the emphasis was directed at the international level. Even in the discussion of domestic policy agendas, there was a distinctly transnational flavor. The vigorous debate over exchange rate policy epitomizes this tendency. The issue is not limited to a choice between flexible and fixed exchange rate systems but between national and supranational currencies. In fact, perhaps the biggest question posed in this book is whether the failure of exchange rates to go global in an otherwise globalized world may not be contributing to international financial turmoil in the first place.

We have come a long way in the course of this book. At the first conference in October 1998, we tried to decipher the nature of the beast. We called it contagion, stared into its fierce eyes, and saw mostly ourselves—individual countries, trying to implement rational policies and to protect ourselves from the financial storm raging around us. We emerged from that encounter with a near consensus on the global nature of the crisis—its origins and its ramifications—but little in the way of responses, other than a stock of prudent domestic policies to help insulate individual economies and a vague call for reform in international financial institutions. In the months that followed and at the subsequent conference held in Paris in conjunction with the IDB annual meeting, a constructive discussion of creative alternatives got under way, particularly for redesigning the international financial architecture and rethinking the role of exchange rates in a global economy. This book chronicles the progress in our collective thought process, the points of consensus and those that remain fiercely contentious.

Assuring the House Is in Order

While achieving international financial stability may be beyond the control of individual countries, preparing for bouts of instability is very much within reach of national policymakers. The key seems to be to consistently apply three principles: solvency, liquidity, and credibility. And a country must apply these principles in three areas: fiscal, financial, and exchange rate policies. About fiscal and financial policy there is a solid consensus; in exchange rates, for very profound reasons, there is no such consensus.

In the fiscal area, the starting point of the consensus is to be solvent and virtuous. The country must have balanced budgets, and these budgets should be adapted to the economic cycle. In good years, a balanced budget is not enough: Surpluses are needed so the fiscal deficit can be allowed to deteriorate in times of crisis rather than react procyclically to fluctuations in the economic cycle.

Second, a country has to be liquid, with a relatively flat public debt profile. Borrowing requirements have to be prefinanced, especially in election years. When the markets are open, countries should borrow heavily and accumulate liquid assets because markets may not always be open. Markets tend to be especially difficult to enter at election times. It is wise, therefore, to have a contingent credit line to protect the Treasury from having to make destabilizing adjustments at difficult times.

Third is credibility, which is based on institutional status. This is particularly obvious in electoral moments because it is then that markets must trust the system, not the qualities of the outgoing minister. Markets must have confidence in an unknown future finance minister, which is why it is better to rely on sound institutions rather than exceptional individuals. In the interest of strengthening institutions, it may be necessary to change budget rules and procedures, adjust the powers of the executive in relation to parliament, and assure fiscal transparency, which can often be achieved by giving a measure of independence to the agency that prepares the budgetary estimates.

In the area of financial policy, it is also important to be solvent. The banking system has to be highly capitalized. From this point of view, the Basle requirements are too low for Latin America. Latin America needs a liquid banking system with remunerated liquidity requirements, even though OECD countries have eliminated them. The credibility of the banking system is very dependent on the credibility of the watchdog agency that tells the public that banks are in good shape. The supervisor must be credible. Credibility also depends on the internationalization of the domestic banking system. With consolidated supervision from the head office, there are many more supervisors looking at the domestic system.

The Exchange Rate Debate

On these two policy areas—fiscal and financial—there is little discussion. Where the debate heats up is on exchange rate policy. Latin America has generally abandoned fixed exchange systems. However, arguably Latin America is not very satisfied with the performance of more-flexible exchange systems. This is why the idea of supranational currencies is under discussion in so many countries at this time.

Why has Latin America been shifting from fixed to flexible exchange rate systems? What did the flexible exchange systems promise? Ostensibly they offered the possibility of a more stabilizing monetary policy. The exchange rate could be used to absorb some of the shocks the economy receives and lighten the burden on the interest rate. They also promised a more independent monetary policy. When hit by an adverse shock, floaters can let the exchange rate take the hit so that interest rates need not be jacked up and output is protected through increased competitiveness and more favorable financial conditions.

Unfortunately, this is not how it works in Latin America. When a Latin American country receives a negative shock, it tends to jack up interest rates more than fixed rate countries, while the depreciation tends to generate contractionary effects due to the presence of dollar liabilities whose value goes up with the depreciation.

This raises some interesting questions. First, why do things work differently in Latin America? And if Latin America is floating its currencies, why does it keep its exchange rates so steady?

Latin America has been buffeted by a sustained sequence of shocks: the financial crisis in Asia culminating in the attack on Hong Kong's currency in October 1997; the subsequent fall in the terms of trade; the devastation of El Niño; the Russian crisis and the hurricanes of mid-1998; and finally the Brazilian devaluation in 1999. How did central banks react to this series of shocks? Interestingly, central banks used exchange flexibility very little while they moved interest rates a great deal, even in countries with floating exchange rate systems. The idea that countries with exchange flexibility move their interest rates less than countries without flexibility is not borne out by recent history. Interest rates fluctuate more in countries with flexible rates than in those with fixed rate systems. Moreover, empirical evidence has shot down the notion that monetary policy is stabilizing in flexible regimes. It was found that monetary policy is more procyclical—that is, less stabilizing—in flexible than in fixed exchange systems, at least in Latin America.

If exchange flexibility does not provide for a more stabilizing monetary policy, does it at least allow for a more independent one? Undoubtedly countries with fixed exchange systems import international fluctuations in interest rates. However there also is significant evidence that exchange flexibility, rather than shielding the domestic economy from the effects of fluctuations in external rates, actually amplifies their impact.

There are other problems with exchange flexibility as well. One is that countries with flexible exchange systems tend to have much smaller financial systems. An econometric study, using data for the last 25 years in Latin America, compared average financial depth over GDP in countries with fixed and flexible exchange rates. The results were stark. Depth increases much more in fixed than in flexible systems. The difference is 11 points of GDP, which means there is a substantial difference in the size of the financial systems.

Why is this? In a floating economy that receives many real shocks, there is no incentive to save in national currency. The exchange rate moves with national income so that in bad times the currency is weak and the value of previously accumulated savings goes down. Savers are better off keeping their money in foreign currency. Ergo, a stunted financial system.

Not only do countries with floating currencies have smaller financial systems, they have substantially higher real interest rates as well. In the 1990s, countries with fixed exchange systems had an average real interest rate of 5 percent, while countries with flexible exchange systems had a real interest rate of 9 percent. This is a large and econometrically very significant difference.

Another finding was that countries with flexible rates tend to have more wage indexation. Union leaders who are negotiating a labor agreement denominated in a currency that is likely to fluctuate greatly will either want a shorter contract and more frequent negotiations or an indexed contract. If they signed a contract in a more stable monetary unit, their fears would be allayed. This explains why there was extremely high indexation in Argentina in the late 1980s and early 1990s, but after convertibility, wage indexation disappeared. The same pattern is noted in Brazil where there was considerable wage indexation before the Real Plan and afterwards there was none. And inflation cannot be blamed for this indexation. Low-inflation flexible rate countries like Chile and Peru also have high wage indexation. Let us look at Mexico in two periods: 1970–1975 when it had a fixed exchange rate and inflation was around 10 percent; and the recent period with flexible exchange rates, when inflation was more or less at the same level. Interestingly, under the flexible exchange system, there is considerable de facto wage indexation.

A Matter of Perspective

Given the disappointing performance of flexible exchange rate arrangements, it is interesting to consider why they are still promoted in much of Latin America, and elsewhere for that matter. Essentially the answer lies in differing views of the world and of the relationship between exchange rates and financial fragility.[1]

One popular vision, which has also shaped much of the discussion on financial architecture, stresses moral hazard and the distortions engendered by implicit guarantees. Governments that bail out domestic financial-market participants and international financial institutions that come to the rescue of countries in distress implicitly provide these guarantees, which give investors a false sense of security and an incentive to indulge in risky endeavors. In the eyes of moral hazard proponents, this excessive risk-taking fosters financial fragility.

From this perspective, the answer lies in reducing moral hazard by more closely supervising and regulating financial systems and replacing international rescues with workouts based on private-sector burden sharing. As far as exchange rates go, the moral hazard viewpoint sees fixed rates as an implicit guarantee and, thus, part of the problem. Fixed rates induce unhedged foreign borrowing and, since they are rarely fixed for long, encourage the accumulation of short-term liabilities. This kind of financial profile—unhedged, short-term, foreign-currency-denominated borrowing—casts a menacing

---

[1] See Eichengreen and Hausmann (1999) for a discussion of the relationship between exchange rates and financial fragility.

shadow over these economies. It follows that more-flexible rates would shift capital flows to the long end and boost overall stability.

The problem with the moral hazard thesis is that it fails to explain the facts. Were the financial system distorted by moral hazard, one would expect markets to be awash in capital flowing from overconfident investors operating in an artificially low-risk environment. Not only should capital flows be abundant, but if moral hazard is at play, then lending should be heaviest to borrowers likely to be bailed out. Banks, which are perceived as a threat to overall macroeconomic and financial stability, and governments, who can run to the sheltering wing of the IMF, are the most likely bailout candidates and should, therefore, lead the borrowing roster.

Actually, however, capital flows are not excessive in today's world. Mobility of capital is less than in the age of the gold standard. With all the apparent mobility of today's world—globalization, the Internet, and all the rest—there is less movement of capital today than in the 19th century. Furthermore there is very little movement of capital from the point of view of economic theory, which says that the capital/labor ratio should equalize at the world level, when in fact it does not. With capital flows at 5 percent of GDP (i.e., less than 2 percent of the capital stock of the recipient country), emerging economies will take centuries to catch up to the developed world.

Nor is the structure of capital flows what would be expected under conditions of moral hazard. Interestingly, banks borrow proportionally less in developing countries than in developed countries, and governments borrow in about the same proportions. In Latin America the composition of capital flows is particularly dumbfounding for proponents of moral hazard. Lending in the 1990s has been greatest to Latin American corporations, which are unlikely to be bailed out by anyone.

There is, however, another view that does a better job of explaining the facts. In the eyes of these theorists, financial fragility stems from an underlying incompleteness in markets that can be called "original sin." Currencies suffering from original sin cannot be used to borrow abroad or to borrow long term, even locally. Economies plagued by original sin are doomed to be financially vulnerable. Domestic investors are forced to either finance their projects in dollars, creating a currency mismatch as these projects generate local income, or take out domestic short-term loans to finance long-term endeavors, setting up a maturity mismatch.

In the eyes of believers in original sin, you are damned if you do and damned if you don't since neither fixed nor flexible exchange rates provide salvation. For a government to defend the currency in a fixed regime, it would have to sell reserves and raise interest rates, increasing the risk of default on short-term domestic debts and setting up the conditions for a banking crisis. But in flexible regimes, devaluation raises the specter of bankruptcy for holders of dollar debts who rush to cover their exposures and cause the currency to depreciate further.

Salvation, preach believers in original sin, lies in developing the ability to borrow long term in one's own currency both domestically and abroad or to give up having a currency altogether. In a practical sense, this implies dollarization or the adoption of some other supranational currency à la the Euro. This route eliminates currency mismatches as incomes and liabilities become similarly denominated. It also eases maturity mismatches as long-term lending becomes more available. Domestic financial markets should become stronger and less crisis-prone as both local and foreign investors feel more comfortable about bringing in their money and leaving it there. Internationally, the world would become a safer place for capital mobility if there were just a handful of currencies rather than hundreds.

The original-sin hypothesis offers another challenge to its critics; it goes farther than the current conventional wisdom in explaining the low level of international capital flows. Capital only trickles from rich to poor countries because it trades in a form that causes mismatches, which in turn discourages lending and destabilizes the financial system. Dollarization would eliminate the distortions and encourage more plentiful capital flows. Of course even the staunchest proponents of dollarization warn that it must be supported by fiscal discipline, adequate banking regulation, and supervision—in short, an overall sound policy base.

International Financial Architecture: Back to the Drawing Board?

To date, the discussion of the international financial architecture has been led by those who believe that moral hazard is the spark that ignites financial turmoil. Consequently the fire-fighting strategy has been mainly to improve financial regulation, eliminate bailouts, keep exchange rates flexible, and develop mechanisms that make it possible for countries to default. When a country cannot pay, it should default, and investors should pay the cost because that is the risk associated with lending money. If the problem cannot be tackled at the root because it takes time to improve financial regulations and because the IMF cannot be eliminated, capital should be restricted through controls and taxes. To a large extent, the goal is to limit the potential liabilities to the international community of more and ever-larger rescue packages and to force the private sector to assume more responsibility for its worldwide lending.

But it may be time to go back to the drawing board and begin designing an international financial architecture that better fits the facts. Instead of building responses around the notion that moral hazard is to blame for financial turmoil—a notion supported by little empirical evidence—perhaps today's architects should turn their sights to problems of liquidity, sovereign risk, and original sin, which may play more important roles.

From this perspective, the house that Jack built might look very different. Instead of eliminating the IMF, perhaps it should assume the functions of an international lender of last resort. In the banking system, a lender of last resort covers liquidity crises, but when the world suffers a liquidity crisis there is no place to turn. Offering contingent credit lines negotiated ex ante in the good years and financed jointly with the private sector could be a way of converting existing institutions into lenders of last resort. Or if new regional currencies are developed to overcome the problems of original sin, a local lender for each monetary area may be more appropriate.

International financial institutions (IFIs) may have a further role to play if they capitalize on their comparative advantage in sovereign risk management. Sovereign risk is another imperfection that has taken its toll on the size and stability of international markets. Sovereignty implies that one cannot be forced to pay if one does not want to pay since the sovereign does not have to abide by the orders of any court. Lending to a sovereign state means charging an interest rate that covers this risk of not wanting to pay. This higher interest rate aggravates the state's inability or unwillingness to pay, creating a distortion that makes the market smaller. Because of their long-term commitment to countries and their willingness to suspend operations in case of nonpayment, IFIs can serve as a pressure point to assure that countries pay. This can be a valuable tool to structure financial instruments for cofinancing with the private sector. The strategy is to bail in private investors for crisis prevention rather than bailing them out after a crisis hits.

Lastly, we live in a globalized world with weak national currencies. Is it not time to reform the monetary structure that supports the international financial architecture? Aren't advocates of floating exchange rates asking countries to swim against the global current? Should the debate not be in offering countries attractive supranational alternatives to the dismal national options?

The financial turmoil of recent years is a new phenomenon for the world that demands fresh ideas and answers. Even when it has not provoked an all-out crisis or collapse, it has robbed countries of hard-fought gains and set back their development plans. From Mexico to Chile, Latin America has felt the economic quakes and suffered the social and political aftershocks. This volume gathers together the contributions of experts from throughout the region as they try to shore up their national defenses while helping to build an international structure able to withstand shaky capital markets. Sharing their thoughts and building on this collaborative foundation can help assure that the international financial architecture is not a house of cards.

Ricardo Hausmann is the Chief Economist of the Inter-American Development Bank.

References

Eichengreen, B., and R. Hausmann. 1999. "Exchange Rates and Financial Fragility." Paper prepared for the Federal Reserve Bank of Kansas City's Conference on Issues in Monetary Policy. Jackson Hole, Wyoming.

PART ONE

Diagnosing a New Syndrome: Global Financial Crisis and Contagion

Washington, D.C., October 1998

The New Features of Financial Crises in Emerging Markets

Guillermo Calvo and Eduardo Fernández-Arias

Perspective is required to understand our present dilemma, to diagnose its causes so that effective remedies can be developed. Clearly these are the biggest crises since 1982, with the potential for surpassing that historic benchmark in severity and scope. Unlike the debt crisis of the 1980s, official financial assistance has been available during the 1990s in ample amounts, to the tune of nearly $200 billion. Yet such rescue efforts have not spared affected countries from deep current account adjustments, gigantic output losses, and dramatic real depreciations; and they have failed to contain financial contagion from spreading to other emerging markets.

The latest upheavals took most people by surprise. In fact, risk spreads continuously declined after the Tequila crisis of 1994, with few if any signs of impending trouble. Credit ratings for the Asian countries near the eye of the approaching storm were among the best in emerging markets. The conventional wisdom was once more shaken to its roots by the new realities, and shifting views of what causes crises continued to evolve as events overtook previous explanations.

During the past two decades, crisis conceptualization can be divided into three stages:

• Before 1994, many analysts narrowly focused on small fiscal deficits as the way to avoid new financial crises. Mexico, however, did not have a fiscal deficit problem, and its crisis did not repeat the pattern of the 1980s debt crisis.

• After the Tequila crisis, many analysts thought high current account deficits and low savings were the triggers. However, the Asian countries that formed the first wave of the present crises did not have these problems, certainly not lack of savings or growth.

• After the Asian crises of 1997, some analysts divided the blame between moral hazard induced by implicit public guarantees of several types, and the presence of fixed or quasi-fixed exchange rates. A second current of opinion assigns responsibility to vulnerabilities in the financial sector, sometimes coupled with weak institutions such as over-accommodating central banks.

The debate unleashed by the recent turmoil extends beyond cause to remedy. Even after the cards are face up for all parties to see, there is disagreement about how to deal with crises once they occur. The debate has two aspects:

• Some analysts emphasize that International Monetary Fund (IMF) rescue packages, even when they work locally, induce more crises elsewhere due to moral hazard. According to this argument, the Asian crises were more likely to occur because investors felt protected from risky speculative ventures after the Mexican bailout. It can also be argued that the extremely adverse financial contagion across emerging markets that followed the failure to provide an effective rescue package to Russia reflects the withdrawal of this implicit guarantee for emerging market obligations, and provides a measurement of its significant value. Alternative proposals calling for preventive programs and precautionary lines of credit are now being made to fill the gap.

• Second, the wisdom of IMF recommendations for restrictive monetary and fiscal policies as well as tough bank recapitalization policy in the midst of crises continues to be heatedly debated not only in academic circles but also inside the Washington beltway. Do these policies resolve crises or aggravate them?

So a puzzling question remains. How could such enormous crises take nearly everyone by surprise? Belief that they resulted from weak fundamentals that turned borrowers uncreditworthy has the advantage of simplicity, but it is hard to reconcile with the market's inability to anticipate the downturns. Why didn't market agents perceive in advance the risk factors that we now identify in hindsight as glaring weaknesses, especially since the lessons from the Mexican experience—forced devaluation of a fixed exchange rate, a weak banking system, and bulging short-term debt—were widely known? Implicit government guarantees eliminating private risk, a point emphasized by Krugman (1998), is a possible explanation of why the market did not internalize the imminent risk. However, in most cases, once a crisis erupted the public sector itself would have had to suspend payments in the absence of hastily arranged official rescue packages, which suggests that such public guarantees can not be the only responsible factor for market blindness.

The fact that the crises were unanticipated can be more easily explained by stating that they were unpredictable on the basis of economic fundamentals. In the context of a consistent model, this implies a multiplicity of equilibria: the possibility that a given set of fundamentals can be consistent with more than one outcome. Thus, essentially sound fundamentals could be so damaged by a massive withdrawal of foreign lenders, in ways discussed later in this paper, that the borrowers would be rendered insolvent, which would in turn validate the decision to withdraw. Such a liquidity crisis hinges on the coordination of expectations about the withdrawal because if such convergence of opinion does not occur, access to adequate financing remains available and the economy's potential vulnerability goes unrealized.

This would suggest that the recent crises were precipitated by sudden changes in expectations, a point emphasized by Radelet and Sachs (1998). Such an event is facilitated by large short-term obligations and a large maturity mismatch that together make the system vulnerable to a run by relatively few lenders. This line of reasoning focuses attention on measuring the degree of liquidity in the economy, as well as the strength of fundamentals, which is always an important factor in gauging the prospects for a liquidity crisis. These economic indices, however, only measure the enabling factors. The probability of crisis crucially depends on a convergence of expectations and is therefore largely unpredictable.

The distinction between fundamentals-based and expectations-based crises involves questions of *solvency* and *liquidity,* respectively. The distinction has important policy ramifications:

• A solvency crisis is the inevitable consequence of weak fundamentals. Such a crisis serves a useful purpose by correcting the misallocation of resources. Policy should facilitate this adjustment while addressing the failure that led to the weakening of fundamentals.

• A liquidity crisis results from an unnecessary panic. Such a crisis is inefficient and serves no useful purpose. Policy should try to prevent a panic from happening, and if a panic occurs, should try to buffer the shock until things get back to normal while addressing the factors that led to investor panic.

In practice the distinction is not so clear-cut, and the policy choices remain more judgmental than academic analysis suggests. First, it can be argued that the financial fragility that makes the liquidity crisis possible often is due to weakening fundamentals. That is, borrowers with declining creditworthiness are offered only short-term contracts, which plants the seed for later runs. Second, it may very well be that when fundamentals are sufficiently weak, the imminent solvency crisis is short-circuited by a liquidity crisis that, given the economic conditions, requires almost no coordination. Strictly speaking, this would be a liquidity crisis. However, if the fundamentals were unsustainable, if they would have led to a solvency crisis in the absence of adjustment, it would probably be more useful to classify it as such despite its counterfactual liquidity nature. With these caveats in mind, we now analyze the evidence.

Scanning the Evidence

In this section we briefly review available evidence about the causes of recent crises. The first question that arises is what standard to use in judging the degree to which the evidence supports various hypotheses. Establishing the presence of a factor that theory has identified as a possible cause is clearly a necessary but far from sufficient condition for judging evidence to be supportive.[1] Our approach tests the hypotheses by looking at their ability to discriminate between crisis and noncrisis countries, i.e., the evidence is supportive when the factor is not only present but more associated with crisis than tranquility.

A balanced panel was chosen, containing six crisis and six noncrisis countries, in order to weigh the discriminating power of various factors in predicting whether any given country belongs to one or the other class. The set of crisis countries includes the five Asian emerging markets that fell into crisis in 1997—Indonesia, Korea, Malaysia, Philippines, and Thailand— plus Russia, which fell into crisis in August 1998. All six experienced balance-of-payments crises characterized by extremely large devaluations and, usually, by payment moratoria or IMF emergency packages designed to stop the hemorrhaging. The noncrisis control group includes the largest Latin American economies: Argentina, Brazil, Colombia, Mexico, Peru, and Venezuela.

We first considered the market assessment of country risk before the crises, as of June 1997. The market ranking of country risk is shown in the left column of Table 1, from the riskiest, Peru (No. 1), to the safest, Korea (No. 12). Ranking was based on contemporaneous Standard & Poor's sovereign ratings, supplemented by information from Moody's ratings and secondary market spreads in the case of unrated countries.[2] As is well known by now, the market largely failed to anticipate the imminent Asian crises. In fact, none of the five in our sample were in the high-risk class. This variable only predicts the Russian crisis (see Table 2a).

Since traditional market fundamentals, such as the relative size of external indebtedness, domestic savings, and the fiscal base, are important for market spreads and ratings (Bevilaqua and Fernández-Arias, 1998), it is reasonable to expect that these indices do not correlate closely with the different experiences of our sample. Specific studies, including Radelet and Sachs (1998) and Chang and Velasco (1998), focusing on each kind of traditional economic fundamental, confirm this expectation.

We then considered financial variables that have recently been advanced as important causative agents in the post-Mexico crises. To this end we constructed two financial indexes, one of financial fragility and another of financial weakness, whose rankings are shown in Table 1. If these financial variables were important causative factors, then one would expect them to successfully identify crisis countries; in other words, the Latin American countries in our sample should fare better when measured by these dimensions. In fact, taking into account that a number of the insights underlying the identification of these variables actually resulted from analysis of the Asian crises under study, this test would be subject to sample selection bias and should be seen as a minimum standard.

---

[1] Such reasoning would be a form of *post hoc, ergo propter hoc* fallacy, as Joseph Stiglitz puts it.

[2] It is well documented that ratings are closely related to market spreads.

Table 1. Country Ex-Ante Rankings

	Market Risk	Financial Fragility (Liquidity)	Financial Weakness (Solvency)
1	PER	KOR	PHI
2	VEN	IND	COL
3	RUS	THA	THA
4	BRA	RUS	ARG
5	ARG	PHI	RUS
6	MEX	ARG	PER
7	PHI	MEX	IND
8	COL	BRA	MAL
9	IND	PER	VEN
10	THA	MAL	MEX
11	MAL	COL	BRA
12	KOR	VEN	KOR

Table 2a. Market Risk

	Crisis	No Crisis
High Risk	RUS	ARG
		BRA
		MEX
		PER
		VEN
Low Risk	IND	COL
	KOR	
	MAL	
	PHI	
	THA	

Table 2b. Financial Fragility

	Crisis	No Crisis
High Fragility	IND	ARG
	KOR	
	PHI	
	RUS	
	THA	
Low Fragility	MAL	BRA
		COL
		MEX
		PER
		VEN

The financial fragility index measures how vulnerable the financial system is to a liquidity run. It is based on three different measures of liquidity mismatch: (a) the ratio of money, measured as M2, to international reserves; (b) the share of short-term foreign bank debt in the total; and (c) the foreign-debt service burden, short-term debt plus interest debt service, as a share of international reserves.[3] Information predates the crises, and is pegged to June 1997 or, if unavailable, to end-of-year 1996. Country rankings for each measure were added to obtain the index.

This measurement of financial fragility identifies crisis countries very successfully. In fact, with the exception of Malaysia, which this index did not find highly fragile, all crises are correctly predicted (see Table 2b). The corresponding false warning among the control set is Argentina, which is identified as a marginally fragile, borderline case. A success rate of 10 out of 12 is statistically highly significant and confirms analyses that emphasize the relevance of this fragility factor in recent crises. This finding is in agreement with previous literature on the subject (see Chang and Velasco, 1998, for detailed statistical information comparing East Asian and Latin American countries).

The financial weakness index measures how vulnerable the financial system is to a solvency problem among its borrowers. The index is based on three indicators: (a) the growth rate of bank lending in excess of output growth, to see if there has been a lending boom to the private sector; (b) the share of nonperforming bank loans; and (c) real exchange rates, to see if appreciation has exposed corporate borrowers to insolvency following a correction. As before, information predates the crises, and partial rankings were added to obtain the index.

Table 2c.
Financial Weakness

	Crisis	No Crisis
High Weakness	PHI	ARG
	RUS	COL
	THA	PER
Low Weakness	IND	BRA
	KOR	MEX
	MAL	VEN

This financial weakness index does not discriminate well among countries in our sample. It picks three crises—the Philippines, Thailand, and Indonesia—but misses the others (see Table 2c). Therefore, the implicit warning to Peru, Argentina, and especially Colombia should be taken with a grain of salt. It can be argued that the statistics for nonperforming loans, collected by the Bank for International Settlements (BIS), may not reflect the true state of affairs in some of the crisis countries that were not spotlighted by the index. At the same time, the posi-

[3] The maturity of public debt was not considered due to lack of complete information.

tive correlation with financial weakness found by Corsetti, Pesenti, and Roubini (1998) depends in part on information about nonperforming loans that is arguably contaminated by the unfolding of the crisis itself.

The other two components of the index offer mixed results when factored in separately. Consistent with prior literature, ranking by appreciation of real exchange rates again fails to discriminate satisfactorily, forecasting only half the crises. However, the lending-boom component performs better, picking four of the crises (Korea, Malaysia, the Phillipines, Thailand).

In summary, financial fragility appears to be the key factor underlying most of the recent financial crises. Financial weakness, as predicted by a bank-lending boom, is also a correlative factor to be considered. On the other hand, economic fundamentals such as traditional macroeconomic balances appear not to have played an important role.

The natural interpretation of this finding is that recent crises were typically liquidity crises, which essentially coincides with the conclusion of Radelet and Sachs (1998) and of Chang and Velasco (1998). Strictly speaking, the true measure of the fragility of the financial system should combine both our fragility and weakness measures because liquidity crises are possible only in relatively weak systems and become more likely as the system weakens. Under this interpretation, financial weakness was perhaps a contributing factor facilitating the run but not sufficient by itself to cause a solvency crisis, contrary to the conclusion of Corsetti, Pesenti, and Roubini (1998), following Krugman (1998). Alternatively, an intermediate interpretation could be argued according to which financial weakness was the root problem, perhaps leading to financial fragility, and eventually would have led on its own to a crisis if it had not been short-circuited by a liquidity crisis.

Theorizing the Meltdown

As indicated previously, all recent crises have been followed by a sharp contraction in capital inflows and in the current account deficit. The central objective of this section is to explore the implications of this phenomenon irrespective of its underlying causes.

By definition, and abstracting from errors and omissions, the relation between Capital Inflows (KI), the Current Account Deficit (CAD) and reserves accumulation (ΔR) can be expressed as follows:

$$KI = CAD + (\Delta R) \tag{1}$$

Moreover, the relation between CAD, *Expenditure* or *Absorption* (A), and *Income* or Gross National Product (GNP) is:

$$CAD = Absorption \ or \ A - Income \ or \ GNP \tag{2}$$

Consequently, a sharp contraction in $K1$—keeping R constant—will result in a sharp fall in expenditure, except in the unlikely case in which there is an equally sharp "expansion" in GNP.

Let us divide the set of goods and services into tradables and nontradables or home goods, i.e., those that can and cannot be internationally traded, respectively. Therefore, given the relative price between tradables and nontradables—the real exchange rate (RER)—a fall in A will likely involve a fall in demand for both types of goods and services. Contraction in the demand for tradables need not be of major consequence because those goods can be rechanneled to international markets. However, home goods have no alternative market; so either their price must fall to enhance demand (an increase in the RER), or their output must shrink. This sets the basis for the loss of output and employment that occur after balance of payments crises in emerging markets.

Before proceeding with the analysis, it is worth recalling that,

$$GNP = Output\ of\ Tradables\ +\ Output\ of\ Nontradables\ +\ Transferences \quad (3)$$

where *Transferences* stands for net factor payments and other transferences from abroad. Consequently, since ex post,

$$Output\ of\ Nontradables\ =\ Absorption\ of\ Nontradables \quad (4)$$

then as a result of definitions (2) and (3), the following holds true:

$$CAD = Absorption\ of\ Tradables\ -\ Output\ of\ Tradables\ -\ Transferences \quad (5)$$

Therefore, given *Transferences*, a cut in the *CAD* implies an "equivalent" contraction in the excess demand for "tradable" goods and services (i.e., *Absorption of Tradables – Output of Tradables*). What happens to nontradables is irrelevant from this accounting perspective.

We will now examine the impact of four changes in variables as they ripple through these relationships:

• *Sudden increase in RER*: We will first consider the impact of a relative price change following a cut in the *CAD*, abstracting from demand-determined, or Keynesian, output contraction. This case corresponds to a situation in which all prices (and wages) are perfectly flexible. Abstracting from financial considerations, relative prices will change until market equilibrium is restored. In particular, the demand for home goods will recover until the sector reaches full employment. Simultaneously, the higher relative price of tradables will shift away "domestic" excess demand for tradables until the *CAD* falls to its new lower level, as the earlier discussion of accounting definition (5) outlined.

To assess the impact of a cut in the *CAD* on nontradables, consider the following example. Assume the share of tradables and nontradables in *Expenditure* or *Absorption* (*A*) is 50 percent unless there is a change in RER (in other words, the underlying utility function is assumed to be locally homothetic). Let the initial *CAD* equal 4 percent of *GNP*. Suppose that the country is forced to close the external gap (i.e., reduce *CAD* to 0). Therefore, assuming that the sum of *Output of Tradables* and *Transferences* is constant, it follows from accounting definition (5) that *Absorption of Tradables* has to fall by the equivalent of 4 percent of *GNP*. By assumption, initially

Absorption of Tradables = 0.5 x 1.04 x *GNP*,

and to close the current account deficit, it must fall by 0.04 x *GNP*.

Dividing the latter result by the former result and multiplying by 100 to obtain the outcome in percentage terms, *Absorption of Tradables* must fall by 7.7 percent to reduce *CAD* to 0. Therefore, under the present assumptions, given the real exchange rate, the demand for nontradables would have to fall by slightly less than 8 percent. This illustrates how a relatively modest *CAD* can result in a proportionately much higher decline in the demand for nontradables if the country is forced to close its external imbalance. As the reader can verify, *this magnification effect will be higher as the share of nontradables in total expenditure gets larger.*

The impact of the fall in the demand for nontradables on RER depends on demand elasticities. Short-run demand elasticities tend to be relatively small, and thus an 8 percent decline in the demand for nontradables may result in a major decline in their relative price (i.e., a major increase in the real exchange rate). How this will be reflected in output and employment depends on initial financial conditions and, in particular, on firms' leverage (i.e., the debt-to-equity ratio). Clearly, the larger the leverage and the share of debt indexed to tradables (or foreign exchange) are, the more likely it is that firms in the nontradables sector will run into financial difficulties. Furthermore, these difficulties are likely to be more far-reaching to the degree that the cuts in foreign financing were unexpected. Finally, as will be discussed more fully in the section titled "Financial Turmoil," financial difficulties can have serious effects on efficiency, output, and employment—especially if they affect firms' credit network.

• *Price stickiness*: Alternatively, the fall in the demand for nontradables can be accommodated by a fall in output. Financial complications can arise in this case, too, but if price elasticities are small, price stickiness may result in less financial turmoil. This can be illustrated by using the terms of the example in the previous subsection on a sudden increase in RER. If the real exchange rate is sticky, output of home goods will have to fall by about 8 percent to reduce *CAD* to zero. However, to the extent that price elasticity is less than unity (which appears to be likely in the short run), the revenue loss will be less than under perfect price flexibility. *GNP* would fall by about 4 percent; but if original profits exceeded short-run financial obligations, financial collapse could more likely be circumvented. Over the medium term, prices will fall, but firms will have more time to line up potential buyers and thereby lower the private and social costs of default.[4]

• *Exchange rate flexibility*: RER stickiness is more likely to be exhibited under fixed exchange rates because, as a general rule, nominal prices and wages are not perfectly flexible. In contrast a large devaluation—which has accompanied recent crisis episodes, with the exception of Argentina after the Tequila crisis—would result in a large increase in the RER, opening the door for the financial difficulties in the nontradables sector discussed above, in the first scenario. This would be aggravated if firms' debt obligations were denominated in foreign exchange.

Large and unexpected appreciations are also damaging, affecting primarily the tradables sector. The effect is symmetric to that of a currency devaluation. However, a key difference from a policy perspective is that the government can fight a currency appreciation by buying foreign exchange (i.e., accumulating international reserves), while a depreciation may require international cooperation once the government runs down its reserves to a minimum tolerable level. This policy asymmetry helps to explain why the nominal exchange rate shows more continuity going down than going up (i.e., appreciations are less pronounced than devaluations). As a result, exchange rate regimes in emerging markets exhibit a bias toward "nominal exchange rate stickiness," occasionally ending in large devaluations that, as a general rule, are contractionary (see Krugman and Taylor, 1978; Cooper, 1971; Edwards, 1986).

• *International reserves: an effective cushion?* Accounting definition (1) suggests that a cut in capital inflows can be partially offset by drainage of international reserves. Loss of reserves is certainly a very general characteristic of balance of payments crises, and in several cases, the loss has been triggered by policy. Mexico 1994, Thailand 1997, and Indonesia 1998 are but a few of the many crisis episodes in which the central bank tried to alleviate the credit shortage—and consequent increase in interest rates—by expanding domestic credit through drawing down accumulated international reserves.

Is the accumulation and subsequent loss of reserves an effective way to cushion a cut in international credit? The answer is likely to be "no" because, as a general rule, reserves are accumulated against short-run official financial obligations—high-powered money and short-maturity bonds; and recent experience suggests that holders of those obligations are the first to run. Thus,

---

[4] As will be argued below, however, anticipated bankruptcy may carry serious productivity costs.

the larger the stock of reserves, the larger the capital outflows are likely to be—specifically, the higher the fall in $K1$ in accounting definition (1).

Moreover, a large stock of reserves is likely to encourage reckless behavior by the central bank. For example, reserves that were accumulated against short-term debt—which is typically the case with sterilization operations—are used to bail out the banking system. As a result, the government's financial problems are aggravated if short-term bondholders refuse to roll over debt, as during the 1994 Tequila crisis in Mexico.

Financial Turmoil

This section will further examine the possible financial repercussions of a sudden and unexpected cut in *CAD*. The term *financial* will encompass all intertemporal contracts, including implicit contracts between firms and employees.

We start from the premises that financial markets in developing economies are incomplete and contracts are hard to enforce. These follow from the fact that market institutions are still in their infancy. Another key feature that characterizes this stage is political instability. This appears to have substantially increased in magnitude after the demise of the Cold War, with political institutions that once held undisputed sway being seriously challenged. As a result, political outcomes have become more volatile and, central to our discussion, harder to predict. This impinges on the credibility of policy and policymakers, creating a breeding ground for rumors about likely policy actions that can overshadow substantive information and roil volatile markets quite independently of the fundamentals.

This background helps explain why disruptions in the financial market have effects in emerging economies that may far exceed those in more advanced economies. By nature, financial contracts involve *trust* and are, therefore, strongly affected by questions of credibility. Hence, in a highly volatile environment, financial trouble can catapult into a major political shake-up that, in turn, deepens financial difficulties, delaying recovery.

We will now take a closer look at some deleterious effects associated with financial difficulties. We note, first, that in a perfect world with costless bankruptcy procedures, a bankrupt firm is quickly taken over by its creditors. If, in addition, the new management and personnel were quickly assembled, then the social cost of bankruptcy would be insignificant. However, these are very strong assumptions. For example, unless there is a very effective bankruptcy law system like Chapter 11 in the United States, managers and workers—especially those that expect to be dismissed—tend to cannibalize the firm. These perverse incentives are aggravated by the breakdown of "implicit" intertemporal contracts. Examples include seniority clauses that reward employees for their loyalty to the firm and for past performance. Since there are no legal grounds for these contract provisions, they are easy to repudiate in case of bankruptcy. Thus, firms' reorganization after bankruptcy may involve more labor turnover than called for by efficiency alone. Moreover, the anticipation of premature (and unfair) dismissal may further encourage employees' destructive behavior.

Another aggravating factor is the existence of interenterprise credit. This involves loans that firms extend to each other to facilitate trade, which is why they are sometimes referred to as "trade credit." Thus when some firms are hit by bankruptcy, their whole credit network is implicated. Firm A may be perfectly efficient and have an excellent repayment record; but if it belongs (or is simply suspected to belong) to a credit network in which a set of other firms undergo financial difficulties, then firm A may see its credit rating fall. This is typically reflected in a generalized increase in interest rates, which deepens the bankruptcy problem. At some point, a domino effect takes hold that may destroy credit channels, virtually bringing the productive system to a halt.

The breakdown of financial contracts is at the heart of the collapse in output and employment in recent crises. Investment in bankrupt firms comes to a standstill until property rights are firmly determined. Moreover, new management and employees require some time before they run up to speed. Therefore, the initial cut in capital inflows puts into motion forces that induce a lower *demand* for credit, validating the initial cut in the *supply* of credit. More specifically, the initial cut in the supply of credit induces lower expected rates of return, thereby generating a lower demand for credit. The resulting fall in output and employment is thus an equilibrium phenomenon, which cannot be undone even if credit supply returns to its initial position, unless the restoration takes place before trust and credit channels start to break down.

Financial Liberalization and Expansion

Several recent empirical studies have shown that a number of balance of payments crises have been preceded by crises in the financial sector (see Kaminsky and Reinhart, 1996). Moreover, the latter have themselves been preceded by financial liberalization or, at the very least, large expansion of the financial sector (see Rojas-Suarez and Weisbrod, 1996; and Gavin and Hausmann,1996). The connection between financial liberalization/expansion and crises is not obvious, but there are several considerations that point in that direction.

Financial liberalization allows banks to pay competitive interest rates on deposits,[5] encouraging a larger flow of lendable funds through the banking system. A key attractive feature of bank deposits is high liquidity, which means they can be transformed into cash at virtually no cost. Bank loans, on the other hand, are generally much less liquid. Thus, a sudden across-the-board fall in bank deposits brings about a liquidity crisis. Why would banks expose themselves to a liquidity crisis? First, if the crisis is circumscribed to a few banks, their borrowing in the call or interbank loan market can solve the liquidity problem. Second, if the liquidity crisis is systemic, worldwide experience shows that central banks act as lenders of last resort to prevent massive bankruptcies, giving rise to moral hazard and overlending (see McKinnon and Pill, 1996).

How do fixed exchange rates affect the situation? Under those circumstances, the central bank's ability to behave as lender of last resort is limited by available international reserves. Thus unless reserves are equivalent to a broad monetary aggregate like M3 or M4—a very unlikely case[6]—there is always a chance that central bank loans will drive reserves to their minimum tolerable level and the currency is devalued. Moreover, financial liberalization tends to increase the ratios of monetary aggregates to international reserves, increasing the chances of a currency crisis.

What happens in the case of floating exchange rates? In this instance, international reserves clearly are never depleted, but a bank bailout can lead to a large devaluation that, in turn, can give rise to the above-mentioned financial difficulties.

In sum, bank liberalization/expansion seems to make large currency devaluation—and consequently large financial disruption—possible. The latter, in turn, may lead to deep cuts in international lending that, as previously argued, result in large output and employment losses.

The question that remains to be answered is why there would be a run against bank deposits if the central bank stands ready to bail out financial institutions in case of a systemic liquidity crisis. As previously noted, having a lender of last resort takes care of the liquidity problem, but if the run takes place, it will provoke a *currency* crisis and possibly a major real-sector crisis. Thus, apprehension that a bank run is in the offing builds pressure on investors to withdraw their bank deposits to avoid the risk of *devaluation*.

Two common characteristics of emerging market economies are the high share of corporate borrowing through bank loans (see Rojas-Suárez and Weisbrod, 1996) and the existence of a segmented bond market. The latter may reflect the economic and political uncertainties previously highlighted, while the former reflects the fact that banks enjoy the benefits of explicit or implicit government insurance. This dual configuration may make the whole system more vulnerable to bank runs. In countries with an advanced bond market, a bank run bears little relationship to a credit crunch. If a firm's bank credit is curtailed, the firm can turn to the bond market for equivalent funding.

---

[5] In the present context, the word *deposits* should be understood as covering a wide range of bank liabilities. Thus, depositors range from the standard current account holder to holders of banks' negotiable notes.

[6] For example, no Latin American country has gross international reserves exceeding the equivalent of M2, with many instances in which M2 is two or three times larger than reserves.

However, if banks are the central source of finance, a credit cut has immediate real effects. Consequently the financial sector in emerging market economies becomes, in a way, the mirror image of the real sector. Financial trouble is thus taken to be a key indicator of major disruptions in the real economy. As a leading economic indicator, the state of the financial sector may play a key role in helping to *coordinate* expectations about economic collapse.

The problem does not stop with the fact that a large financial sector and weak bond and equity markets tend to cause financial sector difficulties to be perceived as macroeconomic rather than sectoral. The danger is aggravated by the fact that individual players may not internalize the resulting vulnerabilities, either because they are not well understood or because players expect a government bailout. Consequently, *financial liberalization may contribute to financial vulnerability unless the country has been able to develop a strong and stable bond market, economic agents have a good understanding of the financial sector, and the government's moral-hazard-inducing policies are reined in.*

Crisis Prevention

Given the analysis above, what policies can be adopted to prevent meltdown from occurring? The following subsections briefly explore some policy implications for public debt, capital flows, regulatory prudence, exchange rates, and fiscal rules.

• *Public debt—maturity structure*: Short-maturity debt is dangerous because it increases the size of potential capital outflows. Notice that this holds whether or not there are controls on capital inflows. Short-term debt may be attractive if the country faces a steep term-structure curve. But even under those circumstances, the policymaker should assess the reasons for the market to penalize long-term borrowing. If these reasons are realistic, the government should still consider borrowing long term. Short-term bonds should be issued only if the public is misinformed and has an unrealistically high expectation of default or devaluation, or long-term bonds become momentarily illiquid.

• *Public debt—currency denomination*: Dollarization and, more generally, indexation are effective tools to lengthen maturity structure since they provide the means for the government to insure against devaluation and inflation. However, they should be used only if the risks as assessed by the public are deemed unrealistically high. Thus, countries should not switch to these kinds of instruments simply to lower their debt service.

• *Controls on capital outflows*: Our assessment finds these controls to be largely ineffective in preventing the meltdown and associated financial difficulties discussed in the section on financial turmoil. Controls cannot prevent the exchange rate from suffering a sharp devaluation during a major capital outflow. The parallel or black market rate will skyrocket. This can cause financial problems if, for instance, firms took foreign-currency-denominated loans. Moreover, if the gap between black market and official exchange rates is large enough, controls become hard to enforce.

• *Controls on capital inflows*: This policy has recently been adopted in Chile and Colombia. One rationale for the controls is that they improve the quality of financial intermediation during large inflows of capital. This makes sense, especially if the funds are partly funneled through the banking system and this generates the type of negative externalities highlighted above. However, these controls do not effectively prevent a capital outflow meltdown. Thus, for example, a tax on capital inflows does discourage quick roundtrips, but it does not stop a bank run and the accelerated capital outflows associated with heightened expectation of a meltdown. To prevent that, the government should make sure that financial capital is invested in long-term instruments and that there is no bunching of maturities.[7] Therefore, this policy of capital inflow taxes would have to be complemented with domestic financial regulations that discourage short-term financial contracts.

• *Prudential regulation*: This is essential to ensure the stability of the financial system, especially when faced with a capital outflow crisis. Much has been written about the desirability of Basle-type Capital Adequacy ratios. However, ensuring banks' solvency may not be enough to prevent the kinds of self-fulfilling financial crises highlighted above. It is also important to ensure that banks are not overexposed to liquidity crises. The critical level of exposure to these crises can only be determined after assessing the characteristics of the financial sector, and the government's ability to come to its rescue. As argued above, the latter depends on the level of international reserves, ability to garner international financial support, and policy credibility, among many other considerations. For emerging markets in which banks hold a strong position in the domestic financial sector, the following policies should be given serious consideration: (1) high reserve requirements (preferably remunerated), and (2) lower legal fees for long-term financial contracts. Both policies have been successfully implemented in Argentina. In case of a capital outflow crisis, reserve requirements could be lowered to prevent a credit crunch. This policy is akin to an open market purchase, but it has the advantage of targeting the banking sector more directly.

• *The exchange rate regime—general considerations*: It is very hard to find examples in which emerging markets exhibit a "clean" floating exchange rate regime, i.e., one in which the monetary authority refrains from interven-

---

[7] Interestingly, in response to the slowdown of capital inflows associated with the Asian crises, Chile lowered the capital inflow tax. This suggests that the authorities sensed that the instrument is not adequate for those circumstances.

ing in the foreign currency market or engaging in offsetting open market operations (Calvo and Végh, 1993). This is probably because the monetary authority is aware that, as argued above, exchange rate flexibility could, beyond certain bounds, generate financial disruption. In practice, therefore, we observe fixed rates or a "dirty" float. Even in exchange-band systems, one observes intra-band intervention or open market operations.

• *Fixed exchange rate*: For the sake of concreteness, we will discuss the case in which there is a unified rate for both commercial and financial operations, and there are no major restrictions on capital mobility.[8] As our previous discussion shows, a large fall in bank deposits may lead to a large devaluation and to financial turmoil if the ensuing central bank intervention leads to a depletion of international reserves. Therefore, the success of fixed exchange rates depends on a high stock of international reserves or effective international credit lines, and rules that prevent the central bank from pursuing reckless financial policies. In this respect, we believe that serious consideration should be given to imposing limits on the rate of expansion of central bank credit. This should be considered even in the context of central bank independence. Otherwise, since all fingers will be pointed in its direction if there is a financial collapse, we suspect that the central bank will tend to be unduly permissive with its domestic credit when a serious financial crisis threatens. As a result, speculative attacks on the currency would be more likely to succeed.

• *Dirty float*: After the Asian crises, the opinion of public policy analysts has moved against fixed and in favor of a form of floating exchange rates (for instance, see Reisen, 1998). Sometimes the arguments given border on the naïve or tautological. More sophisticated arguments, though, point to the extra degree of freedom offered by floating rates. Some of the problems with floating have been discussed above. Dirty floating, however, allows greater flexibility. A difficulty is that the system lacks a nominal anchor unless the associated monetary/exchange rate rules are clearly specified and understood by the public. Once a rule is specified, however, much of the desired flexibility is lost. Moreover, contingent rules are not easy to design properly. For example, dirty floating could be useful to accommodate a change in equilibrium relative prices stemming from deterioration in the terms of trade. However, even leaving financial considerations aside, a good rule would have to discriminate between temporary and permanent shocks. A statistician has the instruments to estimate the breakdown between these shocks. But in order to do so, the statistician will have to make very strong assumptions. In particular, the assumption will have to be made that the present is not significantly different from the past. This may be a questionable premise for emerging

---

[8] Although the focus will be on fixed exchange rates, essentially the same points could be made for *tablita*-type systems in which the exchange rate is preannounced.

markets. As a result, rules are likely to give way to discretionary policy and inconsistency over time, which, as is well known, yield undesirable outcomes.

 • *Floating and the dollarization of private debts*: As the recent experience in Indonesia illustrates, dollarized liabilities could cause major financial damage if the currency suffers sizable *real* devaluation (the usual outcome of a capital outflow crisis). Floating exchange rates could be useful to discourage the dollarization of private debts. However, few central banks seem to be prepared to tolerate the necessary exchange rate volatility.

 • *Fiscal rules—the Talvi effect*: In addition to seriously affecting monetary/financial equilibrium, capital flows also have strong effects on fiscal balance. For example, fiscal revenue rises during capital inflow episodes and collapses after capital outflow crises (Talvi, 1996; and Gavin, Hausmann, Perotti, and Talvi, 1996). Because this phenomenon is not well understood by policymakers, higher expenditure has occurred during capital inflow episodes without full awareness of the dangers. Thus, as a capital outflow crisis materializes, governments are forced to cut expenditure sharply and abruptly, in a manner that is inevitably disorderly and inefficient. A possible way to curb this boomerang effect is to develop rules that put a cap on government expenditure as capital flows in. An option would be to set up a Fiscal Stabilization Fund that grows during bonanzas and is drawn down during slack times to smooth out government expenditure.

Guillermo Calvo is Distinguished University Professor of Economics at the University of Maryland, College Park. Eduardo Fernández-Arias is Lead Research Economist, Office of the Chief Economist, Inter-American Development Bank.

References

Bevilaqua, A., and E. Fernández-Arias. 1998. "Accounting For Country Risk Premia in Latin America." *Latin American Economic Policies*, Third Quarter, 1998. Washington, D.C.: Research Department, Inter-American Development Bank.

Calvo, G., and C. Végh. 1993. "Exchange-Rate-Based Stabilization under Imperfect Credibility." In H. Frisch and A. Worgotter, editors. *Open Economy Macroeconomics*. Hampshire, England: Macmillan Press Ltd.

Chang, R., and A. Velasco. "Financial Fragility and the Exchange Rate Regime." RR#98-05, C.V. Starr Center for Applied Economics, New York University, February 1998.

Cooper, R., 1971. "Exchange Rate Devaluation in Developing Countries." In *Princeton Essays on International Finance 86*. Princeton, N.J.: Princeton University Press.

Corsetti, G., P. Pesenti, and N. Roubini. 1998. "What Caused the Asian Currency and Financial Crises?" New York University, March 1998, Mimeographed document.

Edwards, S. 1986. "Are Devaluations Contractionary?" *Review of Economics and Statistics*. 68 (3): 501–08.

Gavin, M., and R. Hausmann. 1996. "The Roots of Banking Crises: The Macroeconomic Context." In R. Hausmann and L. Rojas-Suárez, editors. *Banking Crises in Latin America*. Washington, D.C.: Inter-American Development Bank.

Gavin, M., R. Hausmann, R. Perotti, and E. Talvi. 1996. "Managing Fiscal Policy in Latin America and the Caribbean: Volatility, Procyclicality, and Limited Creditworthiness." Working Paper Series 326. Washington, D.C.: Inter-American Development Bank Office of the Chief Economist.

Kaminsky, G., and C. Reinhart. 1996. "The Twin Crises: The Causes of Banking and Balance of Payments Problems." International Finance Discussion Paper No. 544. Washington, D.C.: Board of Governors of the Federal Reserve System.

Krugman, P. 1998. "What Happened in Asia?" MIT, Cambridge, MA, Mimeographed document.

Krugman, P., and L. Taylor. 1978. "Contractionary Effects on Devaluations." *Journal of International Economics.* 8(3): 445–56.

McKinnon, R., and H. Pill. 1996. "Credible Liberalizations and International Capital Flows: The Overborrowing Syndrome." In T. Ito and A.O. Drueger, editors. *Financial Deregulation and Integration in East Asia.* Chicago: Chicago University Press.

Radelet, S., and J. Sachs. 1998. "The Onset of the Asian Financial Crisis." Harvard Institute for International Development, Cambridge, MA, Mimeographed document.

Reisen, H. 1998. "Domestic Causes of Currency Crises: Policy Lessons for Crisis Avoidance." Technical Paper 136. Paris: OECD Development Center.

Rojas-Suárez, L., and S. Weisbrod. 1996. "Banking Crises in Latin America: Experience and Issues." In R. Hausmann and L. Rojas-Suárez, editors. *Banking Crisis in Latin America.* Washington, D.C.: Inter-American Development Bank.

Talvi, E. 1996. "Exchange-Rate Based Stabilization with Endogenous Fiscal Response." Working Paper Series 324. Washington, D.C.: Inter-American Development Bank. Forthcoming in the *Journal of Development Economics.*

Washington, D.C., October 1998

Financial Contagion in Emerging Markets

Eduardo Fernández-Arias and Roberto Rigobón

During the past six years, the world has been asking itself if it is possible to live under a free capital market. By September 1998, it was nearly impossible to discuss the state of the global economy without touching on the topic of contagion. The Tequila jolt, its even more virulent relative the Asian Flu, and now the Russian cold have turned an anomaly into a household word, generating a series of stock market crashes around the world, especially in developing economies, and surges in emerging-market bond spreads.

If *contagion* is on everyone's lips, neither academics nor economists in the field have yet defined precisely what the term means. A consensus, however, is beginning to form about what it is not. The phenomenon cannot be explained by the traditional standard propagation of real shocks. In other words, one would expect that aggregate world shocks and trade linkages explain some of the joint movements across countries. The excess variation that cannot be attributed to these standard channels is what constitutes contagion, and it is this definition that this paper will explore. A close look at the evidence will yield some counterintuitive conclusions. Although markets do discriminate across countries based on their fundamentals, investor behavior and the circumstances around their portfolio positions play a major role in crisis formation and transmission. Moreover, standard statistical measures suggest that emerging markets move in remarkably uniform fashion at all times, not just in crises. Their vulnerability is not simply due to anomalous behavior by investors but is a permanent feature of international investment institutions.

Mapping Contagion through Evolving Bond Prices and Spreads

The data used to track crisis formation and contagion corresponds to the emerging-market bond data sets, compiled by J.P. Morgan in the construction of their EMBI+ index. The data includes dollar-denominated bonds issued by emerging market economies: Argentina, Brazil, Bulgaria, Ecuador, Mexico, Morocco, Nigeria, Panama, Peru, the Philippines, Poland, Russia, and Venezuela. Bond prices have been normalized at various points to highlight the co-movement in prices.

Bond market pricing in emerging markets, and particularly in our region, displays three key characteristics. First, the spreads are high and volatile.

Figure 1 shows the evolution of the risk spread in the region during the past four years. As a price of risk, this volatility is remarkably high, especially since it is an aggregate price encompassing seven different countries.

Figure 1. Latin American Spreads 1994–1998

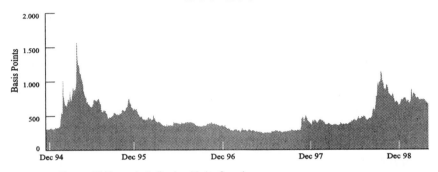

Source: J.P. Morgan Latin Eurobond Index Spread

Second, the data for Latin America show a crisis pattern. Spreads tend to move from relative stability to a sudden surge, followed by a recovery. Three crises are mapped in Figure 2 in terms of their depth. The first surge occurs in December 1994 after the Mexican crisis, which deepens until March

Figure 2. Fall in Latin American Sovereign Bond Prices

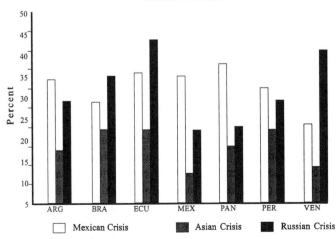

Source: J.P. Morgan EMBI⁺ and Bond Price Index [EMBI⁺]

Figure 3. Emerging Markets Sovereign Bond Prices

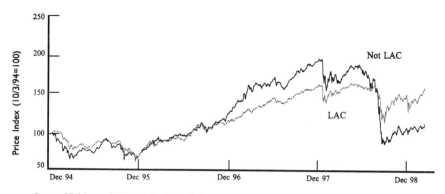

Source: J.P. Morgan EMBI⁺ and Bond Price Index

Figure 4. Latin American Sovereign Bond Prices
1994–1995

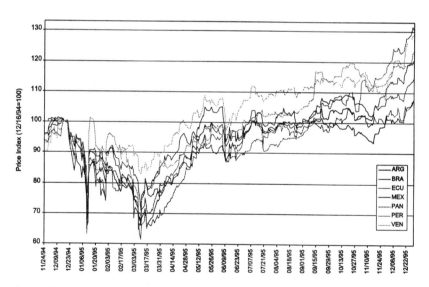

Source: J.P. Morgan EMBI⁺ and Bond Price Index

1995 when the IMF/U.S. rescue package is in place, reaching a reduction in prices on the order of one third. The second, smaller surge occurs by October 1997 when the Asian crisis reaches our region in a significant fashion. The third surge, comparable in size to the Tequila, develops in August–September

Figure 5. Latin American Sovereign Bond Prices
1997–1999

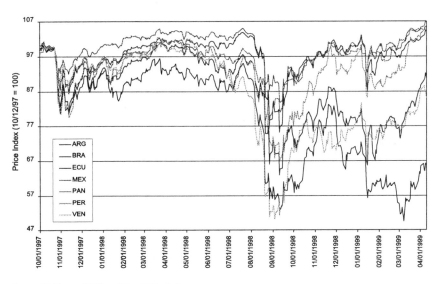

Source: J.P. Morgan EMBI⁺ and Bond Price Index

Figure 6. Fall in Latin American Sovereign Bond Prices

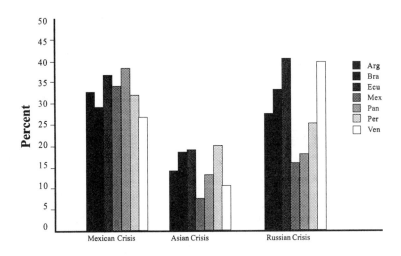

Source: J.P. Morgan EMBI⁺ and Bond Price Index

1998 and is associated with the Russian crisis. In all three cases there is a tendency for recovery, including the current episode since mid-September.[1]

Third, the data are highly correlated across countries, including those outside the region. This co-movement of prices and spreads is remarkable. Figure 3 shows the evolution of bond prices in our region and in other emerging markets during the last few years, which follow generally similar trends throughout. Within our region, Figures 4 and 5 show bond prices for Argentina, Brazil, Ecuador, Mexico, Panama, Peru, and Venezuela around the three crisis episodes. Figure 6 shows the relative fall in bond prices, from peak to trough, in each country during each crisis. The evidence is clear that fluctuations are widespread, both during crises and during recovery.

A more in-depth analysis reveals that the degree of correlation across countries is large even in normal periods before crises. For example, the correlations of returns on bonds between Mexican bonds and other emerging markets were very high before, during, and after the Mexican crisis of 1994–1995. The simple correlations based on two-day returns between each country and Mexico are found in Table 1.

Table 1. Correlation between Mexican and Other Emerging Market Bond Returns, 1994–1996

	Normal	Crisis	Change
Argentina	89.7	92.4	+
Brazil	93.6	94.6	+
Ecuador	93.3	77.1	-
Morocco	69.3	82.0	+
Nigeria	63.4	73.1	+
Panama	92.5	80.5	-
Peru	87.2	93.9	+
Philippines	79.3	57.9	-
Poland	73.9	80.8	+
Russia	82.3	84.8	+
Venezuela	72.8	90.3	+

The sample covers the interval from January 1, 1994, until July 1, 1996. The period of crisis was defined as the two weeks after December 19, 1994, while the normal period comprises the remainder of the time. As is apparent, the correlations of "noncrisis" daily returns are extremely large. All correla-

---

[1] By November 1999, after this paper was prepared, Latin American spreads had returned to within 100 basis points of their pre-Russian level.

tions are above 60 percent, and 6 of 11 are above 80 percent. Latin American countries have correlations above 80 percent for all countries except Venezuela, which has a correlation of 73 percent. The correlations during the crisis period increased slightly in general (in 8 out of 11 cases).

Nonconvergence with Economic Fundamentals

It is extremely difficult to reconcile the above evidence with the notion that spreads reflect economic fundamentals underlying the countries' risks of default.

First, at the individual country level, the high volatility of spreads appears incompatible with a fundamentals-based interpretation in the absence of a real shock to the economy. Even if one argues that it was not the fundamentals but the information available about them that changed abruptly, leading to a drastically altered market perception of risk, this argument cannot explain the recovery that generally follows surges in spreads.

Second, and more generally, it is difficult to reconcile the high level of spreads with the countries' implied risks of default, whether the assessments are fundamentals-based or not. Figure 7 shows the equivalent default loss associated with the levels of spreads in Figure 1. An alternative interpretation is that the surge in spreads reflects, in large part, an increase in the premium that investors demand to absorb a given country risk.

Third, the uniformity of movement across countries during a crisis implies the existence of international transmission mechanisms strong enough to carry a domestic shock abroad despite the wide range of specific country conditions elsewhere. These channels can be divided into three categories.[2]

Figure 7. Loss Equivalent Probability

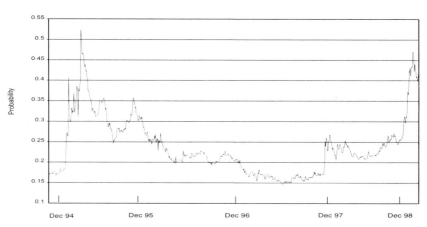

Source: Own calculations based on J.P. Morgan Latin Eurobond Index.

The first two channels—international shocks common to all countries in the system; and a country-specific shock that may spill over to affect another country's economy, like one domino toppling another—are based on fundamentals. Both channels identify real linkages, and constitute standard transmission mechanisms. The third channel—contagion—encompasses those co-movements not explained by standard channels. To understand our present situation, each channel must be examined in turn.

First, co-movement can result from world aggregate shocks. For example, open economies can be affected by the international interest rate, international supply of capital, or international demand for goods, increasing the correlations among emerging markets. In particular, the strong correlation noted in Table 1 may be caused by high frequency movements in the international interest rate. To address this concern, Table 2 shows the correlations of the residuals of the bond returns after controlling for the international interest rate and adjustment lags.

Table 2. Correlation of Mexican and Other Emerging Market Bond Return Residuals, 1994–1996

	Normal	Crisis	Change
Argentina	81.0	87.1	+
Brazil	68.3	89.1	+
Ecuador	53.7	75.6	+
Morocco	69.2	78.1	+
Nigeria	52.5	79.5	+
Panama	40.7	73.7	+
Peru	43.6	77.7	+
Philippines	36.7	65.2	+
Poland	41.8	79.7	+
Russia	32.4	69.1	+
Venezuela	60.0	83.3	+

Compared to Table 1, the estimated correlations fall but still continue to be large. For example, Argentina and Brazil have correlations larger than 68 percent in normal times and almost 90 percent during the crisis. Moreover, all the correlations during the period of crisis increase. This implies that the presence of aggregate shocks plays some role, but it does not account for paired correlations between economies.

---

[2] This subdivision follows the terminology of Masson (1997): aggregate shocks, spillover effects, and contagion.

The second channel addresses the question of why fundamentals in one economy can be affected by shock to fundamentals in one or more other economies. The idea is that real linkages exist among the countries: the preferred example is trade (e.g., Gerlach and Smets, 1995). In this instance, the proposed linkage posits that devaluation in one country affects the multilateral real exchange rate, requiring a real depreciation in the other country. Therefore, a currency attack in one country can drive a currency attack in a trade partner due to increased expectation of a regime shift. However, estimated trade elasticities are far from being able to explain the observed surges in spreads in countries with minor or no direct market linkages. Other real linkages such as monetary policy coordination, research and development, or migration may also be factors, but they are generally less important than trade.

These observations have led to creation of the concept of financial contagion as the nonconventional mechanism underlying the widespread surge in spreads during recent crisis periods. Before analyzing some of the theories that have been advanced to explain the phenomenon, however, it would be useful to see if propagation through contagion discriminates among countries and, in particular, whether fundamentals play a role in such discrimination.

Does the Market Discriminate?

The effect of contagion differs across countries. For example, Figure 6 shows contagion in the Latin American countries of the sample as measured by the relative fall of their bond prices in each of the three crisis episodes. What can

Table 3. Country Rankings

	Vulnerability to Contagion	Ex-Ante Market Risk
1	RUS	NIG
2	KOR	BUL
3	ECU	PER
4	BUL	ECU
5	BRA	VEN
6	VEN	RUS
7	PER	BRA
8	MOR	ARG
9	NIG	MOR
10	ARG	MEX
11	PAN	PAN
12	PHI	PHI
13	MEX	POL
14	POL	KOR

be learned from these country differences?

To answer the question we constructed an index of vulnerability to contagion for the countries in the sample, based on the relative fall of their bond prices. In order to assess the impact of recent upheavals, we added the falls associated with the Asian crises and Russian crisis, in both cases from peak to trough. The composite index ranking for the 14 countries is shown in Table 3, in which the most vulnerable country is at the top (Russia) and the least vulnerable at the bottom (Poland).

Table 4a. Market Risk

	Vulnerability	
	High	Low
Market Risk High	BRA BUL ECU PER RUS VEN	NIG
Market Risk Low	KOR	ARG MEX MOR PAN PHI POL

This vulnerability pattern was compared with the market assessment of risk before the crises, as of June 1997, to see if the two are consistent. The ranking of market country risk is also shown in Table 3—from the riskiest, Nigeria, to the safest, Korea. This ranking was based on Standard & Poor's sovereign ratings at the time, supplemented by Moody's and secondary market spreads in the case of unrated countries.[3]

As is well known, Korea was totally missed by the market, and this discrepancy is highlighted by the total mismatch of Korea in the two columns of Table 3. However, this is the only clear mismatch in the table. In fact, if we classify the 14 countries into two groups, designating numbers 1–7 as the highly vulnerable/risky countries and numbers 8–14 as the rest, we see that there is an almost perfect correspondence between high ex-ante market risk and high ex-post contagion vulnerability. As Table 4a shows, the only exceptions are Korea, which was previously cited, and Nigeria, whose high risk did not fully materialize in contagion.

The fact that when there is contagion in crisis episodes prices fall more deeply in ex-ante riskier countries implies that this phenomenon leads to spread divergence, i.e., the difference in spreads between countries increases. (The reason is that a given increase in spreads in absolute terms has a smaller impact on the price of bonds of high spread/risk countries.) The evolution of spreads in our region during the few months following the Russian crisis exemplifies this trend. The magnitude of increased spread in Argentina, Brazil, Colombia, Mexico, and Venezuela corresponds to their respective initial levels, the lowest in Mexico and the highest in Venezuela (see Figure 8).

---

[3] It is well documented that ratings are closely related to observed market spreads.

Figure 8. Latin American Spreads

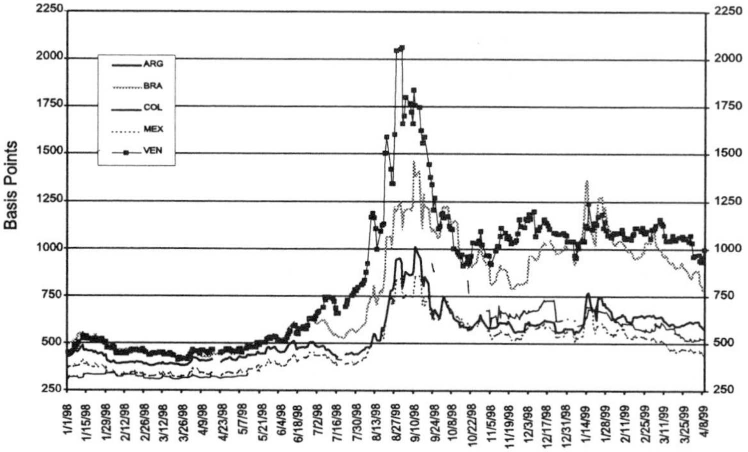

Source: Own calculations based on J.P. Morgan Latin Eurobond Index.

The impressive success rate of market risk assessment in predicting country vulnerability to contagion in 12 of 14 cases means that the market does discriminate, and that it does so in a consistent manner, i.e., in agreement with its own ex-ante assessment of risk. Since market spreads are known to be associated with traditional economic fundamentals (see Bevilaqua and Fernández-Arias, 1998), it also implies that these fundamentals are relevant for the degree of vulnerability to contagion.

Finally, we checked whether specific financial factors that have been proposed as important elements in recent crises also have discriminating power in predicting vulnerability to contagion. To that end we constructed financial indexes for each country, which we call financial fragility and financial weakness. We then conducted the same kind of association analysis between vulnerability to contagion and each of these financial indexes.

The financial fragility index measures how vulnerable the financial system is to a liquidity run. It is based on three different measures of liquidity mismatch: (1) the ratio of broad money, M2, to international reserves, as originally suggested by Guillermo Calvo; (2) the share of short-term foreign bank debt in the total; and (3) the foreign debt service burden, both short-term debt and interest debt service, as a share of international reserves. Country rankings for each measure were added to obtain the overall ranking of financial fragility.

The financial weakness index measures how vulnerable the financial system may be to a solvency problem of its borrowers. It, too, is based on

Table 4b. Financial Fragility

Vulnerability

		High	Low
Financial Fragility	High	BRA KOR RUS	ARG MEX PAN PHI
	Low	BUL ECU PER VEN	MOR NIG POL

Table 4c. Financial Weakness

Vulnerability

		High	Low
Financial Weakness	High	ECU RUS	ARG NIG PAN PHI POL
	Low	BRA BUL KOR PER VEN	MEX MOR

three measures: (1) the prior occurrence of a bank lending boom to the private sector, as measured by an excess in the rate of lending growth compared to output growth; (2) the share of nonperforming bank loans; and (3) the degree of real exchange rate appreciation, whose adjustment may lead to corporate insolvency. As for financial fragility, partial rankings were added to obtain the overall ranking of financial weakness.

Neither financial index performs well in predicting vulnerability to contagion (see Tables 4b and 4c). The financial fragility indicator only helps predict high vulnerability in three of seven cases: Korea, Russia, and Brazil. The financial weakness indicator predicts only two of seven: Russia and Ecuador. The bottom line is that traditional fundamentals, rather than financial vulnerability, appear to be the main factors underlying the degree of contagion. As a result, relative valuations across countries were maintained through the phases of the contagion episode (see Figure 8 in which spread profiles seldom cross).

Accounting for Financial Contagion

Several theories attempt to explain contagion through the observed evolution of spreads in emerging markets. They all share the belief that contagion occurs because of the way investors in emerging markets operate. For the purpose of discussion, we classify these accounts into four roughly generalized groups:

• *Multiple equilibrium.* As it is by now well understood, a coordinated run of foreign investors may cause a payments crisis for liquidity reasons that need not occur with adequate financing. If the run is sufficiently massive, the crisis created renders the country uncreditworthy and thereby validates the investors' withdrawal. Such a liquidity crisis is possible when fundamentals are strong but not invulnerable. In that case, country risk also incorporates the subjective probability that the investor coordination required for a liquidity crisis takes place.

The multiple equilibrium theory assumes that a crisis in one country may become a sunspot for another (Masson, 1997). The idea is that the crisis in one country affects the probability that investors coordinate to move to the bad equilibrium in another economy. This theory not only explains the bunching of crisis but also speculative attacks to economies that look, in principle, healthy. The causative agent from this point of view is the change in investors' expectations during a crisis and not real linkages. The fact that financial fragility is not important for contagion is not supportive of this theory.

• *Information updating.* An alternative hypothesis posits that realizations in one country are actually informative about other countries as well. In this theory agents have uncertainty not only about the fundamentals in an economy, but also about the effectiveness of the country's policies and reforms. So if two countries initiate similar processes of reform (e.g., financial liberalization with inadequate regulation or measures to control fiscal imbalances), the outcomes in one country are informative about the particular state of that economy and the effectiveness of the policies implemented. If a domestic crisis results, it transmits the ultimate bad signal about the quality of policies and reforms in other countries with similar structures that have yet to slip into crisis.

Using this line of reasoning, the Asian crises would have affected countries with potentially similar financial weaknesses, and the Russian crisis would affect countries with a large fiscal deficit defending a fixed—or quasi-fixed—exchange rate regime with high interest rates, etc. More generally, it suggests that countries with large uncertainty about their fundamentals and with similar policies might be affected by common shocks.[4] (However, it is worth mentioning that Eichengreen, Rose and Wyplosz [1996] study the collapse of the fixed exchange rates at the end of 1993 and find that the propagation mechanism across countries was based on trade spillovers rather than country similarities.) The uniformity of contagion and recovery across countries is not supportive of this theory.

• *Political economy.* Drazen (1998) studies the 1993 European devaluations and argues that there are reasons to think of them as products of political contagion. Assume that political pressures existed on central bank presidents to maintain the exchange regime. When one country decides to abandon ship, it reduces the political costs of the next country in line. Thus, bunching in exchange rate abandonment should be expected. Similar to the case of

---

[4] Rigobón (1998) has a similar story for a single country, and extrapolating the result to several countries is easily understandable in his context.

multiple equilibria, the bunching of crises is produced by political considerations rather than real economic spillovers.

In the present context, it can be argued that sovereign decisions not to
pay, as in the Russian case, diminish the political cost for others to follow suit,
thus increasing default risk for all. In a similar vein, it has also been argued
that the IMF's failure to prevent the Russian moratorium and crisis with a
rescue package also increased private risk by signaling that such implicit guarantees are less likely to be available in the future. However, the uniformity and
universality characteristics of contagion across countries are not supportive
of this theory.

• *Weakness of financial intermediaries.* Here the main idea is that liquidity shocks to market participants can drive a sell-off, causing co-movement in prices. In particular, liquidity issues have been raised as an important
component of contagion in the recent Russian crisis. Valdés (1996) analyzes
the impact of a liquidity shock on portfolio recomposition across asset classes.
He finds that a crisis in one country, accompanied by a liquidity shock to the
investors' capital, drives resources out of other countries. The supposition is
that investors require capital in order to operate in the market. A crisis in one
country generates a capital loss that requires a portfolio adjustment. Hence
investors sell their holdings of other assets to make up for their shortage in
capital. In particular, it has been argued that the debt market for noninvestment-
grade countries has "dried up" in the recent Russian crisis primarily because
market participants were caught in this kind of capital crunch.

The question of course is why their selling would lead to a significant
drop in prices. This theory and its variants assume that investable funds are
somehow constrained in such a way that emerging country bonds are allowed
to be underpriced without triggering buyers' demand. For example, such an
outcome could occur if the investment intermediaries who engage in fire sales
after becoming liquidity constrained due to equity losses are also highly specialized in emerging markets and have little competition for that market. This,
in fact, is the case in noninvestment-grade countries for institutional and regulatory reasons. Short of these fire sales, generalized falls in equity from losses
reduce the capacity to bear risk and may lead to large risk premiums on top of
default risk. The maintenance of relative valuations across emerging countries
and the fact that developed markets were also affected during contagion add
support for this theory.

The weakness of financial intermediaries, mentioned earlier in this section, may also spring from flawed decision making on the part of investors.
Within a fully rational framework, principal–agent differences may lead to
herding behavior on the part of agents, magnifying the cycle through extreme
risk aversion at times of crisis and risk indulgence at times of boom (see Calvo
and Mendoza, 1998). Other theories point to the psychological motivations of
investors, suggesting co-movement in prices can be generated by changes in

investor sentiment. For example, Mullainathan (1998) proposes a model in which investors have imperfect recall and a crisis in one country triggers the memories of previous crises. Investors recompute the priors about debt default, assigning a higher probability to bad events recurring. Here, again, the co-movement in prices occurs because memories are correlated even if the fundamentals are not.

Super Virus or Impaired Immune System?

A natural corollary to most of these theories is that contagion takes hold or is most virulent only at times of crisis. However, there is evidence to suggest that contagion is equally active in periods of normality. In other words, the phenomenon under study can be interpreted as a permanent vulnerability of emerging markets to contagion from outside conditions, i.e., low immunity rather than the outbreak of a distinctive virulent disease called "crisis."

Forbes and Rigobón (1998) study international stock market prices and are unable to reject the hypothesis that contagion in return correlations remains constant over time, whether in crisis or in tranquility. Given the hypothesis that the contagion mechanism is always present, they note that observed correlations across countries would be larger during a crisis simply because the relative size of country specific shocks is less important at those times. They then explain the methodology to be used for the downward adjustment of observed correlations in crisis periods.

The work in progress that we are conducting shows that if the same kind of methodology is followed to analyze bond returns around crises, a similar result is obtained. Once adjusted, high bond return pair-wise correlations are statistically the same in all periods: normality, crisis, and recovery. In fact, such a result obtains for all parameters of the contagion mechanism, after controlling for international interest rates and lags. Is it important that contagion is a permanent feature as opposed to specific of crises? Not from the point of view of investors, who would only care about observed returns and their correlations at various times. However, from the government's and policymakers' point of view, the distinction is important because it may shed light on the kind of mechanism that is at work and refine the evaluation of the various theories mentioned above, throwing light on the efficacy of existing and proposed policies. In particular, it would change the focus from crisis management to the permanent features of international financial architecture.

Eduardo Fernández-Arias is Lead Research Economist, Office of the Chief Economist, Inter-American Development Bank; and Roberto Rigobón is Assistant Professor at the Sloan School of Management, Massachusetts Institute of Technology.

References

Bevilaqua, A., and E. Fernández-Arias. 1998. "Accounting For Country Risk Premia in Latin America." *Latin American Economic Policies*, Third Quarter, 1998. Washington, D.C.: Inter-American Development Bank.

Calvo, G. 1998. "Capital Flows and Capital-Market Crises: The Simple Economics of Sudden Stops." Univeristy of Maryland, College Park, MD, Mimeographed document.

Calvo G., and E. Mendoza. 1998. "Rational Herd Behavior and the Globalization of Securities Markets." In Sebastian Edwards, editor. *Capital Inflows to Emerging Markets*. Cambridge, MA: National Bureau of Economic Research.

Drazen, A. 1998. "Political Contagion in Currency Crisis." University of Maryland, College Park, MD, Mimeographed document.

Eichengreen, B., A. Rose, and C. Wyplosz. 1996. "Contagious Currency Crises." NBER Working Paper 5681. Washington, D.C.: National Bureau of Economic Research.

Forbes, K., and R. Rigobón. 1998. "Not Contagion, Only Interdependence: Measuring Stock Market Co-movements." MIT, Cambridge, MA, Mimeographed document.

Gerlach, S., and F. Smets. 1995. "Contagious Speculative Attacks." *European Journal of Political Economy.* 11:45–63.

Masson, P. 1997. "Monsoonal Effects, Spillovers, and Contagion." IMF, Washington, D.C.: Mimeographed document.

Mullainathan, S. 1998. "A Memory Based Model of Bounded Rationality." MIT, Cambridge, MA, Mimeographed document.

Valdés, R. 1996. "Emerging Market Contagion: Evidence and theory." MIT, Cambridge, MA, Mimeographed document.

Washington, D.C., October 1998

Capital Market Contagion and Recession: An Explanation of the Russian Virus

Guillermo Calvo

This paper will offer a brief overview of the role information gathering plays in international financial markets for emerging market (EM) economies. It will then offer a hypothesis of how structural weaknesses make this system susceptible to local viruses that the system itself then transmits and magnifies rapidly into international contagion.

I will begin with four general observations about what makes information gathering unique in financial markets for EMs.

First, a prominent difference between advanced and emerging capital markets is the much higher cost that investors face in assessing the economic prospects of EM countries.

Second, information costs are higher in emerging markets for several reasons (each of which may not apply to all economies). They include a narrow production base of tradable goods (e.g., copper for Chile, oil for Venezuela), short and sometimes not very successful track records in capital markets, young democracies, or political systems that are prone to polarization (e.g., the presidential campaign of Cardoso versus Lula da Silva in Brazil). And the list goes on.

Third, information costs are high in the following two senses: Entry costs are large and informational value decays rapidly. This implies that information gathering is subject to *large economies of scale.* Consequently, there are a few clusters of international (rather than local) specialists that are on top of events in EMs. The rest of the capital market remains blissfully ignorant.

Finally, these informational economies of scale, in combination with other economic and political factors, induce the formation of *specialist* clusters that are knowledgeable about whole regions, e.g., Asia, Latin America. Sometimes a cluster encompasses the whole spectrum of EMs. These clusters are the operators of those mutual funds, hedge funds, etc., which focus on *large* EM subsets.

The Logic of the Russian Virus and Sudden Stops

How does this structure set the stage for contagion? In particular, what role might it have played in spreading the Russian virus of 1998? Suppose that a large EM defaults on debt obligations held by these funds. As a result, and in line with fundamentals, the funds' market value shrinks by exactly their capital losses on the defaulted debt. This shock, however, could be magnified and spread to other EMs by contagion mechanisms like the two that follow.

Default Rumors. Upon observing Russia's default, investors raise their subjective probability that other EMs will follow suit. One explanation for the fear of additional defaults is that the G7 sent a signal by letting Russia collapse that they would not be ready to bail out other EMs in case of financial stress, increasing suddenly the exposure risk of investors elsewhere. Another line of reasoning is that Russia's default lowered the credit market stigma on defaulting. Such conjectures are very difficult to assess in the short run due to the high costs and short-lived nature of information. As Calvo and Mendoza (1998) explain more fully, a rational investor could choose to believe the worst-case scenario and play it safe, causing a fall in EMs' security prices.

The Lemon Problem. If the funds are leveraged and get margin calls because of Russia's default, they will be forced to sell some of their long positions. In perfect information markets, the price of those assets need not change as a result of the sale. Money from loans that were withdrawn as a result of margin calls will be invested in the securities sold by EM specialists. However, if *most* specialists in Russian debt are subject to margin calls, then these securities will have to be sold *outside* the specialists' circle. The latter investors are less informed than the specialists and, therefore, will be willing to buy only if the securities are sold at large price discounts (a situation that echoes Akerlof's celebrated Lemon Problem). Moreover, given that, as argued above, Russian investment funds may likely hold other EM paper as well, these holdings will also suffer a substantial price decline.

As long as the contagion problem is not resolved, EMs will face much higher interest rates or outright exclusion from the capital market, causing a "sudden stop" in capital inflows. As a result, aggregate demand will suffer a sudden collapse, which will likely cause a sharp output slowdown. This might be the "kiss of death" for EMs *because it would tend to validate the uninformed investor's fear that EM financial obligations are actually Lemons.* Consequently, interest rates will remain high and the possibility of deep recession will arise because there would be no end in sight for the sudden stop (for a discussion of sudden stops, see Calvo, 1998).

To sum up, then, the logic of the Russian virus outlined here does not rely on multiplicity of equilibria. The liquidity problem faced by specialists due to Russia's default, for example, kicks them out of the game at the margin. Therefore, prices *are* set by the uninformed, or blind, investor. These, in turn, are willing to hold EMs' paper only if traded at deep discounts (due to the Lemon Problem), which provokes a sudden stop in EMs. Under those circumstances, the "blind" investors have every reason to continue thinking that EM financial obligations could be lemons. Therefore, the fundamental exogenous shock to the system is Russia's default, which, in turn, provokes a loss of *effective* human capital in financial markets—causing a negative output shock in other EMs.

Lessons

What conclusions can we draw from this?

First, emerging markets far from the source of the initial shock can be victims even though they are *innocent bystanders*. Because contagion is possible and even likely for EMs, the costs of capital market contagion could be major.

Second, *lemons are worse than rumors*. False rumors have a short life span (although false rumors may not fade so quickly when elections are impending). In contrast, the Lemon Problem is much harder to uproot. To stop this type of contagion, one or more steps may have to be taken. Specialists could reenter the market, but this is unlikely since it presupposes the Federal Reserve will restore EMs' paper liquidity. A new set of specialists could also step up to the plate and enter the market, but that is unlikely to occur fast enough to halt the contagion. Or the G7 could organize a massive bailout operation for EMs, which is also unlikely.

Third, regional financial coordination is required. EMs must realize that the risk of capital market contagion makes them interdependent. Therefore, they should devise ways to discourage individual countries from following risky financial policy. This can initially be implemented through existing free-trade blocs. If such mechanisms were in place, Brazil might not be running such a biased short-term maturity structure.

Finally, the G7 countries have a major role in stabilizing EMs. This is perhaps a good time to start thinking about a World Central Bank.

Guillermo A. Calvo is Distinguished University Professor of Economics at the University of Maryland, College Park.

References

Calvo, G. 1998. "Capital Flows and Capital Market Crises: The Simple Economics of Sudden Stops." In a forthcoming *Journal of Applied Economics.*

Calvo, G., and E. Mendoza. 1998. "Rational Herd Behavior and the Globalization of Securities Markets." Forthcoming in a National Bureau of Economic Research book edited by Sebastian Edwards.

Opening Remarks

Ricardo Hausmann

The idea for this seminar began in the aftermath of the East Asian crisis. We thought that its impact on Latin America was being channeled through very real mechanisms. Contraction in East Asia would lead economies there to lower their imports of Latin American goods and commodities. That decline in Latin American trade might deepen if East Asia became more competitive with our exports in third markets. What began as concern became, in fact, a source of significant impact.

Now we are seeing the consequences of the Russian crisis. One would expect the direct impact on Latin America to be minimal. After all, the Russian economy represents less than 1 percent of the world's gross domestic product (GDP), and Russia is not linked to Latin America in any particular way. None of its 30,000 nuclear weapons were pointed, the last time I checked, toward Latin America. One would not expect a major disruption of financial flows to the region, yet that has been the case. What has happened clearly shows a mechanism of transmission that can be aptly called a "financial contagion."

In organizing this seminar, it seemed reasonable to focus on three questions. What has caused this financial contagion? What can be done at the national level to prevent its spread or minimize its effects? What can be done at the international level? Three sets of papers and panels will respond: the first panel focusing on the sources of financial contagion; the second focusing on domestic policy options, and the final panel focusing on international policies.

I will open the discussion with a few general remarks. Latin America is integrated to world financial markets through a very specific channel. Most of the region is essentially noninvestment grade. We are dependent then on that relatively narrow segment of the world financial market that specializes in noninvestment-grade emerging markets.

That segment recently has received three major shocks to its capital base. First, it lost money in East Asia. Second, East Asia was downgraded, forcing people who can buy investment grade paper but not noninvestment paper (mainly pension funds, insurance companies) to dump their paper on the small set of participants who do buy. And finally, this segment lost money in Russia.

Having purchased a portfolio of diversified emerging markets when it had money, it had to sell a diversified portfolio of emerging markets to cover its losses. So the relevant question is not about what the fiscal sustainability of Mexico or of Argentina looks like, but what the balance sheet of J.P. Morgan or Goldman Sachs looks like. Because the latter have gotten into trouble, our access to financial markets has become problematic.

This is a pretty novel form of contagion. Steps the region can take to differentiate itself from other regions, and show its comparative value, are unlikely to be helpful because the people who have been selling Latin American paper are doing so with tears in their eyes. They would much prefer to hold onto the paper, but lack the capital base to do so. We are in a different ball game.

Obviously, given this context, G7 monetary policy is likely to be more effective. It is likely to have a bigger impact on the financial situation of those that got in trouble.

Ricardo Hausmann is Chief Economist of the Inter-American Development Bank.

Author's Remarks

Eduardo Fernández-Arias

My remarks will focus on the subject of financial contagion. There are three points to be covered. One concerns the evolution of risk spreads. That leads to the question of whether fundamentals or contagion are behind the present crisis. Since the answer is the latter, of course, the third area looks to the reasons for this contagion and its prospects.

I will start by tracking the evolution of spreads in Latin America over the last four years. One can see the Mexican crisis, the Asian episodes, the Russian crisis, the Brazilian jolt, and the present situation. Highly volatile, these episodes of crisis are very large events involving expected losses of up to 50 percent. Using the Emerging Markets Bond Indices (EMBI) throughout, risk spreads and bond prices have been highly correlated across regions and across the countries within our region at all points of the crisis cycle.

For the Mexican crisis, with bond price indices at 100 on the eve of the turmoil, all the Latin American countries simultaneously suffered falling prices during the crisis that followed. They also recovered together. The same is true for the recent crises, beginning with Hong Kong's shock on October 22, 1997. They all fell together, recovered somewhat, and hit a big slump with the

Russian crisis. Today's market finds them increasing in prices, again recovering simultaneously.

Can these phenomena be explained through fundamentals or not? I argue that they cannot. First, because country fundamentals change slowly, it is difficult to rationalize the volatility that has occurred. Second, the fundamentals tend to be diverse across countries while the volatility is closely correlated. The traditional mechanisms for explaining such correlation are either world fundamentals, for example, changes in world interest rates, or perhaps a crisis in one country spilling over to other countries through real channels like trade. But it has been well documented that these effects do not help or are not nearly strong enough to explain what we see. In the absence of any traditional explanation, this phenomenon can be given the name of "contagion."

But what accounts for this contagion? The first hypothesis, perhaps half jokingly, asks whether Wall Street is off the wall? This would be my mother's hypothesis, so I must take it seriously.

When the percentage fall in bond prices in each country is tracked for each crisis, we see that financial contagion is recurrent over time and is widespread across countries. However, countries also show different immunity levels to contagion. This means they suffered the disease to different degrees. The next step is to ask whether this differential immunity makes sense based on the markets' evaluation of potential crisis for these countries before crises actually occurred, as of June 1997, using credit ratings at the time. When countries are divided into high and low risks based on that market evaluation, and compared with their measure of vulnerability to contagion, there is almost a perfect match. Countries that have high risk also suffer more contagion. The same is true for less-risky countries, which are also less vulnerable. The only mismatches are Korea and Nigeria, and then only marginally.

This suggests a rationale for the way in which countries are affected by contagion. One can think of this contagion as being the realization of some of the risks that the market was anticipating beforehand. All countries have larger spreads and they differ more than they once did, but they maintain their relative valuations. This may be wrong, but at least the market is consistent with itself. We cannot reject the hypothesis that there is a consistent logic in the market.

I will close with four possible rational explanations for contagion, trying to encompass those that have emerged and gained a following. The first says that the market learns from one case and then generalizes to all emerging markets. There is a crisis in one country; that country is similar to other countries; its downgrading results in a downgrading of everybody. The Russian crisis, in particular, speaks to this. One may think that the Russian default or debt moratorium will make other defaults or moratoriums less costly and more likely, or at least that the likelihood will be greater in the minds of most investors. Or maybe the Russian crisis shows that an official rescue may not be there all the time to buffer the fall. That uncertainty again causes a downgrading for everyone. In each example, there is some learning from an experience that is generalized to the rest of the markets that are presumed to be similar. While this may very well be part of the story, it is difficult to reconcile with the global nature of financial turmoil, which includes mature markets, and with the fact that recovery is already under way.

A second explanation, which I will not fully elaborate, involves a simple meeting of minds. If all investors think at once of withdrawing, it will cause a crisis to materialize that would not otherwise happen. It is, in effect, a self-fulfilling prophecy. The presumption that crisis in one place acts as a focal point to shape expectations of what will happen elsewhere makes the likelihood of such a possibility occurring greater. That gets factored into the marketplace, providing another rational, if still unproven, explanation for contagion. One problem with this explanation is that, at least in its pure form, it is difficult to disprove empirically.

The third explanation is the herd mentality of managers. In actuality, managers are the people who move money and make investment decisions. To avoid being exposed as the only one who loses money, they tend to move in herds. If everyone is losing, each can plausibly argue the fault is no one's and escape punishment. That applies to a time like this, when it may be particularly risky to lose money in markets in which lots of money has been lost. So managers sell bonds along with the herd, even if the bonds are underpriced. The same herdlike behavior applies during booms, when eagerness to keep up with the earning curve may foster imprudence. This hypothesis, however, is better fit as a transmission mechanism than as a causal explanation.

The fourth explanation repeats what Ricardo Hausmann explained. The specialized groups that invest in noninvestment grade countries, such as those in Latin America, took a big hit in Russia, in many cases a *coup de grâce* after accumulated losses in other emerging markets. Capital losses put a constraint on the liquidity these groups have to invest in emerging markets, or constrain their portfolio allocations through a lower capacity to bear risks, leading to sell-offs at fire-sale prices that do not reflect country risk. In a market characterized by risks and limited channels of capital, contagion is easy. Market turmoil can be expected to be temporary as constraints ease and new channels are established to arbitrage the over-pricing of country risk.

Eduardo Fernández-Arias is Lead Research Economist, Office of the Chief Economist, Inter-American Development Bank.

Author's Remarks

Guillermo Calvo

I fully agree with the view expressed by Ricardo Hausmann and emphasized by Eduardo Fernández-Arias that we are facing a massive loss of financial liquidity. Explaining it is a key to unlocking the causes of the present crisis. Progress toward that understanding is being made, but the process is just beginning. The second key is deciphering how a financial crisis from loss of liquidity leads to recession. In our paper, Fernández-Arias and I call this process a "meltdown."

I begin my comments on the origins of the crisis by referring to the bond market, half-jokingly, as "sovereign junk bonds." The bond market, as everybody knows, was badly shaken by Russia's default. How can Russia, so far removed in so many ways, generate a tidal wave that hits Latin America? Think of Russia as a focal point, the site of a seismic shock that ripples outward and seems to gather force rather than diminish. How is this possible?

The leading explanation for this transmittal is contagion. Rumors multiply that other countries will soon follow suit. Another feature to this explanation points to the element of moral hazard. Because nobody expected the major powers to let Russia go so quickly, fear spreads that less visible countries like Brazil are even less protected. At the moment these rumors have proven unfounded, and personally, I find them unpersuasive. There are good grounds to believe they are going to be proven false. When that occurs, the present crisis should disappear.

But we are not there yet, and we need to send the right message to the public. Let us go out into the street and tell the world that our countries do not intend to let the drift continue. That would be enough to calm things. I suspect that what we face now is a market failure of some sort in the financial system. In the next sessions, we are going to be discussing policies for dealing with this. Before doing so, we must understand the context for action. If there is a market failure, one must realize that simply turning around and saying let's rely on the market to correct things will not work. That is why it is so important which explanation you buy.

I call this crisis the lemon problem because there is a line of explanation that does not have to do with the lack of knowledge. The first explanation offered is that people do not know, so they run from all markets. In fact a lot is known, but not a lot of people know it—the knowledge is confined to a few clusters of specialists. The reason is simply because countries are very costly to monitor. So you have small clusters of experts and a not-too-large group of people who rely on those experts for advice about whether or not to invest in a given country. The Russian shock tested the reputation of the experts, and people were not reassured. All of a sudden they lost money, a lot of money.

The specialists or those who consult them use leveraging for investment, because when you know better, you borrow more freely. The expectation is that this leveraging is sound. It is a natural outcome of an equilibrium, as economists say. So there is this leveraging, which the Russian shock exposes to sudden risk. There are margin calls, the collateral is too low, and one must liquidate. Is that a problem? Yes, in practice it is a problem. Everybody knows that it is a problem. The question is why *is* it a problem.

If we had perfect information or everybody had the same information, on average, then the groups that are forced to dump paper into the market would find an equivalent group that is willing to buy it from the market. Fundamentally, nothing happens.

So why doesn't that occur? The problem is that the group dumping the paper has to create liquidity. They cannot create liquidity from each other, but must sell to people who do not know the paper's value. That raises the lemon problem. A *lemon*, in the U.S., means a used car that does not work.

The situation gets even more complicated as it develops. In the first place, the seller has to dump his holding by selling it to people who know much less and will presumably take it if the price is low enough. But the buyer must wonder why the expert is willing to sell this used car now, and why at such a discount. Maybe he knows something I don't. So the tendency is to demand much deeper discounts. If buyer reluctance persists, these become fire-sale discounts. One sees how the lemon problem can be incendiary.

Is the market failure traceable to the devaluation of human capital that has taken place in the financial sector? Yes. The credibility of the experts is crucial. Can they go out to buyers and say, "let me explain, trust me"? Their reliability has been, at least momentarily, shattered. Would you turn to someone responsible for getting us into Russia and readily believe their assurances that the Argentinean paper they are now eagerly selling is really good? That, as they say, is a really tough sale.

If that were the end of the story, it would be only a matter of waiting a couple of weeks before we could get back to business. It is a matter of the uninformed becoming informed, getting themselves up to speed. There is lots of human capital there among potential buyers. They do not know about Argentina, but they have the training to learn about Argentina very quickly. Why shouldn't the market recover its footing on its own?

Here is the potential problem. The sudden jolt of *el frenazo* may lead to a meltdown, which is defined as a sharp fall in capital inflows. This is not necessarily because a region or its countries are being rationed, but because the marginal lender is uninformed. The informed person has a liquidity problem and is no longer a player. The uninformed are in charge and have to make a decision. This duality need not be expressed as two institutions, but can arise within an institution. A credit supervisor, for instance, may demand that a position be liquidated because he no longer trusts the people who had been managing it. As the uninformed take charge, interest rates in borrowing countries go up, the demand for loans falls, and there is a sharp contraction in capital inflows. This has a sharp effect on aggregate demand, by definition, and that falls on tradables and nontradables. The price of nontradables has to collapse. There is no need for inflexible prices to tell the story. Prices collapse.

But here is the problem. You may have flexible prices, but an inflexible financial system. We have a very primitive financial system for loans. The interest rate is given. It is not the function of a state of nature, where interest rates are high or low depending on the state of nature. Therefore, when prices fall, the *real* interest rate that the borrower has to pay could be enormous. But this raises a problem that preoccupied U.S. economist Irving Fisher in the 1930s, a problem that has been forgotten because we have not faced it for a number of years. This situation can generate bankruptcies, which make banks more cautious, setting off a chain reaction that soon produces a real effect.

Once that happens, as things sour, the fear of a possible lemon becomes a reality. People start reading that unemployment has increased to 13, 14, 15 percent and more. There are strikes. There are bankruptcies all over. In the immediate term, you have an economic lemon, and the market prices it accordingly. This is the main concern we face.

In sum, there is an international element that has solely to do with liquidity but that can be transmitted into a real shock for the domestic economy. There is nothing that individual countries can do about international elements. The real shock is a reflection of inflexibilities and, therefore, of market failure at home—of incomplete markets as an economist would say. We have to think very, very hard whether or not this is reason enough for governments to do something. I don't think that what might be right in the medium and long term under normal conditions—in effect, saying let the market solve the problem—is the right response because now we are facing a market failure.

Guillermo Calvo is Distinguished University Professor of Economics at the University of Maryland, College Park.

Comment

_____

Guillermo Perry

A host of questions have been presented about crisis prediction and prevention, about the nature of the current financial crisis. I will try to synthesize them into three major queries or propositions. First, this is not just an emerging market crisis but rather a global financial crisis. Second, it takes two to tango. Third, how much does domestic policy matter if the fundamentals did not cause the contagion?

A world crisis, by definition, has regional impact. Latin America, certainly, is suffering a crisis in the financial markets. Many Organization for Economic Cooperation and Development (OECD) investors and financial institutions have become either illiquid or insolvent. Some are suffering a credit crunch. A vicious circle is in motion: The credit crunch has raised fears of a global recession, amid symptoms of a sharp slowdown in world growth. These fears reinforce the credit crunch, leading to extreme risk aversion and preference for liquidity among investors. Spreads have increased for triple-A ratings, even more for nontriple-A U.S. corporate ratings, and even more for emerging market bonds; while U.S. Treasury rates are at a 30-year low, at least in nominal terms. As Ricardo Hausmann has noted, actions by G7 countries to dispel doubts about a global recession and to help Latin America bridge the present disarray of global financial markets may be every bit as important as the domestic policy responses of countries in the region. Another question to answer is how big an impact Japan has had in all of this, not only in limiting the recovery of East Asia but also in triggering the problem in the first place. The world might not have caught just Asian flu but Samurai pneumonia.

It takes two to tango. I think the crisis has revealed great flaws in the regulatory supervisory systems for financial markets in East Asia. It also has revealed major flaws in the regulatory and supervisory systems of OECD countries. Unregulated hedge funds led to excessive risks elsewhere as regulated OECD banks' exposure to hedge fund risks spilled over to affect their exposure in emerging markets. Even if it were true that emerging markets have to improve their financial institutions, it is probably even more important to improve international OECD rules for financial institutions to avoid repeating the crisis in the future.

In looking at the third question, we see that Latin American economies have been faced with both a current and capital account shock. These shocks may be temporary, but they are not very short-run. Countries have no alternative but to adjust; the shocks have affected the fundamentals. Current account deficits that were sustainable are not sustainable now. Real exchange rates that might have been in equilibrium are no longer so. Because Latin America lacks many policy options in the short run, it is important to highlight the need for a coordinated global policy response and a change in the international financial architecture.

Guillermo Perry is the World Bank's Chief Economist for Latin America.

Comment

Guillermo Ortiz

Guillermo Perry has noted that there are many questions that need fuller discussion. I will focus my comments on two points. The first one has to do with the origins of the crisis. A lot has already been said about it. Some of the solutions proposed today (namely changes in the architecture of the financial system) have to do with the diagnosis of financial crises. Knowing why they happen can give us a hint about how to cope with them. The second topic I will discuss is contagion, and I would like to share some reflections on where we stand today.

In terms of the causes of crisis, let me remind you that in the wake of the Mexican crisis there was a lot of soul searching in international financial organizations. Both the International Monetary Fund (IMF) and the World Bank produced several studies trying to explain why the Mexican crisis happened and why international financial institutions did not see the early warning signs of the turmoil soon to follow. There were fairly long discussions throughout 1995 in the international financial institutions, as well as in academic and research circles, and among bankers and institutional investors. One of the conclusions they reached was that there was insufficient information and a lack of transparency. As a result of that analysis, the IMF established the Special Data Dissemination Standards (SDDS), which were supposed to give further information to markets about developments in emerging economies. I understand that Korea, Indonesia, and Malaysia, among other countries, subscribed to the SDDS in 1996. Apparently, this was not sufficient.

Then the question is why did the Asian crisis occur after we were supposed to have learned the lessons from the Mexican crisis? Even though there are certain differences among the causes of the crises, there are a lot of common features within the Asian region, and between that region and Mexico.

One common feature was the tendency to have an overvalued exchange rate. For example, it was widely perceived that exchange rates were overvalued prior to the crises in Mexico, Thailand, and Korea. Other similarities include accumulation of short-term debts, massive capital inflows in the years prior to the crisis, and asset price inflation. All of this combined with weak financial systems that were unable to cope efficiently with the inflows and unable to transform them into productive investments.

In view of the similarities between the Mexican and the Asian crises, one wonders why the lessons from Mexico were not learned and why similar mistakes were repeated. I think, in the case of the Asia crisis, a lot of complacency prevailed. The record success of the Asian countries led investors to believe that they had found the magic formula for growing at 8 percent annually forever. The fact that exchange rates were fixed, and that it was believed they would remain fixed, produced very attractive yields in the presence of ample liquidity in world markets. Some observers have mentioned that Mexico recovered quickly and that it was able to tap international markets just a few months after the crisis. This probably helped to ease the minds of investors regarding emerging-market risk. All this leads to the issue of moral hazard.

Let me now turn briefly to the question of contagion. One may ask why contagion was avoided in the Mexican case. One important aspect in the case of Mexico was that the stage of denial was very short. Immediately after the devaluation of the peso, President Zedillo went to the Mexican people and told them in no uncertain terms that we were heading for very rough times and that strong adjustment measures were needed.

The second point was quick action. Seven weeks after the crisis erupted, we had an IMF program amounting to US$17 billion, and we had negotiated with the U.S. Treasury a financial package of US$20 billion. This came through after a larger financial package of US$40 billion had aborted in the early stages of Congressional discussion.

On the 21st of February 1995, I was sealing the deal and shaking hands with Secretary Rubin. That is exactly seven weeks after the crisis erupted.

Third, we took immediate steps to prevent the collapse of the financial sector. The financial sector played a central role in explaining both the Mexican crisis and the Asian one. Macroeconomic imbalances were not really the culprits in these crises. I think they were much more a financial crisis than a typical macro-disequilibrium situation.

Fourth, an important reason why contagion was avoided (only Argentina got hit by the Mexican crisis) was that in 1995 we were living in a benign world. The U.S. economy was growing strongly. This allowed Mexico to increase its exports rapidly and, thus, to get out of its economic contraction. In Asia, on the contrary, the Japanese economy, instead of helping to pull out the affected economies, has, in fact, represented a drag on the recovery of the whole region. It has contributed to a vicious circle that has led to further deterioration in conditions in Southeast Asian countries. Therefore, a big, big difference is the difficulties posed by Japanese stagnation.

The Russian situation is a completely different story. Guillermo Calvo has already mentioned that contagion in the Asian case was a type that initially had to do with evaluation of fundamentals. Once a country was hit, analysts searched to see whether other countries shared some of the similar fundamental weaknesses. Investors reevaluated their portfolios by comparing the economic fundamentals of different countries.

The whole picture changed completely with the Russian crisis. There was a discontinuity, a blip. The rules of the game were broken. It would be interesting to contrast two hypotheses: one dealing with the issue of moral hazard, the second with the so-called "lemon" problem. They are both interconnected in the sense that the second hypothesis goes much more into the detail of market structure and the human capital component of the problem.

In my opinion, the situation in Russia originated due to some sort of moral-hazard-type assessment. As I have said before, Russia was treated as the most important country after the G7 countries, and, in fact, attended the G7 meetings. There was widespread belief by the markets that Russia would not be allowed to "fail." However this belief is hard to reconcile with market developments prior to the crisis. If you look at interest rates and spreads on the Russian debt in the months prior to the crisis, you observe that the risk indicators were flashing high. Still, the Fund supported Russia with US$11.2 billion. It was a very important country in geopolitical terms. Markets believed that if something happened in Russia, at least there would be an orderly workout. This is an important point. When Russia defaulted, of course, it completely changed the rules of the game. You have already heard from other speakers how these events have contaminated Latin America and how they have already hurt U.S. financial institutions.

The crisis has come full circle: first Asia, then Russia, afterwards Latin America, then financial markets, and finally back to Asia. One of the problems now is that the Asian recovery is being pushed farther and farther away. With the new information we have, even in countries like Thailand and Korea that are doing well in terms of stabilization, which is the first part of getting back on their feet, the prospects for recovery have been pushed farther back.

This leads me to my final comments. I was planning to talk about the short-term prospects and the architecture of the financial system. However, I will skip the architecture because to get there, first we have to survive the short term. In order to be practical, immediate steps, which are known to us all, have to be taken. Because this is a crisis of confidence, confidence has to be built into the markets again. Toward this end, an increase in IMF capitalization is essential. We have high expectations that the U.S. Congress will approve the proposed quota increase in the near term. We are very happy about President Cardoso's clear mandate to continue with the kind of economic program that will promote market confidence and, over time, higher levels of well-being to the Brazilian people. That is another very, very important point. The markets will probably react favorably to that.

In addition, a movement to lower interest rates would certainly help to stabilize financial markets. After four days of meetings here in Washington, my impression is that there is a growing awareness of the graveness of the situation, and thus the need to move in a coordinated manner. I will end my comments by saying that the situation obviously looks very complicated, but there is ample understanding by all the actors on what the situation is and what needs to be done. As central bankers say, we have a feeling of cautious optimism.

Guillermo Ortiz is Governor of the Central Bank of Mexico.

Comment

Marcos Caramurú de Paiva

The general evidence, of course, about contagion is that it represents markets compensating themselves in new places for losses incurred somewhere else. It is a market reaction requiring a market response rather than some other kind of response. But the aftermath of the Russian crisis has put the issue in a new perspective. This shift in perceptions is the essence of many of the discussions taking place here. I will focus briefly on three main points, which are closely related to Guillermo Ortiz's previous remarks.

First, there is extreme fear that emerging market countries not in trouble are doomed to repeat the experience of those that are. After the Russian crisis, there was a general fear in the markets that Latin American and other countries would resort to unilateral debt workouts and impose or reimpose various state controls over their economies, as if a chain reaction were about to be set off.

Brazil felt the impact of this confusion very strongly in the association that was drawn between its internal debt and what happened with Russian T-bills (GKOs). The conventional wisdom was that the Russian situation could be easily repeated. Well, it could not occur under any circumstances in Brazil. Why? Because we have an internal debt market that has been working for 28 years. This internal debt market is basically in the hands of Brazilians. It is basically in mutual funds and pension funds that follow rules and cannot leave the markets easily or at all. The average internal maturity of debt, in fact, actually has increased rather than decreased since 1994. All of these factors made Brazil strikingly different from Russia. We, as well as the multilateral institutions, have a lot of work to do to show our houses are in order and to inform the markets better about the individualities of each economy.

The second brief point I want to make concerns the huge gap that has opened between Foreign Direct Investment (FDI) flows and prices in the secondary market of instruments by a number of emerging market countries. Companies in Latin America that had been able to borrow at reasonable spreads had their terms of market access changed considerably by the Russian crisis. They had to pay much higher rates or found the markets closed to them entirely, even though their operations had not changed and the fundamentals of the country in which they operate had not changed. FDI is an indicator of confidence and an indicator of market perception by long-term investors about a certain economy. It deserves more attention and should be integrated into any international discussion about contagion.

The third point to be made has to do with the absence within the multilateral institutions of a clear instrument, a clear product, to deal with contagion. One of the big gains of these meetings is the general recognition that there must be some kind of public sector action and some kind of action through the multilateral institutions to prevent a crisis from happening and limit the effects of contagion. We cannot live securely in a world in which these institutions are bystanders during a contagion.

We are very confident. There has been a change in perception by the multilateral institutions about how to deal with the contagion phenomenon. We have had very interesting and productive debates during the past few days, but there is still much to be done. In the next month or so, we undoubtedly are going to see action by the parties concerned—including Brazil definitely, the international organizations, and G7 and other leading countries—in a direction that will strengthen the possibilities of dealing with the phenomenon of contagion.

Marcos Caramurú de Paiva is Secretary for International Affairs in the Brazilian Ministry of Finance.

Comment

Ernest Stern

Discussion has focused on the financial turmoil affecting emerging market and transition economies—how it has started and spread, and the relative importance of economic fundamentals versus investor psychology. Gradually, the view has solidified and become accepted that the turmoil is global.

The world is at the end of a long period of sustained growth. Historically, booms lead to excesses—by consumers, lenders, investors, and borrowers. Eventually there is a correction. The global nature of the ongoing correction is a reflection of the virtually worldwide scope of the preceding boom. The recent deleveraging of the financial system is affecting asset values in all countries. For instance, the spreads on Brazilian bonds rose by 52 percent between June 30 and September 25, 1998; while the spreads on U.S. A-rated and B-rated corporates rose by 52 percent and 92 percent, respectively. The Bovespa Stock Index in São Paulo declined by 31 percent for the same period; the DAX in Germany by 23 percent.

There is another reflection of the general nature of the global deleveraging. The implied volatility of U.S. interest rate swaps had a correlation of 0.1 with the Emerging Market Bond Index (EMBI) in the two years prior to June 30, 1998; in August it was 0.9. The correlation between U.S.-asset-backed securities and the EMBI was 0.2 in the past two years; it also was 0.9 in August.

The crisis may have been triggered by the events in East Asia last year, but there are many contributing elements. These include the continued deceleration of growth of the Japanese economy; concerns about the overvaluation of the U.S. equity market; the implosion of Russia; the low prices for primary commodities, especially energy prices, which sharply reduced export prospects for a wide range of countries; and the failure of a highly leveraged fund. At every stage, uncertainty increased and investors began to search for greater security, moving out of major asset classes. Lenders reduced exposures; and as asset values declined, collateral and margin calls increased and further depressed asset values. The financial system, global in scope—with a much larger number of participating investors and borrowers, and a broader range of products—transmitted the effects of economic problems and amplified them.

What are the ramifications of this? First, I suppose all or virtually all of us believe that free capital movements will benefit both the users and providers of capital. This proposition is not based on the assumption that the system will behave flawlessly, or without costs due to disruptions, but because it is a more efficient allocator of capital over the long term. Those who have not been significantly affected by the current crisis, and who believe this is due to a more controlled environment, rarely calculate the inefficiency costs of their current systems. Assuredly these, too, are a large percentage of gross domestic product (GDP).

Markets are heavily influenced by perceptions, short-term analysis, rumors, and a herd instinct that is aggravated by the prevalence of benchmarks. In addition, we have today a large proportion of market participants who have not experienced crisis or prolonged downturns. So, yes, there are tendencies toward overreactions. But it would be a mistake to consider all market reactions as psychological, having no foundation in fundamentals. In part, these reactions are fueled by the collateral and margin requirements I mentioned earlier; in part, they reflect a heightened concern about the risks embedded in economic management issues.

This leads to my second point. Fundamentals are fundamental. The appetite for risk among investors will vary; but unless a borrower can demonstrate sound, sustained economic management, flexibility in light of changing circumstances, and a financial system that is moving toward international standards, access to markets will always be more difficult and the costs greater. When the world is on the down slope of a cycle, this becomes more pronounced.

It is not useful to try and isolate specific policy issues such as the exchange rate. There are many points of vulnerability, and most of the macroeconomic issues are linked. It is possible to have a fixed exchange rate or a currency board system—but each has costs. Investors need to be convinced that a country has the political will and the capacity to bear those costs.

Third, there has been a great deal of talk about transparency. The concept usually is understood as the need for better and more timely data. And that is important. Equally, however, I would emphasize the importance of contextual communications. Information needs to be digested and integrated in the decision-making process. Investor confidence is a particularly fragile thing in times of turbulence. Access to government officials and policymakers is an important ingredient in investor confidence. Guillermo Ortiz, in Mexico, built up a regular system of teleconferences with investors that were held in conjunction with data releases and special developments. The system has served Mexico well.

Fourth, markets are not consistent disciplinarians. They are by far too erratic and volatile for that. It would be a mistake to rely on them to provide detailed feedback on individual policy issues, particularly in a time of high liquidity. Judgments on risks are not absolutes—they are taken by credit managers and investors in the context of a specific economic and competitive situation. Spread volatility is likely to be high in times of crisis or looming problems, which may reflect perceived or real changes in country risk or changes in the global economy. Volatility, too, is not necessarily a reliable commentary on the economic policy framework. Policymakers and academics know that well enough—it is frequently pointed out—but when capital availability is easy and spreads are low, there is a tendency to believe the situation is rationally sound. Yet what is taken as confirmation of a good performance may simply be an excess of liquidity. There is, of course, a lesser tendency to equate scarce capital and rising spreads with poor performance.

From this dynamic flows an important conclusion—countries need to have more robust barriers against market behavior because investor assessment of the economic fundamentals will vary with external conditions. Appropriate measures would include minimizing dependence on debt, whether denominated in domestic or foreign currency; reserves measured in terms of capital volatility not trade flows; effective debt management to reduce risk; and a domestic banking and corporate sector that is not excessively leveraged. On the institutional side, it includes a well-supervised, robust banking system and a domestic capital market that can absorb shocks as well as provide instruments for hedging risks. One important lesson is not to underestimate the potential severity and speed of downside scenarios in this new high-tech environment.

Fifth, a commitment to free capital movements is not at odds with the need to focus more explicitly on ways to reduce the dependency on, and volatility of, short-term capital. Once we recognize that this is a systemic issue, we can move beyond the theological debate of capital controls versus prudential regulations. The attractiveness of short-term external debt to the borrower is a function of price—reflecting inefficiencies in the domestic financial market. For the providers of capital, its liquidity and mobility is of great value. That, too, has a price. So I believe that by focusing on measures that affect the price, we can deal with the issue short of comprehensive capital controls. This might involve early-withdrawal penalties, as in Chile, or other price-based mechanisms. We need to keep in mind that for most countries the combined assets of the banking system and the domestic capital markets are small in relation to the international flows of short-term capital.

Sixth, debtor countries need to appreciate better than they now do that official sector support will be limited, even after the IMF Quota increase is finally approved by the U.S. Congress. The bulk of these countries' external financing is coming, and will continue to come, through private, largely non-bank channels. In times of crisis, spreads increase—sometimes substantially. And unlike official institutions, with which the volume and price of support may be negotiable, private financial institutions do not control market spreads. There is a view among officials in the debtor countries, and sometimes among those in OECD countries, that the cost of capital is prohibitive in times of crisis and that, therefore, the market should not be used. This is misguided. If there is a sensible domestic program, flexibility to adjust it as circumstances change, and adequate implementation capacity, the spreads will decrease as the crisis wanes. One can either look at these costs as temporary and thus to be averaged out over time; or one can look to instruments, such as floating notes linked to spreads, in which costs will decline as market conditions improve.

In conclusion, it is important to keep the global context in mind throughout this process as countries of the region struggle with current market conditions and consider how to adjust their economic policies and restore investor confidence. The deleveraging of the global system has not yet run its course. Capital markets have not yet reopened for emerging market borrowers. Minimum steps that might serve under normal conditions will not suffice. And concerted action on a global scale by political and financial leaders is an essential supplement to national action, as Latin American ministers have been stressing during these past weeks.

Ernest Stern is Managing Director of J.P. Morgan.

Open Discussion

Guillermo Perry: The papers and respondents have given us much to think about. Is the crisis truly global, or still mainly one of emerging markets? We have the issue of capital-constrained investors and credit crunches. Guillermo Calvo has explained a particular market failure as a kind of asymmetric information of financial markets. Then, there are the effects of the Russian default; and the regional character of the Asian crisis, particularly the role of Japan. Finally, there is the role of public institutions, the effect that good institutions have on liquidity cushions in less-developed countries. With only limited time available for questions, let us begin immediately.

Judy Devans (from *Emerging Markets*)**:** Mr. Stern, you previously served for many years at the World Bank. After this crisis and the questioning of decision making at both the IMF and the Bank, do you think that these institutions can survive with the present leadership?

Ernest Stern: I was always a little puzzled while at the Bank, and I remain puzzled, about the common perception that the IMF and the World Bank are independent entities. They have major shareholders—the G7, G8, G12, G22, G47, and so on. There is no doubt that these two institutions will follow the policies that the major shareholders are prepared to support and, indeed, finance. It was a positive step when several weeks ago Latin American finance ministries proposed a new approach to contagion by establishment of a contingent facility that would allow the IMF to step in earlier. Progress is being made in this direction as the idea has attracted a fair amount of support from some of the major shareholders. Some details are still on the table and need to be thrashed out. The mechanics are not that difficult. The problem of changing major policies has always been, and continues to be, that the major shareholders are rarely in full agreement about what to do; and some of them are more averse than others to paying the bill for what has to be done. That impedes quick action. But I have no doubt that the managements of both institutions are perfectly capable of coming up with the ideas to implement the new authorities they may be getting.

Noel Sacasa (Nicaragua's Minister of Industry and Trade, and Chairman of the Board of the Superintendency of Banks)**:** I see three conclusions from what you have been presenting. One is that we have a very deep crisis of confidence by investors, which feeds on itself. This can cause a lot more damage than it has so far. And this investor behavior seems rational to me.

Confidence has been lost in specialists in emerging-market governments and in international institutions and in the domestic banking systems. This crisis of confidence would imply the possibility of bank failures not only in the emerging economies but also in the larger economies. And that would possibly do massive damage to liquidity worldwide. My question is, can we put a figure to the potential destruction of liquidity, which could endanger the world economy in a short period of time? Are there any realistic moves that the international community can take to counter that potential because recovering investor confidence is going to be a slow process that will not provide a solution in the short term?

Ernest Stern: Well, I don't know the exact total, but this week I heard somebody say that the disappearance of liquidity thus far is as if you had wiped out the economy of Canada. So, if that is anywhere near being right, there is no doubt that a serious liquidity crunch has taken place and is continuing.

There has been lots of discussion this week about easing monetary policy and about increasing fiscal expenditure. The problems with both of these remedies are numerous. One is that monetary authorities, particularly in the United States and Europe, have a very clear focus on their domestic inflation rate, which has become increasingly narrowly defined and now hovers somewhere around zero. Anything beyond that is perceived to be evil. So the prospects of substantial monetary easing is a little doubtful.

And on the fiscal side, everybody again in Europe and the U.S. has been dedicated for many years to restoring a balanced budget. The United States is now in budget surplus. In Europe, under the Maastricht criteria, budget deficits are shrinking. The political prospect of any of those countries deciding to increase demand—for the sake of what they still see as something occurring largely outside their own borders—is very dubious. In Japan, monetary policy has run its course. Interest rates are essentially zero. Fiscal policy stimulus, cutting taxes, has had no or very little effect on consumer confidence in spending. Therefore, the prospects for concerted action to increase liquidity are limited.

However, I wouldn't be so pessimistic about investor confidence. Investors have short memories. That is a very good thing. There is an increasing recognition that there are differences among countries, and that Latin American and East European countries are not going to follow the route of Russia. Here is another sign. J.P. Morgan took Swiss Telecom to the market over the weekend. It got the largest equity yield so far this year, in Switzerland, to be sure. But still, equity markets have been terribly depressed, and the offering was three times oversubscribed. I am quite confident that when Brazil has its program worked out and in place, it will by no means be impossible to take Brazil back to the market in a meaningful fashion. That is true for other countries. So liquidity size is important and prospects for official actions are limited. We should not give up hope that the markets will now function and that the emerging markets of countries in Latin America, and generally the good performers everywhere, can go back to the market within the next six months.

Marcos Caramurú de Paiva: I would like to make a very brief comment. I would approach this whole issue as if it were about the issue of financing for developing countries. That is what counts in the long run. Of course, developing countries will have to be able to accumulate savings and be more attractive to mature economies in order to finance their development. The most important phenomenon of the 1990s was that there was access to private financing from mature economies. I tend to believe that Ernie Stern is right, in the sense that markets do not have good memories. This is where the long-run source of financing for the developing economies will be. But during this transition period when there is a deep shortage of liquidity, what role can the multilateral institutions play to keep investments going forward in these economies, and especially to keep social investments going in areas where the private sector has no interest. These are the issues. Resources of the multilateral institutions must be used flexibly if our hope for a successful transition is to be realized. For example, the rules on disbursement by borrowing countries in order to qualify for possible multilateral financing could be adjusted. The goal of whatever policies were taken would be to restore the climate that prevailed in the early 1990s when the private sector actually financed development.

Guillermo Perry: Just one brief word about liquidity. I do not think anyone knows or is able to predict with certainty what the impact will be, because all of the information has not yet surfaced. Or if it has surfaced, it has yet to be analyzed properly. In the case of Brazil, for instance, one finds very different opinions—from those of informed Brazilians to some crazy economist's notions, vis-à-vis caps.

I agree, however, with the view that Latin America is very well positioned in the medium term. That is why whatever the G7 can do to help the area is a very, very good investment. We have seen a very deep financial deterioration of Asia. They are now going through a period of head-over-heels debt that is much like Latin America's experience in the 1980s. An Asian recovery seems unlikely, unfortunately, anytime soon. The problem is deeply rooted. As for Russia, nobody knows. But given the present information, one cannot be optimistic. A vast area of the world that either was receiving funds or about to do so is going to be totally shut off from capital influence. When one looks at the global numbers at the beginning of the Asia crisis, one sees a little widening of current account deficits in Latin America. But now it looks like the capital sources are going out of Latin America. The other place receiving funds was the U.S., which is reflected in its current account deterioration. That is where the funds have gone. U.S. interest rates are extremely low, however, and obviously not very attractive to investors. The moment the financial turmoil in Latin America subsides, funds must flow back to that region. One advantage of Latin America is that, on the whole, it has had a very poor growth record for many, many years, and countries have done their reforms. So it is perched to jump, ready to take off. I am very optimistic about that, although, of course, a bad transition can delay the process.

PART TWO

Domestic Policies for Crisis Prevention

Preventing Crisis and Contagion: Fiscal and Financial Dimensions*

Michael Gavin and Ricardo Hausmann

Recent economic developments highlight Latin America's vulnerability to economic and financial turmoil that is triggered by events in distant corners of the globe. The Asian financial crisis that began in 1997 and the more recent Russian crisis have left the region profoundly shaken, and living in fear of a full-scale collapse. As the papers presented in the first section of this book explain, this "contagion" has occurred through a number of channels. The collapse of Asian demand has contributed to a slide in world commodity prices, cutting income for a region dependent on commodity exports and undermining the public finances in a number of countries. The Russian devaluation has raised the spectre of sovereign default, making investors around the globe warier of increasing their cross-border exposure. And the financial crises in Asia and Russia have severely undermined balance sheets of emerging-market investors, reducing their capacity to invest in the region and forcing them into fire sales of their Latin American investments.

In this paper we lay out the fiscal and financial policies that can help protect economies from the kind of global financial turbulence the world is now experiencing. Exchange rate policies are discussed in a separate paper, which is included in the final section of this book.

Domestic Policy Makes a Difference

The crisis in which Latin America is now embroiled is a global one. The economic and financial strains that were generated by the Asian crisis that began last year, and that have intensified with the more recent Russian collapse, have spread seemingly without discrimination, leaving no region and indeed no major economy of the world unscathed. It seems not to have mattered whether the economic and financial fundamentals were sound or unsound. Most economies of Latin America do not suffer from the underlying

---

*An earlier version of this paper was delivered to the conference meeting in Washington, D.C., in October 1998 and formed the basis for the panel comments and open discussion that are included in Part II of this volume. The final section of the 1998 paper has been expanded substantially and is included in Part III of this volume.

weaknesses that brought down Thailand, Korea, or Russia, yet the entire region suffered a collapse in asset prices as investors have fled, and international financial markets are essentially closed for all of the region's borrowers. In light of this, it might well be asked—Is there any real point in discussing domestic policies other than, perhaps, those that seek to completely isolate the economy from the vagaries of the international financial system?

Although sound domestic policies have not insulated Latin American economies from the current international financial turmoil, it would be a mistake to conclude that policies are utterly irrelevant. Even if financial markets were completely undiscriminating, treating well- and poorly managed countries identically, the impact of the financial disruption on the local economy will depend upon the domestic policy regime.

Furthermore, though they have seemed to act indiscriminately during periods of extreme turbulence, financial markets do seem to discriminate between countries on the basis of macroeconomic fundamentals once the panic begins to subside. There is some evidence for this in Figure 1. There, the September 29, 1998, yield on countries' long-term dollar debt is plotted against an estimate of the countries' overall fiscal balance in 1998, measured as a share of gross domestic product (GDP).[1]

Figure 1. International Bond Yields and the Fiscal Balance

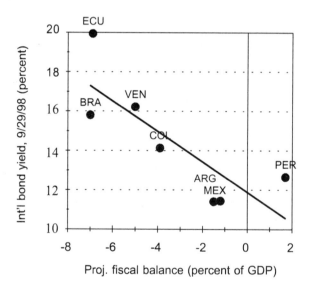

[1] Recently issued global bonds that mature in either 2026 or 2027 were used except for Ecuador and Peru, for which only Brady bonds were available. This may help explain why yields for Ecuador and Peru were higher than would have been expected on the basis of fiscal outcomes.

A strong negative correlation is shown between the fiscal balance, which is an imperfect but relevant indicator of the strength of domestic policy fundamentals, and the bond yield. The relationship suggests a significant payoff to sound fiscal policies: While a balanced budget is associated with an international bond yield of about 12 percent, a deficit of 6 percent of GDP is associated with a yield of over 16 percent.

None of this is to suggest that fundamentals such as the fiscal policy stance explain all, or even most, of the contraction in international credit that now afflicts Latin America as a whole. After all, the region's fiscal and other fundamentals were much the same in, say, July of 1998 as they were in August and September. But, whereas asset prices were relatively high and the markets were open for the region in July, bond yields skyrocketed and the financial markets slammed shut for the region in August. However, Figure 1 supports the idea that, as markets return to some semblance of normality, countries with better economic fundamentals will be among the first to return to the market, and will therefore be better placed to avoid major economic disruption.

Three Objectives for Policy

There are a number of policy arenas in which policymakers must act and dozens of decisions—some large and others small—that affect an economy's vulnerability to crisis. Each decision involves a different set of difficult analytical issues, and different economic and political tradeoffs. But despite these complications and this heterogeneity, we can organize our thoughts more effectively by evaluating policy alternatives in terms of three broad policy objectives: (1) Be solvent, (2) be liquid, and (3) inspire confidence. Often these imperatives involve no tradeoffs but are instead mutually reinforcing. For example, fiscal reforms that reinforce the public sector's solvency are likely also to inspire greater confidence about prospects for the economy. However in other contexts there may be difficult tradeoffs, such as those discussed below.

1. Be solvent. The first of the three imperatives is also the most fundamental. If policies imply insolvency or—in terms more appropriate for some contexts—are not sustainable, then liquidity can do no more than postpone the inevitable. And it goes almost without saying that insolvency precludes confidence. The important point here is that, in the volatile economic and financial environment that faces Latin America, solvency has as much to do with what *might* happen as what is *expected* to happen. That is, protecting an economy from financial contagion requires more than solvency under existing or normal circumstances; it is also important to be solvent under the more difficult circumstances that may very well be down the road if the world financial system comes under unexpected stress.

2. Be liquid. Solvency, or "sustainability," is essential but it is not enough. It cannot be assumed that international financial markets will always be available for individuals, businesses, or countries that are solvent. As is now on vivid display in every corner of the globe, financial markets occasionally seize up and credit vanishes for reasons that have nothing to do with borrowers' actions or circumstances. When this happens, those borrowers who rely upon the normal operation of financial markets need to have alternative ways to finance themselves if they are to avoid a disruptive payments crisis. They need sources of liquidity to ensure that they can roll over their debt and finance their deficits during these temporary interruptions of access to financial markets.

Coping with these liquidity shocks is a particularly important challenge for the economies of Latin America, and should be a key consideration in all dimensions of policymaking. For various reasons, including most notably their vulnerability to external shocks, public and private borrowers from the region are considered risky; and only a few countries of the region have investment-grade ratings. Because of regulatory structures in the industrial countries, this leaves Latin American borrowers (and borrowers in emerging market economies around the world) reliant on a relatively narrow range of potential investors who are themselves highly vulnerable to portfolio shocks in other regions of the world. Thus it was not a fundamental reassessment of Latin American risk that caused emerging-market investors in the North to conduct a fire sale of assets in, and interrupt normal credit flows to, the region, but the need to raise capital quickly to cover their portfolio losses in Asia and Russia. Consequently, even while fears about the region's stability are low, an interruption of credit can occur, carrying with it the danger of capsizing those economies lacking sources of liquidity sufficient to ride out a potentially prolonged period of global financial turbulence.

3. Inspire confidence. It is almost always far easier to maintain a stable macroeconomic and financial environment when there is confidence in the credibility of the fiscal and monetary policy framework, and in the robustness of the domestic financial system. In fact, all economies are at least theoretically vulnerable to confidence crises, if only because financial crises can so easily be self-fulfilling. Even the best-run bank would be brought down if depositors lost confidence in the institution and ran. Similarly, even sound and conservatively managed economies would find themselves in a crisis if, for some reason, holders of the public debt lost confidence in the government's ability or willingness to repay and refused to roll the debt over.

Confidence also is essential in other less-extreme but no-less-relevant circumstances. It is, for example, well understood that the inflationary costs of a move in the exchange rate or other inflationary shocks depend upon the credibility of government promises not to accommodate wage inflation. To raise another example that will be discussed in some detail below, we all understand that there are very good reasons to allow the budget to move into deficit during recessions. But financial markets will finance such deficits only if market participants have confidence that when the recession disappears, the government will be able to generate the fiscal surpluses that are required to service the higher public debt.

What is required to inspire the confidence needed to maintain economic stability in a volatile environment? Certainly the solvency or sustainability of the current policy stance and sufficient liquidity to survive periods of international financial turbulence are essential. Yet they may not be sufficient. The public needs to worry not only about current but also future policies; and if the right institutional framework is not in place, policymakers have no way to commit themselves (much less future policymakers) to a given course of action. This means that policy actions and institutional structures need to be established with an eye toward inspiring confidence tomorrow, as well as ensuring solvency and liquidity today.

Arenas for Policy Action

These general objectives must guide action in two key arenas in which policymakers must make decisions: fiscal policy and policies toward the financial system. This paper will concentrate on these two policy arenas, leaving exchange rate policy for separate discussion in the context of transnational remedies discussed in the concluding section of this book (see Hausmann, Gavin, Pages-Serra, and Stein, 1999). While this may exclude some relevant areas of domestic policy action here, it allows us to cover most of the key decisions and to highlight the ways in which decisions may affect solvency, liquidity, and confidence. In Table 1, we summarize the discussion that follows, highlighting the solvency, liquidity, and confidence problems that need to be addressed in each area and how they might be resolved.

The Fisc

Although both the Tequila crisis of 1995 and the ongoing crisis in Asia demonstrate that a responsible fiscal policy is no guarantee of economic stability, few would deny that incautious fiscal policies increase vulnerability and, if carried too far, can become an independent source of economic instability. The most obvious problems arise from insolvency, when fiscal imbalances are large enough to generate doubts about the public sector's actual or prospective capacity to repay the debts implied by current and anticipated future imbalances. When these doubts become severe enough, financing for the deficits vanishes and the government is forced into either a fiscal adjustment or inflationary finance.

Table 1. Overview of Policies to Promote Economic and Financial Stability

	Be Solvent	Be Liquid	Inspire Confidence
The Fisc	**Problem:** Precarious access to noninflation-ary sources of financing creates the need for a large and destabilizing fiscal adjustment during bad times. **Response:** Run a precautionary fiscal surplus in good times. Introduce fiscal rules or stabilization mecha-nisms to cope with large fiscal shocks.	**Problem:** Need to refinance existing debt stock creates "rollover risk" if financial markets disappear. **Response:** Issue debt well in anticipation of cash flow needs, especially around the time of elections. Avoid short-term debt. If necessary to extend the maturity of the debt, and if the public sector is solvent, issue indexed debt.	**Problem:** Inability to credibly commit to future surplus under-mines confidence in medium-term fiscal viability. Danger of self-fulfilling inflationary expectations. **Response:** Institutional reforms to buttress credibility of medium-term fiscal management.
The Banks	**Problem:** A volatile macroeconomic environment poses major threats to bank solvency. Large capital inflows may generate bank-lending booms that lead to impaired balance sheets and a vulnerable financial system. A weak information base and limited regulatory capacity undermine the effectiveness of bank supervision and regulation. **Response:** Impose capital requirements for credit risk appropriate for the volatile economic and financial environ-ment. Institute mechanisms to promote market-based discipline over banks. Internation-alize the financial system.	**Problem:** Volatile money demand creates large liquidity shocks for banks. **Response:** Substantial (and actively managed) liquidity requirements for banks, held in the form of foreign currency (or backed by a high level of international reserves). Discourage intermediation of short-term capital inflows. Encourage development of international standby credit facilities. Internationalize the banking system.	**Problem:** Lack of confidence and limited information create the potential for self-fulfilling panics. **Response:** Create adequate financial safety nets. Promote transpar-ency in the domestic banking system.

But this extreme situation of insolvency is not the only, or even the most important, challenge faced by Latin American governments, almost all of which have debts and deficits that are manageable now, and are perceived to continue being so in normal times. Problems arise during bad economic times, when the economy decelerates, fiscal revenues decline, and a previously manageable deficit begins to grow. It is widely understood that such an increase in the fiscal deficit is stabilizing and desirable as long as the bad times are expected to be transitory. And if holders of the government's debt had confidence that these transitory deficits would be followed by surpluses sufficiently large to service the implied debt, all would be well. Unfortunately this confidence is often lacking because policymakers cannot commit themselves (or future governments) to running the requisite future surpluses. As a result, noninflationary finance often vanishes just when it is most needed, and governments are forced into highly destabilizing fiscal contractions just when a more stabilizing fiscal policy would be most valuable.[2] The interaction of solvency and confidence problems thus generates a highly destabilizing fiscal response to adverse economic shocks.

Liquidity concerns pose an additional challenge to fiscal policymaking. No matter how small the fiscal deficit, any government with an outstanding stock of debt needs to roll it over as it matures. The amount that needs to be rolled is normally large, in the sense that generating a fiscal surplus sufficient to redeem the debt as it comes due would be economically and socially difficult and often politically impossible. This makes even solvent governments highly reliant upon the normal operation of financial markets. But as we have seen, the financial markets available to Latin American governments are not completely reliable, and have in recent years suffered periodic breakdowns that result in temporary closure of access to credit. Unless governments of the region plan for these episodes, they may find themselves forced to take highly disruptive, emergency fiscal measures; and even these may fail to generate the resources required to redeem the debt that cannot be rolled over.

How can the region's governments address these problems? To promote solvency, governments can do at least three things:

• *Run very small deficits or precautionary fiscal surpluses during normal times.* These reduce the precariousness of the region's access to credit by lowering, over time, the public debt and thus improving over time the public sector's perceived capacity to run deficits during bad times. More immediately, a precautionary fiscal surplus provides a fiscal cushion so that the bud-

[2] Gavin, Hausmann, Perotti, and Stein (1996), and Gavin and Hausmann (1997) provide evidence that (in sharp contrast to the industrial economies) fiscal policy has been highly procyclical in Latin America, particularly during "bad times" (roughly speaking, recessions).

get can absorb an adverse economic shock without generating a deficit large enough to be perceived as threatening.[3]

• Because these surpluses are difficult to sustain in a competitive political environment in which fiscal decision making is plagued by the well-known traps associated with the process of social choice, it may be desirable to *develop appropriate rules for the conduct of fiscal policy.* The logical basis for such rules is the same as the case for an independent central bank or for autonomous regulatory authorities. The distortions inherent in the process of collective choice about aggregate spending or borrowing decisions imply that outcomes can be systematically improved if participants in the decision-making process agree ahead of time to bind themselves to a set of rules.[4] Simple balanced-budget rules are highly inappropriate for the region since they essentially would legislate the procyclicity that we seek to eliminate. But rules expressed in terms of a fiscal balance that is adjusted for the "cycle," or other economic factors such as a key commodity price, may improve matters.

• Where the public finances are highly reliant upon certain key commodity prices, governments can also *develop well-designed fiscal stabilization funds,* which combine a fiscal rule for spending commodity-based income with an investment policy for the excess portion of actual commodity-based revenue above what is spent in a given year. Once it has accumulated a sufficiently large balance, the stabilization fund not only promotes solvency, but also provides a stock of liquid assets for handling liquidity problems created by a temporary loss of access to financial markets. Stabilization funds can also be complemented with policies to *use financial markets to insulate the budget from fluctuations in commodity prices.* While financial markets as they now stand provide only limited protection, this is no reason not to take advantage of what protection is offered.

As we have noted, solvency is a necessary but not a sufficient condition to prevent crises. Even solvent governments can experience liquidity problems, either because of an unjustified (but self-fulfilling) panic or because international financial markets temporarily freeze up for reasons completely unrelated to the country involved. This means that a government trying to decrease its national economy's vulnerability to financial shocks should concern itself with liquidity as well as solvency. Potential responses to this objective include:

---

[3]Gavin and Perotti (1997) provide evidence that Latin American countries that entered a period with a relatively small fiscal deficit tended to exhibit less procyclicity than countries that entered the period with relatively high deficits.

[4]Eichengreen, Hausmann, and von Hagen (1996) discuss in detail the distortions inherent in collective decision making about fiscal policy and explain why imposing some constraints on the process may improve outcomes.

- *Avoid short-term debt.* Of course, this is easier said than done when economies come under stress and the market for medium- and long-term public debt begins to evaporate. Under these conditions, there is a strong case for indexing or dollarizing the public debt if that permits governments to issue longer-term debt, and thus reduce rollover risk, and *if* the public sector is solvent. If the public sector is not solvent, then issuing indexed debt merely postpones the inevitable adjustment, and will make the adjustment much more expensive when resolution of the unsustainable fiscal position involves, as it often does, a major move of the exchange rate, prices, and interest rates.

- *Issue debt in advance of cash flow needs,* even if this means paying a significant difference between the cost of borrowing and the return that can be earned on deposits. Insurance is never free, but the security that is provided when the public sector's cash flows are covered for several months may prove invaluable if financial markets vanish. This insurance policy is particularly crucial around the time of elections, which have tended to be problematic periods for fiscal policymakers since their access to financial markets may be reduced until the nature of the future government is ascertained.

- *Seek contingent sources of credit.* Last year the Mexican Government entered into an agreement with 33 international banks that committed them to provide the government with a total of roughly US$2.7 billion should the financial environment deteriorate for Mexico. Recently the government drew upon that line of credit. The banks involved were somewhat dismayed, but the experience shows that insurance policies against international liquidity crises can be purchased in the market, at least in limited quantities.

Finally, fiscal policymakers need to inspire confidence. Achieving solvency and ensuring adequate liquidity will obviously go far; however they may still fall short because investors need to be confident not only that the current fiscal stance is adequate, but that future fiscal policies will adequately service the debt the government is trying to issue. It is difficult for governments to create this confidence, if only because they cannot commit the actions of future governments. Thus to increase confidence in the nation's fiscal stance, it may be desirable to:

- *Implement institutional reforms to buttress confidence in fiscal management over the medium term.* Fiscal rules are one way to do this. But confidence can also be created through reforms of the budgetary process that provide for greater transparency and that ensure the budgetary debate will not be skewed by unclear or flawed assumptions or by misleading fiscal accounting. Policymakers could think about going further, and create an autonomous scorekeeping institution with responsibility for ensuring adequate fiscal accounting, forecasting fiscal developments under alternative policy assumptions, and perhaps making recommendations about the appropriate fiscal stance.

The Banks

It is only a slight overstatement to say that, during the 1990s, the conventional wisdom shifted from "It's mostly fiscal" to "It's mostly financial." We have learned that fragile banking systems can act as powerful amplifiers of external shocks. And because domestic banks are an important interface between the international financial system and the domestic economy, the banking system is particularly exposed to international financial turbulence.

When the banking system is fragile, an economic or financial shock can lead to a loss of confidence in its stability, prompting a disruptive flight from the system. A robust banking system is thus built upon the same three pillars discussed earlier: solvency, liquidity, and confidence. Policy choices are somewhat more complex than in the case of fiscal policy because policymakers' influence in these three areas is more indirect. There is, nonetheless, much that can be done.

Solvency of the banking system is a concern because the volatile macroeconomic environment in which Latin American banks must operate creates major shocks to the profitability of banks' borrowers, and therefore the quality of the banks' portfolios. Here it is worth noting that banks do not benefit when their borrowers experience a positive shock because, for the most part, banks make loans rather than equity investments; but banks do lose when their borrowers experience an adverse shock large enough to result in default. However solvency can also be threatened by good times, such as when a surge of capital inflows is intermediated by the banks, creating a lending boom that results in impaired balance sheets and a vulnerable financial system.[5] Finally, ensuring that banks remain solvent is more difficult in Latin America because supervisors must work with a weaker information base, and the scarcity of relevant skills undermines the effectiveness of bank supervision and regulation. What can governments do to ensure that banks are solvent, and will remain solvent even after the economy is hit by a significant shock? They can:

• *Counteract bank-lending booms* by "leaning against the wind" with countercyclical liquidity requirements.

• *Impose significantly higher capital adequacy ratios than may be appropriate for banks located in less volatile environments.* The 8 percent capital adequacy ratio that was enshrined in the Basle Accord was designed for major, internationally active banks operating in industrial economies. Banks operating in highly volatile environments like Latin America need more capital; luckily this is being recognized in many countries of the region. Argentina's

---

[5]Gavin and Hausmann (1996) argue that bank-lending booms have preceded every major banking crisis in Latin America and the industrial countries, and provide reasons why the lending booms contributed to the subsequent crises.

requirement of 11 percent, for instance, is more attuned to the economic and financial environment in which that country's banks must operate.

• *Institute mechanisms to promote market discipline of domestic banks.* Market discipline is no cure-all; but in an environment that is relatively information-poor, it is particularly useful to complement official supervision with the efforts of informed investors who have a financial stake in the bank's soundness. The requirement that a significant portion of a domestic bank's capital base be in the form of subordinated debt is particularly useful since this structure creates a set of informed investors with an incentive to monitor bank behavior in order to protect their own holdings. This in-built alarm mechanism adds an informal watchdog to the formal watchdogs of the official regulatory apparatus.

• *Internationalize the domestic banking system.* Banking firms are national not because national borders define natural market limits but because national authorities have granted bank charters in order to regulate in-country activities. Internationally active banks promote robustness because they are diversified geographically, which makes them less vulnerable to country-specific macroeconomic and financial shocks. When they are hit by such a shock, local branches or subsidiaries of major international banks have access to the parent company's stock of capital. Furthermore, international banks from well-supervised financial systems with well-functioning capital markets bring supervisory efforts of the world's most effective regulators, and the market discipline imposed by the world's most demanding capital markets.[6]

Promoting solvency, however, is not sufficient to protect the domestic financial system. Banks are preeminently vulnerable to liquidity crises that are generated by runs by their depositors, or by reserve outflows associated with an interruption of international capital flows during a temporary breakdown of the international financial system. Liquidity shortages caused by these events may force banks abruptly and unexpectedly to contract credit, putting both their borrowers and the economy under strain, and eventually undermining the stability of the financial system.

In the relatively tranquil economic and financial environment of the industrial countries, where official safety nets are relatively broad and strong, such runs have become a subject of interest mainly to economic historians. If bank reserve or liquidity requirements are thought of at all, they are considered mainly as tools to improve monetary control. But in the more volatile Latin American context, the risks of systemic bank illiquidity are much more real and are far more difficult to handle. In the event of a run on a banking system, depositors are likely to avoid domestic currency and flee into a foreign currency, which the national authority cannot devalue by printing more money.

---

[6] Gavin and Hausmann (1997) discuss these ideas at substantially greater length.

How can authorities minimize the risks of systemic illiquidity in the banking system? They can:

• *Build bank liquidity requirements as an essential element of the prudential regulatory framework*, whether they are needed for purposes of monetary control or not. Where the volatility of the demand for bank deposits is high, liquidity requirements should also be high. And to prevent these requirements from unnecessarily raising the cost of credit, they should be remunerated. A substantial portion of the reserves should be in the form of liquid foreign currency assets that can satisfy the sudden demand for international liquidity in the event of a shock.

• *Discourage intermediation of short-term capital inflows* by requiring that banks hold substantial reserves against all of their short-term liabilities, foreign and domestic. If international deposits are more volatile than domestic, they should attract higher reserve requirements.

• *Encourage the development of international standby credit facilities.* Although there is no true international lender of last resort, the banking system can protect itself from the danger of systemic liquidity crises by entering into contracts with private international lenders that provide a source of contingent credit in the event of a liquidity crunch in the domestic banking system. The Argentine Contingent Repo Program, for instance, gives the Central Bank the right to obtain short-term credit from a collection of 13 international banks in the event of a liquidity crisis like the one that hit the country in 1995. It is an innovative example of how markets can be utilized to protect the financial system from liquidity shocks. Such programs need not be limited to the central bank but could also be extended to domestic banking institutions.

Finally, the domestic banking system needs to inspire confidence. Solvency and liquidity are essential elements, but they may not be enough since a bank run can bring down even the most prudently run banking institution. To promote confidence in domestic banks, governments can also:

• *Promote transparency* by setting high standards for bank disclosure and working with the private sector to improve accounting standards.

• *Create adequate safety nets* so that small depositors will be relieved of worries about the safety of their deposits and be less likely to flee on the basis of vague anxieties or wild rumors. Certainly such safety nets create potential problems of moral hazard, which must be controlled through a prudential regulatory and supervisory framework. But in our view the costs of such moral hazard are easily overstated and are almost certainly very small compared with the costs of a bank run that could have been prevented.

Michael Gavin is the Director of Economic Research for Latin America at Warburg Dillon Read; Ricardo Hausmann is Chief Economist at the Inter-American Development Bank.

References

Eichengreen, B., R. Hausmann, and J. von Hagen. 1996. La Reforma de las instituciones presupuestarias: Argumentos a favor de un consejo nacional de asuntos fiscales.Washington, D.C., Inter-American Development Bank, Office of the Chief Economist, Mimeographed document.

Gavin, M., and R. Hausmann. 1996. "Securing Stability and Growth in a Shock Prone Region: The Policy Challenge for Latin America." Working Paper 315. Washington, D.C.: Inter-American Development Bank, Office of the Chief Economist.

——. 1997. "Make or Buy? Approaches to Financial Market Integration." Working Paper 337. Washington, D.C.: Inter-American Development Bank, Office of the Chief Economist.

Gavin, M., R. Hausmann, R. Perotti, and E. Talvi. 1996. "Managing Fiscal Policy in Latin America and the Caribbean: Volatility, Procyclicality, and Limited Creditworthiness." Working Paper 326. Washington, D.C.: Inter-American Development Bank, Office of the Chief Economist.

Hausmann, R., M. Gavin, C. Pages-Serra, and E. Stein. 1999. "Financial Turmoil and the Choice of Exchange Rate Regime." Paper presented at the Inter-American Development Bank seminar New Initiatives to Tackle Financial Turmoil. Paris: France.

Comment

_____

Carlos Massad

Why waste time discussing what measures should be taken to avoid an economic crisis that is already upon us? It is very difficult to define a coherent set of policies to face a crisis without considering the starting point. It is fundamental for our analysis to know about banking system strength, public finances, and the balance of external payments. So let me focus my remarks on two areas, briefly touching a few points that seem relevant in light of the Chilean experience.

First, the composition of external liabilities does matter. A composition too geared to the short run will increase the potential volatility of financial resources, and may result in higher financing costs. Relying on short-term financing also affects the credibility of economic policies, limiting the range of options available to monetary authorities. Emphasizing long-term external financing may provide substantially more elbowroom for central bank and fiscal authorities to influence domestic macroeconomic and financial conditions.

The instrument that we have used in Chile is a mandatory, noninterest-bearing, one-year, dollar-denominated deposit in the Chilean Central Bank. Under this system, all capital inflows, except for direct investment and a few other flows, were subject to the mandatory deposit, without regard to the maturity of the inflow. The one-year requirement has an implicit financial cost that becomes lower as the inflow maturity increases, making external financing based on repetitive short-term inflows very expensive. As a result, short-term debt went from about 18 percent of total debt in the early 1990s to about 4 percent in the late 1990s. Use of this instrument allowed us to change the structure of maturities in Chile's foreign debt toward the longer end of the market.

The instrument was necessary when external financing was excessive, but not when external financing dries up. So it has been used like an umbrella: When too much external capital rained into the Chilean economy, we opened the umbrella to protect the economy from excessive financing and to divert the flow of water toward the driest areas. Now that the rain has stopped, we decided a few weeks ago to close, snap shut, and put away the umbrella. Some people have asked why, since this will facilitate short-term inflows. My answer is that when you close your umbrella after the rain, you are not calling for more rain. That is exactly how we look at it. At this time, the cost of financing has already increased and we don't need to make it even more expensive for Chilean borrowers. The system is useful when you have short-term inflows of capital larger than those that the economy might be able to digest prudently.

Additionally, the one-year mandatory deposit instrument has resulted in a composition of liabilities heavily weighted toward direct foreign investment. Indeed, at the beginning of the 1990s, approximately 25 percent of foreign capital inflows were in the form of direct investment, while 75 percent represented borrowing. Currently, the composition has been reversed: Between 78 and 80 percent of inflows are foreign direct investment, while 20 percent or less come from borrowing.

During this year, capital inflows other than direct investment have diminished, and seem to have fallen substantially below the level that would have been possible without the mandatory deposit requirement. Direct investment inflows, meanwhile, have increased significantly. Some theorists, relying on a handful of limited empirical studies, can argue that the substitution between different types of flows is not perfect, and that changing the composition of inflows also affects the sum total. Yet the highest total is not always best because the positive and negative impact of inflows varies by type. Different flows do not have the same characteristics: From the point of view of stability, permanency, and long-term commitment to the economy, foreign direct investment is not the same as borrowing. The current composition of liabilities gives the Central Bank much more elbowroom to apply domestic policies.

The second point that I would like to make is that the fiscal position has also been very important for the Chilean success. Chile's strong fiscal position, with sizable surpluses in the public sector balance for about 12 years in a row, should not be forgotten. Moreover, the surplus position will be maintained during this year and 1999, the years of the international financial crisis. And it will probably continue after that, but such projections are beyond our scope since the Chilean Congress approves the public budget annually.

The surplus in the public sector account implies that the Chilean government has not needed to borrow in domestic or external financial markets. Indeed, quite the opposite has happened, and public debt has been reduced to a very low level. This, in turn, permits the Central Bank to increase domestic interest rates in order to cool down the economy, as we have been doing this year, without having an impact on the fiscal deficit. In other words, high interest rates do not increase the fiscal deficit; and as a consequence, the monetary policy becomes more credible and may be more permanent. This is true also from the point of view of the banking system. Indeed, our banking system is very strong and well financed. I will give just one figure to indicate that: Nonperforming loans are 1.2 percent of total loans, compared to something like 8 percent, on average, in Latin America and over 20 percent in Asia.

The Central Bank has room to maintain high interest rates for a longer period of time due to the quality of banks' loan portfolios.

All these structural conditions have given Chile a wide range of policy alternatives in responding to the present crisis. During this year we have combined a very tight monetary policy, increasing interest rates to relatively high levels; and a moderately tighter fiscal policy, in the context of a managed float for the exchange rate.

As for exchange rate systems, our experience shows that there is no single recipe. The important issues are the fundamentals and consistency among exchange rate policy, fiscal policy, and interest rate policy. As long as there is consistency in the set of policies, the choice is almost open.

In our case, we have chosen a managed float within a band. The band was widened over time and became almost like a free float. Then, when speculative positions against the peso were increased, we decided to narrow the band, contrary to some theoretical recommendations. If you maintain very wide bands during a highly speculative period and the exchange rate is expected to move only in one way, it is likely that speculators will have a field day, and the value of the currency may over- or undershoot its equilibrium position. Then, in response to the speculative pressure, and as a way to make a clear statement about the policymakers' intentions, we narrowed the exchange-rate band and increased interest rates sufficiently to discourage speculation and avoid undershooting the peso. On September 16, when evidence showed that speculation had been defeated, the band was widened again, but to a lesser extent and gradually.

The kind of policies that one may implement—fiscal, monetary, exchange rate—hinges on where the starting position is, in terms of the economic fundamentals.

In Chile, given our fundamentals, the main channel of crisis transmission has been trade rather than capital markets or capital movements. Indeed, we have been mainly affected by a deterioration in the terms of trade that has translated into a sizable loss in national income and a widening in the current account deficit. On the capital account side, the effects have been less significant, in part because we had taken some preventive measures so that the shock was partially absorbed by the reduction in the mandatory deposit.

The Chilean economy has been subject to terms-of-trade shocks before, so several systems have been devised to cushion the blow. First, Chile has a large stock of net international reserves: one of the world's largest in relation to the size of the domestic economy. Second, the public sector has a system to compensate for changes in the price of copper that affects public sector revenue. When the price of copper goes above a certain limit, the incremental revenue is put into a fund in the Central Bank; and when the price goes below a certain limit, the government draws on the fund for revenue to maintain regular spending. Chile is an oil importer, and there is also an oil fund that is used to stabilize the domestic price of petroleum. When the international price goes below a given benchmark, the price difference is taxed and revenue deposited in the fund. When the international price of oil goes above a given benchmark, the government draws from the fund to offset some of the higher cost in the domestic market. Naturally this does not avoid the final transfer to the domestic market of a permanently high international price once the fund is depleted, but it does stabilize the domestic price against short-term shocks. None of the funds are allowed to exhibit a negative balance. This system of funds has allowed us to compensate, at least partially, for the effect of changes in the terms of trade.

Obviously, however, no fund can compensate for the loss of income involved in a terms-of-trade deterioration of more than 10 percent such as the one that has affected Chile in 1998, producing an implied loss of income equivalent to approximately 2 percent of the gross domestic product (GDP). To absorb the shock, some use of international reserves (and of the funds) has been made, but the main reaction has been in reducing expansion of domestic demand and reducing the rate of GDP growth. In this way the loss of income is accommodated, and an excessive imbalance of the external sector is avoided.

Carlos Massad is President of the Central Bank of Chile.

Comment

Miguel Kiguel

Prevention should be our primary focus—prevention of crisis and prevention of contagion. This concern for prevention has been at the core of policymaking in Argentina for many years now because we have experienced too many crises and know firsthand how very damaging and painful they are. Moving beyond damage control means asking how we can avoid the next crisis.

There are two main aspects to our efforts at prevention—both of them geared toward macroeconomic stability. We have taken policy positions to strengthen the solvency of the government and the banking system, and to strengthen liquidity. These are the areas where we believe good policies can make a difference.

Crises have too many dimensions to attack all of them effectively. One can try to isolate the country from trade shocks caused by world recession. Given the emergence of a global economy, such policies cannot be airtight when times are bad and mean lost opportunity when times are good. So we decided to concentrate on buffering our country from financial shocks, from financial disturbances like the one we experienced in 1995 following the Mexican devaluation. Our banking sector lost 17 percent of deposits during this bank run, an experience comparable to that of the U.S. in the 1930s. We faced a loss of international reserves of $6 billion, or one third of our total. This ratio exceeds Brazil's during the current crisis.

This experience taught us that three things matter during a financial crisis: liquidity, liquidity, liquidity. So what did we do? The first step was to generate liquidity in the banking system so that enough cash would be on hand to prevent any run on deposits. Usually one thinks of reserve requirements or liquidity requirements as a tax on the banking system. We don't. We think it is a precautionary measure. We imposed a 20 percent liquidity requirement on all bank deposits and liabilities. To make sure that the money was there, banks were required to deposit it abroad or at the Central Bank of Argentina.

What else did we do? The Central Bank negotiated a contingent trade facility equivalent to 10 percent of total deposits. Combined with the requirements financial institutions had to meet, this particular line of credit brought liquidity levels up to an equivalent of 30 percent of total deposits. That is a pretty sizable amount, especially since during times like today's crisis, banks usually take their own preventive medicine and generate additional liquidity. The amount of liquidity that banks have relative to deposits now is between 30 and 40 percent. So that's the first thing we have done. We generated a lot of liquidity in the banking system.

The second element we zeroed in on was to minimize our vulnerability to short-term debt. Argentina is a relatively unique case. Our system of convertibility is a fixed exchange rate of 1 peso equals 1 dollar. For us, there is no difference between borrowing pesos or borrowing dollars. Most of our capital market, in fact, functions in dollars. That, for a long time, has been a matter for serious discussion, especially with the rating agencies. They tend to think—even though we have fixed exchange rates and a convertibility law that prohibits devaluation—that we need the backing of a monetary base. That line of thinking does not see short-term debt in pesos as a problem because we could always print pesos. They forget that we need the dollars to back those pesos. Having short-term debt in dollars can not be treated lightly; it creates big problems.

Experience has shown that with fixed exchange rates the denomination of the debt is not as important as its structure. Today Argentina has a small amount of short-term debt—just 3 percent of total debt, or $3 billion. That is less than 1 percent of gross domestic product (GDP), which means we have a relatively small amount to refinance.

So another way of ensuring adequate liquidity is to prevent the accumulation of short-term debt, to have most of our debt be long-term and spaced out so there is not undue concentration of amortization.

But we also know that liquidity, however vital, is not enough. One can be liquid but insolvent, and be in big trouble. So we have been improving our fiscal accounts and making sure that the banks are extremely solvent. Central Bank President Pedro Pou will more thoroughly address later what has been done on the banking side, but I will briefly touch on two factors. First, our capital requirements are well in excess of the basic. Second, a large number of our banks are subsidiaries of foreign banks. Although the stocks of the parent firms are down significantly, their institutional soundness has been verified by supervisory authorities abroad. Domestic depositors have clearly been provided with enough reassurance to make them feel comfortable.

As for public sector solvency, we have consolidated our fiscal accounts by reducing the budget deficit from around 2.5 percent of GDP in 1996 to less than 1 percent today, with a balanced budget planned by the year 2000. So we are also working on preventive medicine there.

Does this preventive policy work? The proof of the pudding, as they say, is in the eating. One indication can be found by looking at how Argentina has performed during the present crisis. It is interesting not only to compare this performance with that of other countries, but with the baseline of our own performance during the Tequila crisis of 1995.

These comparisons reassure us that our preventive policies are bearing fruit. Look at international reserves. I mentioned earlier that in 1995 they fell by a third, from $18 billion to $12 billion. During the first phase of this crisis, from October 1997 to midsummer 1998, our international reserves increased at a steady rate of 10–15 percent. During the second phase, starting in August after the Russia default, our capital outflows started to stabilize while elsewhere they were falling. *They have merely stabilized, not fallen.* The first test for us is very reasonable behavior of international reserves, and we have at the moment full confidence in the convertibility of the Argentine peso.

The second test is interest rates. Interest rates have two components, as you well know. There is what we call the country risk, or the spread Argentina pays over U.S. Treasuries; and there is the currency risk. In Argentina we have pesos and dollars. We can differentiate very clearly what is the country risk, which is the spread over U.S. Treasury bills. The domestic currency risk is the spread between pesos and dollars. We have seen a significant rise in country risk since the Asian crisis. It has probably doubled, reaching ridiculously high levels. But the increase is in line with other emerging market countries, Mexico for instance. The peso evaluation risk has also increased, but very little. For comparison one can look, for instance, at the interbank rate. At the height of the Tequila crisis, almost overnight, it reached 70 percent. In October of last year, following the East Asian devaluations, the interbank rate increased to 15 percent. This is much less, and shows much more confidence. Since the Russian crisis, the rate has been hovering around an increase of 10 percent. It is difficult to say that our preventive policies are the sole reason for this greater confidence in the peso, in its convertibility. But surely they deserve much of the credit.

Miguel Kiguel is Undersecretary of Finance in Argentina's Ministry of the Economy and Chairman of the Council of Economic Advisors.

Comment

José Antonio Ocampo

The fundamental issue in crisis prevention and resolution involves the size and composition of the imbalances or deficits that build up during the boom period that precedes a downturn. There is, however, a fundamental difference in this regard between crises of the "old" type, which were associated with fiscal deficits, and the "new" sort, which are associated with private deficits. Let us examine how the nature of the problem has changed.

In a crisis caused by private deficits, the fundamental issue is the degree of strength of the domestic financial system prior to the crisis, particularly the size and nature of the risks that have been assumed by private banks and financial institutions but also by private nonfinancial institutions. A major problem with these private risks is that, if excessive, they will force state intervention during the ensuing crisis. Thus, in a sense, fiscal risks are always assumed during a boom period. If they are not properly managed, they effectively become fiscal costs during a crisis. The most familiar example of this is the bailout of banks during a crisis, which may involve huge sums of money. Although the actual costs appear only with the onset of the crisis, in a sense they were incurred as subsidized risks during the boom.

Two fundamental issues are involved in better risk management. The first involves information. How can the quality of information be raised and how is it best used? By definition, better information is useful, but I would argue that its impact is greater in dealing with fiscal crises of the old sort than with the new sort of crisis fueled by private sector debt.

Transparency of fiscal information is certainly an asset, and that applies across the board throughout the international community. Unavoidably, however, the nature of the information coming from the private sector will always be incomplete. It tends to become fully available only with significant lags, after a crisis has exposed real positions. Thus, efforts to build and disseminate information cannot offer the same degree of warning about preventing the new sort of crisis that information offered in preventing a traditional fiscal crisis. Just look at any private bank or company, and the evaluation of risks and the nature of bad investments only become apparent when they have to be cashed in. The sheer volume of information to be weighted about the quality of banking assets and private sector investments means that both regulators and risk-grading private agencies are always behind the curve and cannot anticipate how sound the underlying exposure to systemic risk is.

For this reason, information remains valuable and must be improved, but action here will not be a panacea. Perhaps the best proof for this is that major problems remain despite the forward strides that have already been made. The quantity and quality of information have been increasing over time. Today, we have grading agencies, investment banks, and multilateral institutions, all with very qualified staffs. Market analysts multiply almost as fast as the computers they use. Yet despite all of the sophisticated programs, their predictions sometimes crash. The best-informed institutions and agents, private and public, are not foolproof. For this reason, I think the problem requires us not only to look at information flows, but also beyond them.

That is why we believe strongly that crisis prevention must be a cornerstone of policymaking during boom periods. The basic problem is how to let a multitude of private agents know that the indirect collective risk they are assuming is more dangerous than the private assessment of their own direct exposure might suggest. In this regard, I think there is no alternative but to avoid the overly expansionary monetary policies implicit in the way that capital market flows push economies during periods of financial euphoria. A massive influx of foreign capital can push economies into expansionary bubbles, with widespread reductions in interest rates accompanied by some real appreciation. The authorities must stop the bubble before it gets out of hand.

Before proceeding, let us acknowledge that traditional instruments are probably insufficient for the job. Traditional monetary and exchange rate policies are not enough. Additional instruments are required. For that purpose, the Economic Commission for Latin America and the Caribbean (ECLAC) has long defended the idea of using some sort of taxation on capital flows, and particularly on short-term capital flows

As Carlos Massad and Miguel Kiguel have indicated, the primary objective of these policies is to improve the debt profile. They may also affect the magnitude of flows. Several actions can be taken to avoid unsound expansionary effects. One instrument, used by both Chile and Colombia, is a reserve requirement on capital inflows. Argentina's liquidity requirement is an alternative. It is a different system, which is not targeted at capital inflows but has a similar effect on the debt profile. One can also use a targeted form of taxation. The reserve requirements of Colombia and Chile are, in effect, an implicit tax paid by the borrower seeking capital abroad.

Another set of actions must be undertaken during boom periods. This is the time to force a capitalization of financial institutions, to enhance prudential regulation overall. This is also the moment to explore policy options that seek to limit the use of fixed assets as guarantees for credit by lowering the proportion of fixed-asset values that can be committed for the purpose. This will reduce the risk exposure and force greater prudence on investors and borrowers alike. Let me emphasize that any regulation must be as general as possible. There are loopholes that need to be covered, in particular the well-known ones associated with hedge and mutual funds.

The Chilean and Argentinean experience during the recent crisis demonstrates the usefulness and flexibility of some of the instruments of indirect taxation and liquidity requirements we have been discussing. Proposals have been made, particularly in Chile, to use explicit taxation to moderate private demand during boom periods. The problem with this proposal is a legal one. Tax rates are the prerogative of legislatures, and are thus difficult to modify. Besides, any codified system is likely to be inflexible.

For these reasons, reserve requirements are preferable. They are a form of taxation that is totally flexible and can be managed anticyclically. Liquidity requirements do not have the same indirect tax ingredient, but they may have similar effects on private-sector debt profiles.

Finally, I would like to look briefly at stabilization funds. One reason why they should be used much more widely has to do with the side effects of our tradition of targeting the current fiscal deficit rather than the structural deficit, as the OECD countries do. I think the targeting of annual fiscal deficits should be gradually changed, particularly because tax revenues have become increasingly procyclical. A more general stabilization fund that forces authorities to save some temporary tax revenues when times are good would be very useful for offsetting problems when times are bad. This would, indeed, be a move toward targeting structural deficits, which is clearly needed to eliminate the procyclical character of the traditional targeting of the annual deficit.

The devices available today are commodity stabilization funds. Colombia has long had one for coffee, and Chile has more recently started one for copper. Venezuela is starting an oil stabilization fund, as Colombia did a couple of years ago. These experiences must be extended, however, to the design of stabilization funds for *tax* revenues rather than being limited only to those associated with fluctuations in commodity prices. They are one of many instruments that must be available as policy options if we are to better manage boom periods and prevent them from sowing the seeds of the next crisis.

José Antonio Ocampo is Executive Secretary, Economic Commission for Latin America and the Caribbean (ECLAC) and former Minister of Finance in Colombia.

Washington, D.C., October 1998

Author's Remarks

Michael Gavin

The paper I presented here with Ricardo Hausmann grew out of a fairly substantial body of research conducted by the Office of the Chief Economist of the Inter-American Development Bank, and by other scholars working on these issues. I will begin my response to comments heard today by reinforcing a point that was made emphatically in the previous session. Although this is a global crisis and global actions must be part of its resolution, it would be a serious mistake to conclude that domestic fundamentals are unimportant. This can be shown in a very rudimentary yet convincing fashion. One simply has to look at countries in the region and ask whether the so-called "risk premium" charged by investors on long-term, dollar-denominated paper is or is not related to fundamentals, which are approximated by measuring the projected 1998 fiscal balance as a share of gross domestic product (GDP).

The picture that emerges strongly suggests that while fundamentals of the region cannot explain the sudden and catastrophic loss of access to financial markets that occurred after the Russian default, there is some measure of discrimination in the market reaction to the crisis. It holds out hope that the better-managed countries within the region and the region as a whole—which is generally perceived to be among the better-managed parts of the emerging-markets universe—will be able to get back to international financial markets on something like normal terms sooner rather than later.

But which fundamentals will matter in making that happen? Surely, the fiscal deficit is only a small part of the picture. Since the present crisis is breaking new territory, we might begin simply by compiling a long list of policies likely to be productive. But we wanted also to provide an initial conceptual framework to help focus and refine policy analysis. We say that in order for economies to be robust to international economic and financial shocks they need to satisfy three key objectives, which if we consider Miguel Kiguel's comments, actually can be counted as five.

The first is to be solvent, whose importance seems self-evident. What needs to be said in the Latin American context, however, may not be so obvious. A region that is subject to large and frequent external shocks cannot afford to look at solvency one-dimensionally. One must go beyond asking a particular sector (whether the public sector, the banking sector, or some other) if it is solvent under current and expected future circumstances. One must ask if its financial position is robust enough to remain solvent after a large external shock? I will return to this question later, when discussing specific policy issues.

The next three points, as Miguel emphasized, are to be liquid, be liquid, and be liquid. And as he adds, that applies to the banking system as well as fiscal accounts.

The final point is that policies need to inspire confidence.

Of course, these three objectives or imperatives, or however one chooses to think about them, are quite obviously interrelated. Guillermo Calvo has pointed out how a liquidity crisis can induce insolvency, whether in the banking system or in the public sector. And it goes almost without saying that without solvency and liquidity it is going to be pretty hard to inspire confidence in an institution or a policy framework. But since there is sufficient room for maneuvering all three of these things, it makes sense to consider each separately.

When applying these general principles, policymakers need to be concerned about three main areas. The first and most obvious is fiscal policy. The region is replete with historical examples of episodes in which a fiscally driven balance-of-payments crisis generated an exchange rate collapse and temporary descent into high inflation or even hyperinflation. That is not the problem, really, in most countries of the region today. The core problem, as previously stated, is contingent solvency. The concern is not that most countries are insolvent under current policies and circumstances, but that a large external shock would bring their fiscal balances close enough to worrisome positions that investors will try to bail out. To stop the panic, governments respond with fiscal measures that are contractional, procyclical, and destabilizing. Works cited in our paper show that this has been a general pattern for destabilization in the region.

The importance of solvency in the banking system also should not need elaboration. But once again, Latin America's susceptibility to very large shocks requires a deeper look. Such shocks affect the banking system at least as much as they affect the fisc. This means that the standards for solvency have to be higher for the banking system in Latin America than in the industrial countries. One has to plan for bank solvency not only under normal circumstances, but also when the ever-looming danger of a large, adverse shock becomes reality. And then, once again, policymakers need to worry about the money, which is obviously closely related to the banking system and to fiscal outcomes. I will return to this scenario a little later.

Our paper essentially works out a three-by-three matrix and tries to indicate how the three imperatives—be solvent, be liquid, inspire confidence— have implications for the three different policy areas just described. Briefly, in fiscal policy "be solvent" implies that it is hyper-useful to have precautionary surpluses in good times. This simplifies enormously the management of fiscal policy in bad times. Chile has shown the importance of this. And because it is so politically difficult to run those surpluses, it is useful to have stabilization mechanisms and fiscal rules that constrain policymakers in good times.

Miguel Kiguel's comments have explored the imperatives for liquidity in some detail. First, there is a need to avoid short-term debt and to conduct cautious public debt management—both of which are easier said than done, especially when times get rough in international financial markets. The option of issuing long-term domestic currency debt is not realistic in many contexts. Our judgment is that as long as the public sector is solvent, the risks of indexation are far lower than the risks of illiquidity. So under these circumstances, we advocate indexing of the public debt if it is necessary to lengthen maturities.

What are the policy implications for inspiring confidence? The complicating factor is that the public needs to be confident not only about the policies of the current government, but also those of future governments. The danger arises that a fiscal deficit that is wholly appropriate to run during a recession will be unfinancible because the private sector lacks confidence in the ability or willingness of future governments to raise the revenue required to service the accumulated debt.

Earlier I promised to return to the question of appropriate policymaking and crisis prevention in relation to the banking system. Does our matrix shed light on the problem? First, solvency requires higher capital requirements. It requires that the authorities avoid bank-lending booms. The Argentine policy framework contains some interesting initiatives to promote the market discipline of private banks. Argentina and other countries of the region also have shown that internationalizing the banking system can make it more financially stable.

Liquidity, obviously, is equally important for the banking system. And measures to promote solvency and liquidity are obviously a key to inspiring confidence in the banking system. But there is also another factor here. People need reliable information. More can be done to promote transparency through complete accounting and disclosure requirements. Finally, authorities should not be afraid to create adequate safety nets for domestic banks.

Michael Gavin is Director of Economic Research for Latin America at Warburg Dillon Read.

Open Discussion

Miguel Kiguel: I would like to clarify my comments and respond to José Antonio Campo's point about capital controls and liquidity requirements. There is an important difference between putting liquidity requirements on bank deposits, and imposing capital controls or reserve requirements on capital inflows. In putting liquidity requirements on bank deposits, we assume that all liabilities can leave. What we are doing is generating liquidity for the banks should they face a run on deposits. That is important because previously, at least in Argentina, the first run came from domestic depositors not foreign ones. So we understand the need for this kind of liquidity.

A second, very brief comment has to do with information. Everyone agrees that information is useful. One always wants more information rather than less. But the quality of this information must also be considered. First, governments have to establish a reputation for transparency, not only in how much data they collect and release, but also in its reliability. We receive numbers about international reserves, for instance. Some people believe those numbers, and others do not. There may be lots of other things going on, unknown to outsiders, that may have influenced those figures. So countries have to be very transparent and establish a reputation over time about the quality of information they supply for international reserves.

Then there is also the matter of interpreting the information. Is the data being read correctly, and is it the data that matters? For instance, in the case of Russia, everyone knew the stock of Russian T-bills (GKOs). There was no mystery. The investment banks would even fax you daily the list of GKOs scheduled to mature every week. But the magnitude of vulnerability was not visible in the size of these numbers. Unfortunately, the G7 does not publish on the Internet whether or not they are going to bail out a country. That hidden decision-making process was really the key to Russia, and shows the limits of only relying on the technical information.

Question: Mr. Gavin, based on your research, what advice would you have for Latin American countries about whether or not to establish some sort of currency board?

Michael Gavin: The history of this crisis is yet to be written. [A paper in the next section will explore this issue more thoroughly, but I will make some preliminary comments here.] No one knows at this point how valuable the option to devalue will prove to be to those countries that have not chosen to establish a currency board. Certainly my own textbook attitudes have shifted radically from the position I held prior to the most recent episode of financial instability. Look at Mexico and Argentina. Their other fundamentals are more or less comparable, but Argentina's domestic financial system has proven itself to be almost totally insulated from the international financial turbulence while Mexico's has been hit hard from the outset in ways unforeseen by the textbook model of exchange rate flexibility.

So countries that wish to adopt a currency board will have to adopt, in tandem, the complementary measures introduced in Argentina. Most countries in the region are far from those policies at the moment. However, I do not think it would take them very long to get there.

Michael Pulmarevan (from the World Bank): I would like to raise a crucial issue that came up during the first session—liquidity contraction in the markets. It is a vicious spiral in which hedge funds and all the players are getting hurt. Their margins are going down; liquidity is drying up. In this vicious circle, countries get downgraded by rating agencies, cutting them off from investments by pension funds and insurance companies, which are forbidden from operating in nations whose risk assessments are unrated or classified as noninvestment grade. Unless something is done, this spiral will continue. I have a suggestion. Most of these instruments are now selling at spreads around 1,600 basis points, according to the current J.P. Morgan index. The idea would be to go out, buy them at prevailing market prices, and put them into a pool, possibly with assistance from the multilaterals. Then enhance their credit rating with a guarantee. By spreading risks across various countries, across various instruments, the pool could even achieve an investment-grade rating. It would inject liquidity and other players into the emerging markets. Perhaps the multilaterals eventually will embrace or are already considering such a solution, but I would also very much like to know the reaction of policymakers from emerging markets to such a suggestion.

Michael Gavin: The proposal sounds interesting. We have been dealing in this session with what can be done to mitigate the crisis through actions on the domestic side. Whatever can be done in the international arena to improve emerging markets' access to liquidity would be excellent. So your question is a good lead-in to the subject of the next session—what is the role of international financial institutions in preventing crisis and contagion?

PART THREE

International and Supranational Remedies

Washington, D.C., October 1998

Preventing Crisis and Contagion: The Role of International Financial Institutions

Eduardo Fernández-Arias, Michael Gavin, and Ricardo Hausmann

International financial volatility increasingly looms as a major obstacle to development. Fallout from the chain reaction of financial, exchange, and payments crises that have resulted is felt disproportionately by the poorest segments of society and threatens the educational level of future generations.

The force of balance-of-payments pressures from imbalances on capital account, the speed with which they mount into a wave when the market loses confidence in a country, and the way it sweeps forward to engulf other economies through contagion dwarf the negative impacts traditionally caused by international trade flows. The enormous magnitude of private capital flowing into emerging markets in recent years thus brings with it new risks that are redefining the mission of international financial institutions (IFIs), whose conventional tools are not adequate for the new responsibilities. By their very nature, IFIs must become involved in supporting crisis-stricken developing countries. To meet this challenge, IFIs must prepare themselves, as best they can, to leverage their limited resources by designing a strategy to dampen international financial volatility and help keep crises from forming. The need has grown urgent at the Inter-American Development Bank because the financial stability of several of our borrowing countries is now being threatened by world financial turbulence.

This paper discusses what such a strategy might entail. As we shall see, a concerted effort is needed that embraces a variety of instruments and methods, ranging from the most conventional to the highly innovative, depending on the circumstances of each case. Some instruments are aimed at overcoming the effects of financial volatility and limiting its impact on development, while others are targeted at creating conditions that reduce volatility, but all of them are intended to forestall the outbreak of a crisis. A precondition for effective crisis prevention is that all recipient countries must have a well-managed economy and prudent financial policies. This strategy is designed primarily to diminish the financial vulnerability of countries in our region. Since a degree of economic and financial restructuring is required to meet the standard that the strategy requires, this strategy has the secondary merit of encouraging prudent policies that are beneficial in their own right.

The next section will analyze the nature of the crises caused by external financial volatility to see what sets them in motion. Subsequent sections will discuss how IFIs can tailor their policies to help neutralize those causes and the instruments required for the strategy to work.

External Financial Volatility: Isolating the Virus of Crisis and Contagion

The existence of high levels of debt creates susceptibility to very costly balance-of-payments crises should the market lose confidence in a country. If lost confidence is not justified by a country's inability to pay—if with adequate financing the economy would be sound enough to service its debts—then a crisis is unnecessary and IFIs must try to prevent one from occurring.

In an extreme case of lost confidence, creditors will seek to minimize their exposure in a country and refuse to refinance debts; and this will provoke a serious short-term liquidity problem, which may even threaten a suspension of payments. Ebbing external financing paralyzes capital flows in the country's financial system, and the goods-producing sector of the economy is forced to adjust inefficiently.

If it is severe enough, a crisis will form in the real economy that seems to justify, in hindsight, the market's original loss of confidence that cut off external financing and exposed the underlying weakness. Even then, however, the loss of confidence may have been unjustified, to the degree that the "prophecy" was self-fulfilling. The country may have been capable of servicing its debt under normal market conditions with adequate financing. In this case, the loss of confidence and the ensuing crisis were not the necessary and inevitable consequence of the economic situation. Most analysts agree that "runs" of this kind, which were sparked by a loss of confidence not fully justified ex ante, have been important factors in most of the crises that afflicted our region in 1994–1995, and that hit East Asia in 1997 (Calvo and Fernández-Arias, 1998).

Today, in the wake of the August 1998 Russian crisis, most emerging markets in the world, including our region, have lost much of their access to external financing, even though their economies lack any great inherent weaknesses. Yet this relative strength has not been enough to shore up the collapse of confidence or reduce its dangers. The generalized loss of financial market access is a kind of contagion caused by the pressures to which investors in certain emerging markets are being exposed at this time. On one hand, the huge losses that have been suffered worldwide threaten investors' own access to financing and force them to close out their positions at any cost. On the other hand, the great uncertainty over sovereign risk in the wake of the Russian moratorium is leading to a wait-and-see attitude on the part of market players. Both of these factors are temporary and will be overcome in due course by the functioning of the market itself; but if they persist long enough, the lack of external financing could precipitate a much deeper crisis that need not have occurred.

In a situation in which a country's economy is basically sound but it cannot avoid a severe and prolonged loss of access to capital markets, there are two possible outcomes: a normal, crisis-free exit; or a crisis of liquidity. Such liquidity crises must be distinguished from traditional "solvency" crises, in which the country's underpinning is unsound and its economic fundamentals are unsustainable. Solvency crises are inevitable unless the economic fundamentals are brought into line, whereas a liquidity crisis can be avoided with suitable mechanisms to ensure continued financial flows. The strategy discussed here focuses on preventing these crises of liquidity.

In the case of a properly restructured economy, the availability of external sources of support to bridge a temporary gap in access to financial markets can ensure that the economy remains on track by forestalling a liquidity crisis. This applies, of course, only if private external flows dry up from short-term market disruptions, such as those that presumably prevail today, and presumes that bridging is needed only until markets recover their balance and the supply of lending returns to normal. In crises in recent years, loss of access to capital has given rise to runs that then validated investors' self-fulfilling expectations of the costs of an imminent crisis. The existence of a support fund would bolster investor confidence because it would avoid those costs, eliminating the source of uncertainty. In this case, the mere existence of such a facility will tend to dampen incipient panic and may preclude the need for any disbursement at all.

Without a strategy for participating in such preventive programs, IFIs would be obliged to act ex post facto. When a crisis breaks out in a country, they would have to examine the situation and provide support in line with prevailing circumstances. Recent experience, from Mexico to Russia, suggests that such a strategy would be insufficient either to avoid enormous damage to the well-being of the country involved or to prevent the contagion from spreading widely, even if there is ample financial support. The regional scope of current financial turbulence makes such a strategy especially risky for contagion regionwide.

The principal limitations of this ex-post strategy can be summarized as follows:

• *Prevention is better than cure.* Once a crisis breaks out, the economic fundamentals swiftly deteriorate through impact on financial channels in all sectors of the economy, and are transmitted internationally through contagion. Damage may be caused that is not easy to repair.

• *Emergency support will probably be uncertain and come too late.* It is important that IFIs act before the crisis-induced lack of financing causes irreversible damage to the economic fundamentals. Even with emergency procedures in place, IFIs need time to analyze the situation and arrange for disbursements, and this leads to delays and uncertainties that will exacerbate the damage.

• *Conditionality probably would be hastily conceived and ineffective.* The pressure to quickly devise effective emergency support would put at risk the quality of the technical analysis underlying the loan recommendations, and conditionality would likely be weakened by the need for swift disbursement.

• *Private investors would benefit without shouldering any of the burden.* At times of crisis it is unrealistic to think that the private sector will cooperate in defraying the costs of an emergency package. On the other hand, the implicit guarantee that such a rescue package represents for private investors tends to undermine market discipline, inducing less caution in future lending and breeding more frequent crises.

• *Traditional financial instruments of multilateral development banks (MDBs) are unsuitable.* Conventional long-term loans are inappropriate for dealing with a short-term liquidity crisis since they unnecessarily tie up resources, hamstringing development-lending programs. And even when resources are not diverted, traditional policy guidelines tend to cut off financial support at times of difficulty because counterpart funding dries up, which further exacerbates the crisis.

The net result is to limit the effectiveness of IFI response to emergencies of this kind, both in terms of helping resolve crises as they break out, and in terms of creating moral hazard by seeming to underwrite risky speculations by investors that sow the seeds of future crises. On the other hand, there is no doubt that once a crisis appears, it will be deeper and costlier if no official rescue packages are available and if countries have to resolve their problems on their own. The argument underlying the discussion of crisis prevention strategy is not that the net results of the current emergency rescue strategy are negative, but that they are not enough. Rescue should be our last line of defense against contagion, rather than the first and only option. To minimize the damage from crises and the costs of repairing them, a preventive strategy is also needed, and that means a new way of thinking. It means devising new tools and adapting old ones to meet the challenge.

There are, however, no magic bullets. A crisis prevention strategy based on providing backup financing during temporary shutdowns of capital markets also carries risks. The primary danger is that a country's economic fundamentals may, indeed, be weak and the market's loss of confidence thoroughly justified, either because of economic policy errors or an excessive level of debt contracted in the past. This situation will inevitably lead to a traditional solvency crisis, which interim financing to avoid a liquidity crisis will be powerless to prevent. In extreme cases, expectations of a major bailout might even cause the required economic policy reforms to be postponed.

Alternative lines of credit against external financial contagion cannot cure weak economic fundamentals and should be designed in a way that avoids exacerbating them. In fact, the opposite should be true. IFIs should support programs only for those countries whose economic fundamentals are sufficiently sound, and whose policies contribute to strengthening, rather than undermining the strategy's aim of preserving market confidence.

Basic Elements of an International Strategy

A crisis prevention strategy requires coordination to work. It requires each of the three sectors involved to play its part. First, the official sector—the IMF and MDBs—must cooperate closely in order to mobilize the leverage to implement the strategy. Second, a participating country must commit itself to maintain and enhance the soundness of its macroeconomic policy if the strategy is to be sustainable. Finally, the private sector must be receptive to participating in innovative approaches that will serve the collective interest for the strategy to be fully effective.

The analysis in the previous section suggests the following five principles as guidelines for formulating strategy. The proper balance in applying them, of course, will have to be determined in light of the circumstances of each operation.

* *Prevention.* The governing principle is to focus on strengthening mechanisms designed to prevent a liquidity crisis, in accord with the provisos detailed in the previous section. This means that the program must be applied only when the economic fundamentals are sufficiently sound to reasonably expect that market confidence and access can be restored to a level that will forestall a crisis.

* *Certainty and speed.* There must be certainty that the support provided—whether in the form of a guarantee, a loan, or a line of credit—will be available immediately when funds are needed. Otherwise, uncertainty about whether the support will be forthcoming, indeed any delay in providing it, will undermine crisis prevention. Therefore the conditionality applied in such operations must not impede urgently required capital infusions; disbursement conditions must be replaced by conditions of approval, or "preconditions," which are discussed in principle three. Ideally, operations will be structured to provide incentives for using the resources only when trigger contingencies arise, after which disbursement would be automatic.

* *Preconditions.* Support should be offered selectively to countries that meet a series of preconditions demonstrating that their economic fundamentals and their economic policy commitments are compatible with warding off a crisis, emphasizing prudential standards and efforts to reduce financial vulnerability. Such preconditions for approval must be reviewed regularly through

periodic recertification to ensure that compliance with standards has not lapsed over time. The IMF would certify that these conditions are met.

• *Catalytic effect.* IFIs' participation in this program will be more effective to the extent that it supplements market mechanisms and can be leveraged through the private sector in a cofinancing mode. In particular, this strategy reverses what typically characterizes ex-post emergency packages, in which official money is almost exclusively used. For the private catalytic effect to work, official international cooperation is essential to achieve the necessary critical mass of seed capital.

• *Short-term and hard-term loans.* Loan terms will be in line with the pricing of private cofinancing. Loans disbursed under this program, including those resulting from guarantees that have been called, will be medium term and may be repaid early without penalty. These loans will carry sufficiently high interest rates that there is an incentive to draw upon them only when there is a financing shortfall. On the other hand, the fee for the IFIs' commitment to disburse the loan, whether in the form of a guarantee or a line of credit, would be held low to promote the use of these prudential mechanisms.

As previously indicated, the major risk in this comprehensive strategy is that financial support will be applied to a crisis whose underlying cause is solvency rather than liquidity. Our principles reduce this risk by restricting program access to healthy economies that meet a series of preconditions regarding sound and prudent management. The arrangement of this program in good times should make it possible for the private sector to participate. Private participation in the program, when it occurs, will minimize the danger further by acting as a watchdog to assure that these conditions will be fulfilled (as well as by imposing market discipline on prices).

The above strategic principles can be seen as an adaptation of the classical principles of lending of last resort to domestic banks (Bagehot, 1873) applied to countries. A key difference is that the solvency ensured by good (illiquid) collateral in the traditional case is replaced by the establishment of adequate country solvency preconditions.

A crisis prevention strategy based on ensuring continued access to external financing during periods of international volatility must come with a broad variety of instruments, which IFIs must be properly prepared and equipped to use. The next section discusses general classifications for those instruments based on how they will be used.

New Modalities

One useful way to think about instruments relates to when they will be used to reduce vulnerability to external financial volatility. *Compensatory operations* seek to counter severe financial volatility and to moderate its impact on development, for example on social spending, through specially designed financing packages. These kinds of transactions are useful only at times of financial turbulence such as we are experiencing today, and consequently IFIs should hold them in reserve as exceptional and temporary measures for use when market access is disrupted. *Precautionary operations* are aimed at reducing volatility through providing financial support to mechanisms that bolster market confidence and avoid runs, such as those arranged in Mexico and Argentina. This kind of operation addresses a permanent market weakness and hence may be conducted at times of heavy capital inflows.

Since crisis formation centers on financial volatility, it is to be expected that the IFI strategy for dealing with it will involve *contingent measures* designed to become operational only if and when a shortfall of liquidity or financing occurs. Consequently, many of these operations will feature instruments such as guarantees and standby lines of credit. These measures are particularly appropriate in the case of precautionary transactions, in which support mechanisms automatically become available once certain conditions arise. Because those contingencies are unlikely to occur, contingent financing will not normally lead to actual disbursements.

Since the problems that generate volatility in financial markets are intimately linked to lack of private financing, IFI operational strategy should try to encourage greater contribution from the private sector wherever possible. Most operations under this program will therefore most likely be explicitly supplementary to the private sector, either in terms of engineering complex financial structures or providing straight cofinancing. These structures will require flexibility in the use of financial instruments to absorb a high proportion of the private sector's country risk through the use of guarantees, lines of credit, or other methods.

Any financial instruments, whether credits or guarantees, that are used to mobilize private funds and obtain a critical mass may require *complementary financing*, whereby IFIs syndicate financial operations with the private sector and implicitly extend their privileged creditor status to participants in the "B" portion of the package. This of course is an exceptional approach that must be used only in cases when official support of any lesser quality would be insufficient to achieve a satisfactory degree of private participation. In such cases this tool presents clear advantages, and the IFIs' financial leverage can be expected to be substantial. After all, the value to private partners from official participation in a package is not so much the share of official resources being contributed as it is the IFI's overall relationship with the country as major creditors.[1]

---

[1] This leverage may well be greater than what MDBs can achieve in private-sector lending, in which case this argument is only partially valid because the borrower is not the sovereign.

Deciding Which Instruments to Use

IFIs could use a number of instruments to participate in support programs, consistent with the strategic elements discussed earlier, and the selection will depend on the specific conditions of each operation. These instruments fall into two broad categories:

• *Financial support loans.* This conventional form of financial support is intended to minimize the negative impact of international financial volatility on public spending and policies to avoid cutbacks that will undermine the country's economic and social progress. In addition to mitigating immediate distress, this compensatory instrument has the long-term preventive goal of reinforcing critical areas of the economic development process that may suffer when access to external financing is closed, and that if damaged may lead to dangerous weakness and future structural crises.

• *Instruments to help maintain the flow of private capital.* In contrast to the previous class of instruments, this type of support is precautionary in nature and can be implemented even when access to financing is still unimpeded. Clearly, precautionary instruments that attack volatility at its roots are the first and best line of defense against crises. Maintaining private capital flows completely protects economic and social gains that can be only partially safeguarded by compensatory instruments such as those described earlier. Lines of credit negotiated with commercial banks, like those Argentina and Mexico opened after the Tequila crisis in order to forestall runs and ensure the continued flow of private capital, are examples of approaches that IFIs could find it attractive to support. More generally, all official support cofinanced with the private sector through highly leveraged mechanisms implicitly helps maintain the level of private capital flows. As discussed earlier, complementary financing ("A/B") offers broad possibilities for implementing this concept, whether through loans, lines of credit, or guarantees.

Eduardo Fernández-Arias is Lead Research Economist, Office of the Chief Economist, Inter-American Development Bank; Michael Gavin is the Director of Economic Research for Latin America at Warburg Dillon Read; and Ricardo Hausmann is Chief Economist at the Inter-American Development Bank.

References

Bagehot, W. 1873. *Lombard Street: A Description of the Money Market.* London: William Clowes and Sons.

Calvo, G., and E. Fernández-Arias. 1998. "The New Features of Financial Crises in Emerging Markets," in Part One of this book.

Comment

Pedro Pou

My comments will focus on the tradeoffs between the problem of moral hazard and the role of international financial institutions (IFIs) in reducing the probability of liquidity shock, spread by contagion. Two very specific assumptions underlay these thoughts. First, maintaining capital account convertibility is a high priority; and second, my concern is with emerging markets, in which *emerging* is defined as those economies that lack permanent access to international capital markets.

Before assessing the tradeoffs, one must first step back and consider what domestic policy stance is appropriate for emerging markets. IFIs, after all, should not substitute for good policies but complement them. A proper foundation obviously begins with sound macroeconomic policymaking characterized by consistency among its monetary, exchange rate, and fiscal components. However, it also includes a second aspect. If emerging countries wish to participate in world capital markets, they need an appropriate financial policy. This financial policy may consist of a number of elements, including strong bank regulations regarding capital, provisioning, and risk management. These elements address a general concern: Because emerging economies tend to be subject to higher volatility, they need strong banking sectors irrespective of their monetary arrangements.

This also means that a liquidity policy is needed, independent of whatever exchange rate regime is in place. By definition, emerging markets may be cut off suddenly from international credit, and government bond markets may simply dry up. Consequently, an emerging country has less maneuvering room than a typical G7 country. The latter, for example, can combat a liquidity problem by injecting liquidity and sterilizing that injection simultaneously so that monetary or exchange rate targets are not jeopardized. An emerging country whose government bond market has become illiquid lacks that option. A monetary injection will not normally be accompanied by increased demand for domestic liabilities; hence the exchange rate instantly will be put under pressure. This means that an ostensibly free monetary policy is less free than it looks. Assume, for instance, that a country has decided to adopt a flexible exchange rate but no liquidity policy. If there is a liquidity shock and the central bank feels forced to inject liquidity into the banking sector, then the exchange rate pressure previously described will quickly expose the "independence" in monetary policymaking to have been an illusion.

To put this another way, whatever macroeconomic rule an emerging economy adopts, whether it is an exchange rate, or a monetary or a fiscal target, the rule may be put in severe jeopardy because of inadequate access to international credit and insufficient liquidity. Of course, an emerging country without a liquidity rule can claim greater "flexibility." What *flexibility* really means in this context, however, is "instability."

Since a liquidity policy is essential, what should it include? I strongly believe it should take into account the liabilities of both the private and public sectors in both local currency and foreign currencies, and should include nonresidents as well as residents. Recent crises have shown that the policy must be overarching and systemic. The exact mix may vary by country context, but liquidity problems have surfaced in public, bank, and other private sector debt, and there have been problems with foreign as well as domestic liabilities. Our experience in Argentina, which covers a range of monetary and exchange rate regimes, is that domestic depositors flee at least as fast as foreigners, and that peso liabilities can be as serious a problem as those denominated in dollars.

Liquidity policy has been unattractive because it is clearly expensive, especially for emerging economies in which the banking system is the largest component of the capital market. Economies in which loans are scarce commodities and in which capital markets are underdeveloped face a strong tradeoff between a prudent liquidity policy and domestic credit creation. The standard solution to finding the best possible tradeoff has been to create a domestic lender of last resort (LOLR). Usually this has meant the central bank, an institutional context in which the tradeoff between providing liquidity to preempt bank runs and contagion and creating moral hazard has been well understood since the last century.

The new scope of crises we face now demands an informed debate of these issues at the international level. A set of rules is needed for an effective international LOLR to improve the tradeoff between liquidity and credit while controlling the moral hazard.

I think we understand the issue of moral hazard reasonably well. It occurs when creditors believe that somebody else will absorb the cost of investment mistakes. In the recent crises, the mistakes were made jointly by borrowers and by creditors and their regulators. To the extent that private banks assumed official assistance would always be available to countries with problems, and to the extent that regulators did not require sufficient capital or provisions to offset those risky investments, then both must share with local authorities blame for what happened.

Clearly, one result has been to cut off most emerging countries from world capital markets at current spreads. This has had a significant negative effect on those economies, and has the potential for turning even groundless fears about their investment risk into self-fulfilling prophecies. So having the kind of domestic liquidity policy previously described is extremely important in buying time for these economies. But this is not a solution. To solve the problem and preserve open capital accounts—which must be one of our highest priorities—the international community needs to develop an international LOLR to protect countries from the maelstrom of contagion.

Such an institution will have to act guided by rules similar to those that govern a central bank's relations with domestic banks. Of course, this is easier said than done, as central banks will attest. A central bank does not like to be too explicit about which sound banks would receive assistance and which would not. This policy has become known as "constructive ambiguity." Whatever its merits domestically, it is clearly insufficient internationally. Something more predetermined, less arbitrary, is needed so that it is crystal clear no political issues are involved. The need for transparency in procedures and practices becomes paramount.

I would advocate a two-level approach. Countries that satisfy a set of criteria—perhaps including Maastricht-type fiscal rules plus benchmarks related to the soundness of their financial system—should gain access to virtually unconditional lending to prevent contagion from other countries' problems. Conditionality, in other words, should be ex ante and not ex post, in order to make this a preemptive program in which everyone knows that funds are available unconditionally when they are required.

Matters are complicated, however, by the changing nature of crises. The recent ones have reflected sharp disequilibria in financial stocks rather than the flow disequilibria that typified the balance-of-payments crisis of the 1970s. This has two major implications. First, it means that IFIs, whether they like it or not, are put into the analogous position of being a financial LOLR. Second, the amounts of assistance required have mushroomed. The total sum committed to the packages for Mexico and Argentina in 1995 and recently to Thailand, Indonesia, Korea, and Russia amount to a staggering $185 billion.

I would argue strongly that the IMF should assume this LOLR role. G7 central banks are constrained by their legal mandates to seek price stability in their own countries. They can only be counted on to internalize worldwide problems, then, to the extent that these problems impact on their domestic economies. Yet if the IMF is to play this role effectively, its standard programs prior to the Mexican crisis will not be enough. IMF standbys and Extended Fund Facilities (EFFs) typically commit amounts on the order of 1 percent of gross domestic product (GDP). The stock of short-term liabilities may be far greater, however; and since stocks and not flows are involved, more than 5 percent of GDP might be required.

Even with the quota increase of more than a third—from $200 billion to $270 billion—being discussed presently, the IMF will lack the needed resources. The IMF in 1945 had quotas equivalent to 4 percent of world GDP, and there were capital controls. To achieve a comparable size today, without considering the impact of capital account liberalization, would mean a quota total of $1.3 trillion. This disparity calls for creative solutions, which I will consider in a moment.

But first there is the matter of those countries that do not meet the specified policy targets and have some fundamental problems. This second tier requires an approach that corresponds to the more traditional approaches of the IMF. A substantial amount of policy dialogue and conditionality needs to be applied at the time of disbursement. Distinguishing which countries fall into the first and second tiers will be complex and require considerable research and involve difficult political decisions. However, taking this approach will send a clear, strong message to countries to get their houses in order.

The recent initiative by President Clinton suggesting and pushing for new Preventative Contingency Funds for countries following sound policies is to be welcomed as a step in this direction. But other steps will be required to compensate for the shortage of resources at the IMF's disposal. At some point, after all, the amount of available official funds will reach their political limits. It is then both beneficial and necessary to "bail in" the private sector to make crisis prevention and resolution credible. The IMF should probably focus on the steps previously described, while the multilateral development banks (MDBs)—the World Bank and the IDB—would assist countries to set up private-sector LOLR facilities. Argentina already has set up a private contingent liquidity repo facility. The unique status of the MDBs implies that they have an appropriate and important role in complementing the private capital in such a facility, and their presence would significantly enhance the quality of private-lender LOLR arrangements. We have proposed such a course for Argentina and are pleased that the management of the IDB and the World Bank will be recommending precisely this to their boards in the very near future.

This facility has played an important role in Argentina to help ensure that credit keeps flowing to enterprises, especially small- and medium-sized firms, when banks suffer a liquidity crunch from some completely external event. Anyone who thinks the facility serves no productive purpose should compare what happened in Argentina during the Tequila crisis, when a sharp liquidity contraction caused a severe recession and large spikes in unemployment and poverty, to the relative calm in levels of deposits and international reserves during the current crisis.

As we survey the landscape of this current crisis, two things are clear. First, we do not yet understand very well the mechanics of contagion. A much better picture of the microstructure of international capital markets is needed, zeroing in on the behavior of hedge funds and mutual funds. For this, information is required. As a first step, position data should be gathered for these funds, and the motivations for their actions should be carefully analyzed. Just as the world has developed complex bank regulations to prevent systemic banking risks, these other markets may have features that imply the need for regulations on players in world capital markets to protect their integrity.

Second, as my comments have stressed, an *effective* lender of last resort must be developed. There is resistance to this idea, but analyzing the costs and benefits of action and inaction clarifies matters. The risk of action is that we might not get it exactly right from the beginning. Since that is likely, the real question is whether action will improve the current overall arrangements. The risk of inaction would be to leave the world in its present peril, a particularly dangerous condition for emerging countries. The progress made in opening capital accounts is frozen. And many may decide the degree of volatility in capital markets is just too great for any exposure and access to them must be rolled back.

Pedro Pou is President of the Central Bank of Argentina.

Comment

Joseph Stiglitz

Two general observations can be made about the problem of crisis prevention and contagion and what international financial institutions can do to help find solutions. First, financial crisis is becoming increasingly frequent and increasingly painful. The number of countries that have faced financial crisis in the past quarter century is estimated at somewhere between 70 and 100. So the problem cannot be confined to a region or a few offenders. It may be a result of human fallibility or failed government policy, but it is a worldwide disease. Our international architecture has to recognize this fact and compensate for it. As someone has observed, nuclear power plants must be made so that ordinary people can run them safely. Our economic system demands no less.

The second observation is that much of the shock triggering the crisis is external to the countries eventually affected. Early evidence for this was revealed in the way a crisis was highly correlated within a region. Now we are beginning to see crisis spreading from one region to another. The most recent crisis has brought this home very forcefully, as Guillermo Calvo has noted on many occasions. Clearly, a number of countries in Latin America have been pursuing good economic policies for several years but still find themselves affected by a political and economic crisis in Russia to which they have no apparent connection. Now that crisis can spread through much of the world, it is paramount that we devise an international architecture and a set of policies

that provide countries with some security against these large external disturbances. If policies or structures leave even well-managed countries vulnerable
to distant disturbances over which they have no control, something is clearly
wrong and corrective action ought to be taken.

In thinking about this broad issue, we have to begin with a certain measure of humility. We know a lot, but there is much we do not know. Reflecting
on the events of the past year suggests that we have yet to make full use of the
knowledge we have, and too often we have not recognized the limits of what
we know. Explanations of what caused the crisis and what ought to be done
about it are descriptive rather than analytical and are at the level of good
business journalism. That is, people who write about the stock market have a
very difficult task. I sympathize. They have to write a story every day about
why the market went up or down. This hindsight is understandable because
most of us know that the stock market is unpredictable. If journalists could
predict its course, they would not be journalists but wealthy. So the explanations that pour forth from the media on a regular basis have little forecasting
power. They are nice stories that amuse people and sell newspapers. That is
an important economic function, but the product, in bits and pieces, has little
intrinsic value. Yet when ex-post interpretations of the facts are assembled
over time, hopefully patterns emerge. They provide material for serious economists to build up a theory, test it through models, and see which statements
make sense and have explanatory power.

Unfortunately, in trying to describe what has caused the East Asian crisis or the Latin American crisis or the Russian crisis, there has thus far been
more journalistic fire and smoke than penetrating scientific and economic
light. Real explanatory power has two dimensions. It must enable you to make
statements that predict a crisis ex ante, but without sounding false alarms.
You want to avoid both type-I and type-II errors. Some famous forecasters
have predicted nine out of every four economic downturns. That isn't such a
good record when you realize that crying "wolf" sometimes lulls people to the
imminence of real danger.

The credit rating agencies, on the other hand, have been criticized for
giving strong ratings in June 1997 to all the East Asian countries on the eve of
their crisis. The agencies respond to this criticism by pointing to the footnotes
in which vulnerabilities were indicated. But of course, these footnotes resemble the footnotes in the reports for almost every other country. Using
footnotes as an indicator of whether or not to invest would mean avoiding the
emerging markets altogether, and in fact, developed markets as well. Just
saying that there are vulnerabilities and we warned you about them doesn't
mean much unless the warning distinguishes levels of risk and has predictive
value.

In fact, some research has looked at financial crisis prediction models
constructed before the East Asian turmoil. One can plug updated information

into the standard models to see if they could have anticipated what happened had more complete data been available at the time. There are lots of different models, and we tested four categories using different variables. The standard models, using the data that was available in 1997, showed that East Asian countries were about or a little below average in vulnerability to financial crisis. They were not the countries of highest risk. Not only did we not predict the oncoming crisis; we ought to admit that we probably could not have predicted what happened because the standard models had blind spots.

Now, ex post facto, the journalists, as well as others, are rushing forward with explanations. One that is frequently heard is the lack of transparency. Let me make clear my view about transparency. Of course it is very important. I also think the international financial institutions have an important role in improving transparency and setting international standards. That was one of the important recommendations that came out of the G22 working party.

Yet transparency as a causative agent must be put into perspective. First, it is interesting that transparency was never used to explain previous crises or to predict this one. And it has not been used to explain contagion to countries with basically sound fundamentals, which has occurred in the aftermath of the Russian crisis. So it seems to be a good journalistic explanation for what happened in these particular East Asian countries, although as the next few points make clear, even this qualification has limits.

Second, there are independent measures for transparency, and the data show that the East Asian countries are about average compared to the rest of the world. The least transparent countries are not the ones in crisis. There is no indication that East Asian countries were, in some sense, fundamentally worse than most countries that did not have a crisis.

Third, the countries in East Asia actually had much better performance over the previous 30 years than did other countries, not only in terms of average growth but also in terms of cyclical variability. They had fewer years of economic downturn than OECD countries. In fact, two East Asian countries had no years of economic downturn, while another two had only one such year. If lack of transparency leads to more vulnerability than why were there 30 years of sustained growth? One might argue that existing transparency was eroding during that period, but the evidence actually points the other way, toward more transparency.

Finally, one must look at the evidence from countries that formed the last ring in the current financial crisis. All were Scandinavian countries— Finland, Norway, and Sweden—that claimed to be and are the most transparent in the world. The lesson, then, is not that transparency is unimportant, but that it is no panacea. It is not a vaccine against this kind of crisis, and to think otherwise is to be lulled into complacency.

In fact, a great deal of theoretical research suggests that more transparency could actually lead to more volatility. The rationales for this are too complex to explore here fully, but we should be aware that a considerable body of supporting evidence has been amassed. One of the interesting sidebars is that many of the more developed countries have, during the past decade, deliberately decided not to be as transparent as was possible. In the wake of the savings and loan (S&L) crisis in the United States, there was a lot of discussion about increasing transparency. That term wasn't used because it hadn't become fashionable yet, but essentially the same argument was framed with a different vocabulary. For example, many of us thought marking to market was the way to go because it would reveal information about the true state of balance sheets. Some of the most-respected regulators at the time opposed this, and for very defensible reasons. One concern was that if they did the marking to market, not all assets could be covered. That is, increased transparencies could lead to distortions because the information was not perfect and there would be asymmetries. Second, there was worry that more transparency would reveal many more American banks below water. This could have sparked a full-scale crisis that dwarfed the situation with the S&Ls. And finally, even in more normal times regulators resist calls for absolute transparency in order to protect their range of discretion. Regulators like more discretion, so even the more developed countries do not push transparency as far as it could go.

So far we have looked at what we don't know. Now it is time to turn to what we do know. We know there is an economic justification for acting. Because there are significant discrepancies between the social and private benefits and risks, there is a real rationale for doing something. In other words, the very presence of bailouts means that investors are not bearing the full consequences of their actions. The fact that bailouts proceed anyway testifies to the need to combat externalities that lead to contagion elsewhere. So if you believe that there ought to be somebody involved in the bailout business, you have to believe that there ought to be interventions to stop the events that trigger it. What do we know about these events?

Let's look at the evidence. We know first that financial crises are systematically related to financial market liberalization. We know this through statistical studies done on a cross section. We also know that a wide body of theory supports that perspective.

We also know that having better financial market regulation can reduce the likelihood of financial crisis. This is tempered by the knowledge that a lot of the frameworks put forward have been, at the least, a little misguided. Let me give you an example. There has been excessive focus on one set of instruments—capital adequacy standards. We all know that the risk adjustments behind capital adequacy standards are inadequate. They really do not accurately reflect risk. Recognition of this is growing and has raised concerns that opportunities have been opened to exploit the distortions between perceived and actual risk and that this can actually lead to increased risk exposure. Speculation about the misalignment of the system in judging true risk can increase exposure.

Overreliance on capital adequacy standards also has a second costly side effect. There is an enormous body of theory, and some evidence, to support the concept of franchise value—that is to say, the value of banks as an ongoing enterprise—and how this leads to prudential behavior. We are just beginning to realize that an increase in capital adequacy standards can lead to a decrease in franchise value, and that in turn leads to less-prudential behavior and more risk taking. Capital adequacy standards are only one tool, and an imperfect tool. They need to be accompanied by other actions, such as restrictions on risky investment opportunities. They have to be used in conjunction with other instruments. Thailand, for example, represents a very strong case for how financial market liberalization is a key factor leading to the crisis that spread throughout the region. In the 1980s, the Thais had restrictions on investments in speculative real estate. Then purists told them to get rid of the restrictions and let the free market reign. It was more important, these experts said, to let people invest in empty commercial office buildings (imitating U.S. S&L investments in Texas) than to invest in education or other infrastructure to boost productivity. When the bubble burst, of course, the consequences were very severe.

We also know that capital market liberalization, when it is associated with heavy short-term capital flows, increases risk and exposes countries to contagion from external shocks. The evidence of the benefits from these flows is much weaker. Instruments to limit the level of risk need to be found.

Finally, I want to conclude by returning to my earlier point that interventions are justified to correct the discrepancies between private and social risks, to correct problems in ways that reduce the likelihood of crisis and the threat of spreading contagion. We have some evidence that there are instruments that can help to correct the discrepancies between private and social returns. Analysis of all these instruments goes beyond the scope of this session, so I will briefly address the topic of what the international institutions can do.

At a minimum, international institutions can play an important role to encourage adoption of needed policies and to clear up misperceptions about them. International institutions can persuade investors that adoption of some restraints on capital flows is not necessarily a sign that a country is unfriendly to investments. The goal is simply to insulate the domestic economy from certain kinds of risk that are not compensated by adequate benefits.

A second set of actions would involve the international community in setting up procedures that parallel, at the international level, the national bankruptcy laws that are so essential to the well-being of domestic economies.

Most importantly, I want to underline the role international institutions can play in trying to complement private markets by providing risk guarantees that can mitigate some of the excess volatility that characterizes the current uncertainty about the degree of exposure and imperfection in the capital market. The history of the World Bank shows that providing these risk guarantees to complement private capital markets was very much on the minds of the founders of the Bretton Woods institutions. Their experience of the 1920s and its consequences in the two decades that followed was indelibly imprinted in their resolve to act. It is now 60 to 70 years since worldwide capital markets have behaved so erratically. Again it is time to act. Recapturing the spirit and wisdom expressed at Bretton Woods, we must think about how international financial institutions can work effectively with private capital markets to reduce the virulence of contagion so that countries pursuing good economic policies for an extended period of time will not fall needlessly into financial crisis.

Joseph Stiglitz is Senior Vice President/Chief Economist at the World Bank.

Washington, D.C., October 1998

Author's Remarks

Ricardo Hausmann

It is a pleasure to be able to respond after Pedro Pou and Joseph Stiglitz's interesting and important contributions. I would add that wrong diagnoses are not limited to journalists. The Bretton Woods institutions, after the fever had passed, argued that low savings had caused the Mexico crisis. A contemporaneous work we did with Ernesto Talvi and Michael Gavin suggested that savings had nothing to do with crises, but the idea seemed so counterintuitive that it never got a serious hearing. Now that countries with the highest savings in the world have gotten into trouble, that issue has hopefully been put to rest.

Continuing to be counterintuitive for a moment, crises are opportunities, as the Chinese proverb says. They generate an abundance of ideas for debate and discussion. The only problem is that ideas for action by the international financial institutions have to be approved by 170 governments at the World Bank and the IMF. The comparative advantage of the IDB is that it only needs the approval of 46 governments. We are much more "dynamic" in that sense.

But before considering how to get these institutions moving, we need to concentrate on ideas for what they could be doing at a time like this. The first imperative is not to do harm. That thinking is quite unconventional. It means not only not giving the wrong policy advice, as Joseph Stiglitz has indicated, but also being willing to adjust our rules and procedures by understanding how their interaction can be counterproductive. The rules say that loan disbursement is contingent on the borrowing country putting counterpart funds into the projects being financed. Yet if the country is also being advised at the same time to do fiscal adjustments, counterpart funds must be cut. In turn, this means the international institution must automatically cut its lending. The net effect of current rules is procyclical, aggravating the crisis. One remedy would be to lend countries the money for counterpart funds (perhaps in the form of shorter-term debt) so that the projects that meet our grade don't come to a halt because countries are adopting prudent fiscal policies. That is one idea: Do no harm, particularly by adopting a more countercyclical approach to project implementation.

A second idea would have international institutions play a compensatory role in regard to capital flows. Two years ago, the talk was that multilaterals were too expensive and slow. That talk has gone silent in the past couple of months as the crisis has deepened. When the markets are there, people don't want to deal with the multilaterals. When the markets have vanished, they want the multilaterals to step in. So multilaterals have a natural sort of anticyclical role to play in this world. We need, and will continue, to provide loans that are, in fact, filling gaps in private markets.

The third idea would have multilaterals supplementing private markets to play a precautionary role in warding off crises. The contingent repo facility that Argentina has built under the leadership of Pedro Pou is a fantastic idea. The notion that you can do it through the market, that a country might be able to construct a market lender of last resort with some leverage or participation by international financial institutions, is a great idea. The "theological" problem that we have in these institutions is that people want to know precisely what the money is buying. Show me the bricks. Show me the mortar. Show me the teachers. Show me something that resembles development and poverty reduction, something I can take a picture of. It is very hard to take a picture of precautionary facilities. Yet reducing the social cost of volatility is as important or more important, in terms of preserving people's livelihoods, than some of the more conventional programs we fund. International institutions are not structured to prevent the house from burning down, but to send some blankets once the house is rubble. So ideas that allow us to prevent disaster should be at the forefront of our attention.

Inevitably this means cofinancing. Multilaterals are too small to be the only source of compensatory flows. The capital markets for Latin America are too big to be replaced by the World Bank and the IDB. If they want to compensate for the declines in private flows, the two institutions should try to leverage their resources with the private sector. This idea was mentioned in a question from the audience at the end of the previous session.

Cofinancing with the private sector has two advantages. First, we get more volume. Second, we bail in the private sector instead of bailing it out. But why should the private sector take up our offer? The reason is our comparative advantage in sovereign risk management.

This concept needs a fuller explanation because it is important. Sovereign risk management is too often hollow. Being sovereign means if you don't want to pay, you don't pay. That is what Russia has just done. Choosing not to pay; that's the end of the story. There is no international court, no seizure of collateral. Understandably this uncertainty about willingness to pay creates problems in credit markets. Markets deal with it by charging a higher spread to cover the risk of default. But this too has limits. When countries with no intention of not repaying face huge spreads because of a generalized anxiety about default, they may decide that the rate of overpayment is so great they might as well not pay it. So an escalation of uncertainty sets in that can very easily make the market disappear.

The multilaterals can manage sovereign risk differently. The IDB has in a country like Argentina 20 ongoing projects. In addition there is a pipeline of loans scheduled to come onstream. All these projects and loans are at below-market rates for Argentina. The IDB's rules stipulate that if Argentina does not repay, disbursements end on the 20 current loans and all processing of new loans also stops. That is called a big hammer. Since they know the hammer exists and will be used, they have always repaid. This held true during the 1982 crisis and during the hyperinflations of the late 1980s and early 1990s. This hammer has been our comparative advantage.

Now it has added value. This is because there are very few ways in which countries can signal their firm plans to repay. A country that signs a contract, despite being subject to the possibility of being hit with a hammer, is saying that the prospect is not frightening because it fully intends to repay. This signaling device has become even more valuable now that Russia has defaulted and received nearly universal applause. People said this is great, this is burden sharing, this is a lesson in moral hazard for investors, and so on. Yet this public reaction to Russia has increased sovereign risk. And that has made the sovereign risk management technology of multilaterals more valuable to others. The multilaterals can structure in financial instruments that make cofinancing more attractive to the private sector.

The final idea I want to mention is that the market for our sovereign debts is very, very illiquid because our financiers got in trouble and had to sell. As Guillermo Calvo mentioned in Part One in describing how the contagion has spread, these investment managers are the knowledgeable ones. If they are selling, even with tears in their eyes, those who don't know the region follow their lead and presume there must also be a good reason not to buy. A fire-sale mentality sets in, and the market disappears. This lack of liquidity in that market is a little awkward.

After all, Latin America is hyperliquid. We have over $100 billion in international reserves that is being invested to create liquidity for the G7 sovereign debt. Some people would say no, for the G3 sovereign debt. Other people would say no, for the G1 sovereign debt. The point is that there has to be some mechanism to recirculate that liquidity, so that we have greater liquidity for our instruments.

That can be done. The idea that Pedro Pou put on the table is very attractive, very interesting. It would require some international concerted action. I think that some agreement at the hemispheric level between governments and their central banks, with some support by the U.S. administration or even Canada, can provide this liquidity support to shore up sovereign debt markets that are now suffering from fire-sale prices. Let me conclude by arguing in favor of an initiative to ease this crisis that does not depend on all-G7 concerted action because as Ortega y Gasset once said, "Other peoples' pain is so much easier to bear." It is our pain, not theirs.

Ricardo Hausmann is Chief Economist of the Inter-American Development Bank.

Open Discussion

Question: Mr. Hausmann spoke of the IDB's support for financing plans and how to complement the private sector. A good example is what the IDB is doing with Argentina. As Mr. Pou said, Argentina is now negotiating a contingent line of credit with a guarantee from the IDB. This is the first time this type of solution has been contemplated. I would like to know what other types of mechanisms the IDB may be studying to help provide financing to these countries. Are there other alternatives? Is this financing only for the public sector, as in the case of Argentina, or is it considering another type of cofinancing between the IDB and the private sector, investment banks, or for the private sector in Latin American countries? The other question regards your comment that when a country is receiving loans for infrastructure projects, if the country does not pay, the infrastructure project is halted and the IDB withholds its loan. I would like to remind you that most countries in Latin America borrow to pay debts, not to execute infrastructure projects.

Ricardo Hausmann: In answer to the first question—what are the international institutions considering—I suppose that since I work for this institution and I made the statement that the IDB is considering various alternatives, then we are considering them. But as I said before, some 46 countries must come to an agreement. But I think there will be great receptivity for the kind of support we are giving Argentina, which is the first of its kind. Secondly, we are already cofinancing investment projects with the private sector. This window is open. Through this window the IDB arranges financing for private investment projects and cofinances them with private investors throughout the world for the private sector in Latin America. We are already offering this product. Finally, most IDB projects are investment projects. We are financing investment programs in education, health, water, roads, etc. This is the bread and butter of our work. I would take exception to the statement that most countries borrow from the IDB to pay debts. Usually, they borrow from the IDB to execute investment projects.

Question: Mr. Hausmann, do you think other regional development banks throughout the world could use the IDB's approach? Could these development banks become more important by exploiting their comparative advantages?

Ricardo Hausmann: The nice thing about the multilateral development banks is their overlapping memberships. The 46 countries that own the IDB are also owners of the World Bank. So there is a natural process whereby ideas get discussed and shared. Documents are sent out to the same capitals. Ideas move around, acquire feet of their own. For example, the Clinton initiative emerged from debates in which the International Financial Institutions (IFIs) participated. Eventually, the owners of these institutions have to decide in which organization to put a plan of action. We are early supporters of the idea of contingent lines of credit, which is now being advocated for the IMF. We are very glad that the U.S. now wants the IMF to assume that role.

Question: You have said that "the hammer" applies when a country considers not making repayments. Have you ever considered using the hammer when a country is not following what you would consider to be sound economic policies? That is, can the hammer be used more effectively by withdrawing all funding for projects when it seems a country is on the wrong path?

Ricardo Hausmann: The hammer is a very clear contractual arrangement. We only use the hammer when those terms are abridged. That is the agreement. Everyone who signs the contract agrees to the hammer. We don't make ex-post judgments about a country's policies. Such appraisals precede making a loan, but are inappropriate later. If we think that a project is well designed, and the country is a member of this bank, we will support the country. We will only stop disbursement if there is a breach of contract. A country signs before the project gets under way, thereby signaling its commitment to repay. That is why we do not have a problem with lack of commitment to repay the IDB. Not one country has a single arrearage with the IDB at the present time. In the last four years that I've been at this bank, there has been no occasion in which any country has delayed payments with us. That clearly indicates the incentive structure is well designed to address the problem of sovereign risk. This is our comparative advantage, and it should not be squandered.

Paris, March 1999

Financial Turmoil and the Choice of Exchange Rate Regime

Ricardo Hausmann, Michael Gavin, Carmen Pagés-Serra, and Ernesto Stein

Financial turmoil is becoming a fact of life in Latin America. The 1990s have been characterized by enormous volatility in the magnitude and cost of capital flows (see Figures 1, 2, and 3). The swings in capital flows have not only been large, but very highly correlated across countries. The disparateness of these countries suggests it is not only the quality of policies in each emerging market but global factors that are responsible. As blame has moved away from inappropriate domestic policies, the paradigm has shifted toward the determination of which policies—domestic or international—are most effective in taming the destabilizing effects of inherently volatile capital flows.

This debate has been raging throughout the decade and some areas of consensus have been emerging. In particular, fiscal and financial policies have been revisited in order to make them more resilient and stabilizing, given the volatility of capital flows. The paper by Gavin and Hausmann in Part Two of this volume reviews these policies. There has been much less agreement on the appropriate design of exchange rate policy. This paper asks what the appropriate exchange rate arrangement for Latin American countries should be. It reviews the theoretical claims made in favor of each regime and checks whether the empirical record is consistent with these claims.

For much of its history until the 1960s, Latin America adopted fixed exchange rate systems (see Table 1). In the 1960s, a few countries, notably

Table 1. Proportion of Exchange Rate Arrangements by Period

Type of arrangement	1960–1973		1974–1981		1982–1988		1989–1994	
	#of Obs	%	# of Obs	%	#of Obs	%	#of Obs	%
Fixed to single currency	322	88.5	159	76.4	110	60	56	35.9
Fixed to basket					4	2.2		
Fixed w/frequent adj.	18	4.9	12	5.8	4	2.2	3	1.9
Forward-looking crawling peg			9	4.3	4	2.2	10	6.4
Forward-looking crawling band							3	1.9
Backward-looking crawling peg	12	3.3	22	10.6	46	25	9	5.8
Backward-looking crawling band							7	4.5
Dirty Floating	8	2.2	6	2.9	5	2.7	28	17.9
Free Floating	4	1.1			9	4.9	40	25.6
Total	364	100	208	100	182	100	156	100

Brazil and Colombia, faced the problem of domestic inflation leading to recurrent exchange rate crises and responded with a crawling exchange rate system. This approach became more common in the 1970s. With the debt crisis in the early 1980s, most countries abandoned fixed exchange arrangements and adopted a myriad of alternative regimes. As inflation became a central concern of monetary policy, Latin America began to explore exchange arrangements that provide some anchor on price expectations but with some built-in flexibility to make them more sustainable. *Preannounced crawling rates* were used as an inflation stabilization strategy in the Southern Cone in the late

Figure 1. Volatility of Capital Flows as a Share of GDP

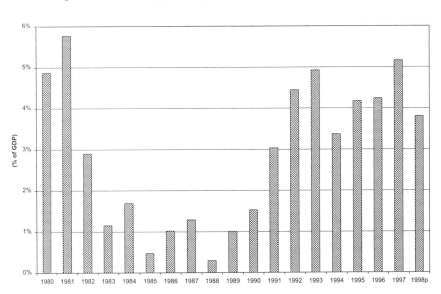

1970s (e.g., Argentina, Chile, and Uruguay). These attempts led to massive real appreciation and were abandoned as the debt crisis set in. Then the mood changed in favor of *backward-looking crawling pegs* in order to protect the real exchange rate from serious misalignment. However, in many countries this arrangement was put under stress in the early 1990s by large inflows of capital. *Exchange rate bands* were then introduced (e.g., in Chile, Colombia, and Mexico) in order to provide some flexibility while creating an anchor for the price level. Other countries adopted managed floats, either in the context of stabilization attempts (e.g., Bolivia in 1985, Peru in 1990) or as a consequence of exchange rate crises (e.g., Mexico in 1994, Brazil in 1999). Hence

Figure 2. Volatility in Yields of Latin American Sovereign Dollar Bonds

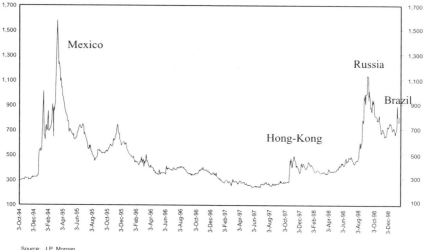

Latin Eurobond Index Spread (1994–1999)

Source: J.P. Morgan

Figure 3. Regional Correlation of Yields on Emerging Bonds Market across Disparate Regions

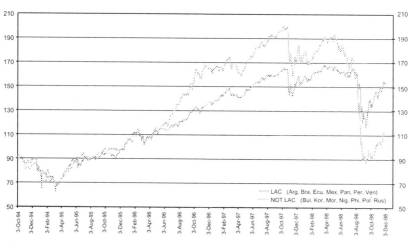

EMBI + Price Index (1994–1998)

Price Index (01/03/94 = 100)

the region has been exploring alternative exchange rate systems, with a growing preponderance of more-flexible arrangements such as managed floats and crawling bands. Only Argentina, which adopted a currency board in 1991, has moved into a highly fixed regime.

This shift highlights one of the major undercurrents behind the experimentation with alternative regimes: the benefits of a clear and strong price anchor to fight inflation provided by fixed regimes vis-à-vis the degrees of freedom in monetary policy and exchange rate outcomes provided by more-flexible arrangements. The crawling band appears as an intermediate regime that attempts to reap some benefits of both objectives.

Although the region generally has been moving from fixed to more-flexible arrangements, there has been very little convergence to a new paradigm. The classification of regimes in Table 1 counts nine different systems. Many of these regimes were adopted not because of their proven success but their theoretical promise. It is fair to say that given the difficult times the region has had to endure in the past decade, these regimes have worked about as well as snake oil. The debate reopens after each experiment goes awry, and one regime is replaced by another in hopes of finding the magic formula. Venezuela fixed its official exchange rate in 1994 but was forced to abandon it in a currency crisis in 1996. Two exchange rate bands have collapsed (Mexico in 1994 and Brazil in 1999) and have been succeeded by floating regimes. Chile and Colombia have kept their currency bands but with frequent adjustments to their parameters. Argentina's currency board was able to survive the Tequila, Hong Kong, Russian, and Brazilian crises, bringing this arrangement to the attention of policy circles throughout the region. However Argentina now is seriously considering the possibility of full dollarization, in the context of the Brazilian crisis. This proposal comes after the launching of the still untested Euro and suggests the possible convenience of supranational currencies. It also has focused attention on the financial experience of Panama, the only Latin American country with a fully dollarized system.

This paper attempts to assess the performance of alternative exchange rate regimes in Latin America relative to the benefits they theoretically are supposed to deliver. We will test empirically whether flexible systems allow for better cyclical management, more monetary autonomy, and improved control of the real exchange rate. We find that flexible exchange regimes have not permitted a more stabilizing monetary policy but instead have tended to be more procyclical. In addition, flexible regimes have resulted in higher real interest rates, smaller financial systems, and greater sensitivity of domestic interest rates to movements in international rates. We also find that flexible regimes tend to promote wage indexation. We show that the revealed preference of Latin America is to allow very little exchange rate movement, even in periods of large real shocks such as in 1998. We explain this preference as a consequence of de facto wage indexation and the high proportion of dollar-denominated financial liabilities. The paper then discusses the problems with fixed exchange rates and reviews the current interest in supranational currencies, including full dollarization.

The Case for Exchange Rate Flexibility

One way to explain the logic behind exchange rate flexibility is by noting that it is a prerequisite for an independent monetary policy. If a country fixes its exchange rate, monetary policy and outcomes will be determined by the exchange rate commitment. Domestic short-term interest rates will reflect the rates observed in the country of the currency to which one's own currency is pegged, plus a risk premium related to the credibility of the peg. There is no leeway to use monetary policy for other purposes, such as demand management or balance-of-payments adjustments. Moreover, a fixed exchange rate implies "importing" the monetary policy of the country to whose currency one's own has been pegged.

This has two unsavory consequences. First, it may be the wrong monetary policy if business conditions in the two countries differ. Perhaps the country to which one's currency has been pegged is undergoing a recession and wants to reduce interest rates in order to stimulate aggregate demand. Meanwhile, your country may be in the midst of an unsustainable boom and need to reduce aggregate demand through higher interest rates. In this scenario, the peg would import the wrong kind of policy. In fact, the theory of optimal currency areas (Mundell, 1961; McKinnon, 1962) is based precisely on this intuition. Two areas that undergo highly correlated economic fluctuations could share the same currency since they would want to expand or contract aggregate demand at the same time. The high correlation may be the consequence of the fact that the two areas undergo similar external shocks or, more likely, that economic fluctuations in one country are transmitted to the other through highly integrated goods and factor markets. For example, a boom in one country spills over to the other through an increased demand for its exports and its workers.

The second problem with pegging is sovereignty. Even if the business cycle in both countries is highly correlated, the polity of each may have different interpretations of current conditions or may have different preferences in the trade-offs among inflation, unemployment, and external competitiveness that monetary policy entails. Canada is a good example. Despite being a country that is often said to be more integrated to the United States than to itself, Canada has opted to float the exchange rate in order to maintain its monetary independence. In this context, exchange rate flexibility—by allowing a country to run its own monetary policy—leaves it with the choice of either mimicking the policies of its trading partners or going its own way by exploiting its sovereignty.

That is, interest rate policy can be used to achieve internal balance while the exchange rate is allowed to move in order to achieve external balance. This additional degree of freedom allows economic management to be more protective of the level of domestic activity and of unemployment.

This and other favorable theoretical arguments may have underpinned the movements toward more-flexible regimes in Latin America. But have the promises been fulfilled? After almost two decades of experience with more-flexible regimes in Latin America, the empirical validity of many of the supporting axioms can be tested.

Exchange Rate Flexibility and Monetary Policy: From the European Aspirin to the Latin American Headache

Suppose a country is suffering from high unemployment and is keeping interest rates high in order to defend a certain exchange rate peg. The policy is costly because all major constituencies are unhappy. Workers complain about unemployment. Manufacturers and farmers are unhappy because the strong currency makes them less competitive vis-à-vis foreign producers. The construction, consumer durable, and financial sectors are upset about the high interest rates. Then suppose that the monetary authority shifts gears and decides to lower interest rates and let the exchange rate weaken. If this can be done, the constituencies that were previously upset will now be happy, and will probably forgive the central bank for reneging on its commitment to a strong and stable currency.

The European experience suggests this latter policy combination can be done successfully. Figure 4 shows the exchange rates and interest rates for the United Kingdom, Italy, and Spain circa October 1992. In the first two cases, the government reacted to an attack against its currency by letting it float and used the opportunity to lower interest rates. In the U.K., rates were lowered from a level of 9 to10 percent to around 5 percent as the currency depreciated by some 30 percent.[1] In Italy, interest rates rose from 12 percent before the crisis to 18 percent in the middle of the attack, and were then brought down to less than 9 percent while the currency weakened continuously in the following months. In Spain, two discreet devaluations in October 1992 and April 1993 "failed," in the sense that they did not allow a reduction in interest rates. Nevertheless the government was not overwhelmed by the attack. In the end, a further depreciation in June 1993 finally allowed interest rates to decline from 13 percent to 9 percent. Overall the peseta depreciated by some 40 percent.

---

[1] All rates of depreciation are calculated in the Latin fashion as the change in the amount of local currency needed to buy a unit of foreign currency.

Figure 4. Nominal Exchange Rates and Interest Rates in the United Kingdom, Italy, and Spain (1992–1994)

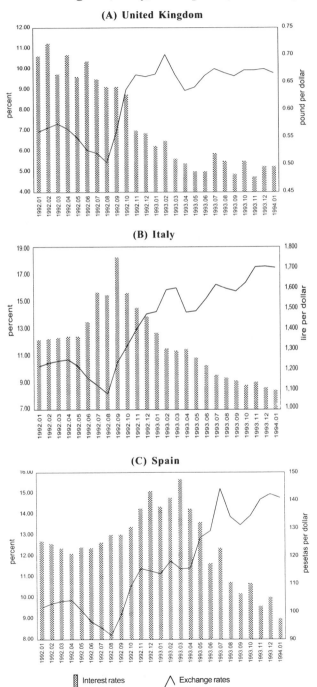

(A) United Kingdom

(B) Italy

(C) Spain

Interest rates   Exchange rates

The European experience of 1992 suggests that it is possible to let go of a fixed exchange rate and reduce interest rates, allowing the economy to gain both from improved competitiveness and from more-expansionary monetary conditions. Moreover, the impact on domestic inflation was minimal in spite of the sizeable devaluations. Letting the exchange rate go relieves the pain.

The European experience suggests that letting the exchange rate go has three benefits. It allows for lower interest rates, has minor effects on the price level, and allows output to recover.

Yet the Latin American experience is quite different (see Figure 5). Take, for example, the case of Mexico in 1994. On December 21, the government announced a controlled devaluation (à la Spain) of some 20 percent. Mexican authorities were only able to defend the new parity for two days before being forced to let it float. The exchange rate depreciated by 70 percent in spite of an interest rate hike from 18 percent before the crisis to over 80 percent at the peak before settling into an average of 50 percent in the second semester of 1995. This increase took place despite massive international financial assistance. Unlike the European experience, output dropped by almost 8 percent in 1995, and the inflation rate accelerated from 8 percent in 1994 to 55 percent in 1995.

Brazil had a very similar experience in January 1999. The government announced a controlled devaluation (à la Spain and Mexico) that it could only defend for a day, in spite of some US$35 billion in reserves and an equivalent amount in commitments of international financial assistance. It was then forced to float. The currency quickly depreciated by some 60 percent, an amount that exceeded everyone's assessment of the previous level of overvaluation. But in spite of this "overshooting," interest rates went up not down. The government has announced that it expects to achieve an inflation rate of 15 percent in 1999 (up from 0.5 percent) and that output will fall by 3 to 4 percent.

Although much less dramatic in nature, the depreciations in Chile and Colombia during 1998 led to qualitatively similar results.

Hence the Latin American experience suggests that letting the exchange rate go results in the following ill effects. It forces an increase in interest rates, has a large inflationary impact, and causes a major decline in output.

The Revealed Preference of Latin American Central Banks

Perhaps these tendencies help explain the choices made by Latin American monetary authorities since July 1997, when a severe sequence of negative external shocks began. First came the financial contagion associated with the East Asian crisis. Then came the major deterioration in the terms of trade caused by declines in the prices of oil, metals, and agricultural products. During this time, the region was hit by devastating natural disturbances such as El

Figure 5. Nominal Exchange and Interest Rates in Mexico and Brazil

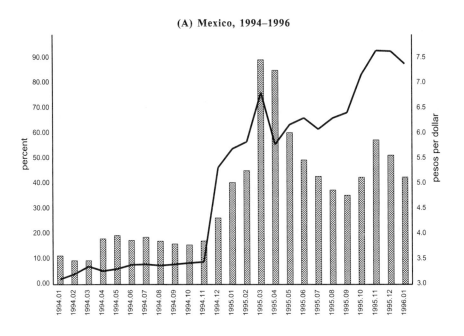

(A) Mexico, 1994–1996

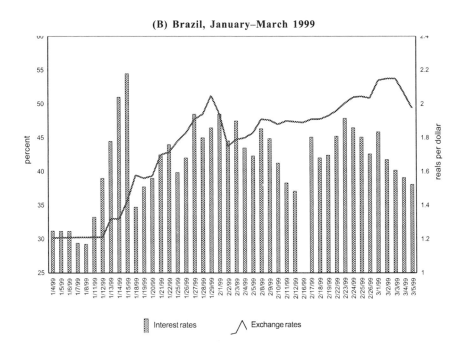

(B) Brazil, January–March 1999

Niño, hurricanes Georges and Mitch, and the earthquake in Colombia. To top it all off, the region felt the impact of the major financial contagion that followed the Russian crisis. How did the monetary authorities of Latin America react to this negative drumbeat of real shocks? In particular, did countries with exchange rate flexibility make use of it or did they rely on higher interest rates and reserve losses to cope with the external shocks (as would be required in a fixed exchange rate regime)?

Table 2 shows the changes in international reserves, exchange rates, and interest rates from May 1997 to October 1998 for 11 Latin American countries. We divided the period into three segments in order to capture the major shock that characterized each period: the Asian financial contagion (May to November 1997), the collapse in the terms of trade (December 1997 to July 1998) and the Russian crisis (July to October 1998). The table includes countries with very fixed (or dollarized) systems such as Argentina and Panama; countries with crawling rates such as Costa Rica and Uruguay; countries with crawling bands such as Brazil, Chile, Colombia, Ecuador, and Venezuela; and countries with managed floating regimes such as Mexico and Peru.

The first stylized fact to emerge from the data is that, in spite of the large magnitude of the external shocks, *most countries used their exchange rate flexibility very sparingly*. If anything, exchange rate depreciations were not used to attempt a real depreciation but were instead used to keep up with inflation differentials, as was the case in Costa Rica, Ecuador, Uruguay, and Venezuela. In Peru—a formally floating rate country that was severely hit by both El Niño and the collapse in the terms of trade—the cumulative devalua-

Table 2. Reserves, Exchange Rates, and Interest Rates since the Asian Crisis

	May 1997– Nov 1997			Dec 1997–July 1998			July 1998–Oct 1998		
	Financial Crisis in Asia			Terms of Trade			Russian Crisis		
	ΔR	Δe	Δi	ΔR	Δe	Δi	ΔR	Δe	Δi
Argentina	4.40	0.00	2.40	0.80	0.00	-2.13	0.98	0.00	0.81
Brazil	-12.11	3.56	18.68	33.79	4.12	-15.31	-40.45	2.65	17.66
Chile	10.72	3.91	6.50	-16.30	5.78	8.29	3.66	-0.58	2.15
Colombia	-2.38	21.06	0.26	-8.57	5.96	8.76		12.87	0.89
Costa Rica	13.27	5.12	-0.75	-14.16	6.13	0.76	-2.79	2.78	0.00
Ecuador	-5.26	10.66	-0.02	-2.62	21.07	9.36	-21.58	25.72	2.96
Mexico	10.25	3.69	1.26	10.01	10.32	1.16	-3.17	13.90	12.94
Panama	-39.94	0.00	-0.26	13.05	0.00	0.03	-2.37	0.00	-0.09*
Peru	4.89	1.87	-0.94	0.64	7.33	7.60	-3.90	4.78	12.44
Uruguay	22.08	5.82	-1.77	9.47	4.94	-6.42		1.40	8.82
Venezuela	22.41	3.41	2.87	-20.66	11.55	19.35	1.37	1.51	2.34

Source: IFS

*August ΔR = Change in reserves. Δe = Change in exchange rates. Δi = Change in interest rates.

tion barely kept pace with inflation. Chile also allowed minimal movements in its exchange rate in spite of a major collapse in the price of copper and in the Asian demand for its exports. The only countries that allowed the exchange rate to move more significantly were Colombia and Mexico.

The second stylized fact is that *countries did use interest rates very aggressively* to defend their exchange rates. Brazil increased interest rates dramatically after the Hong Kong and Russian attacks. Chile, Mexico, Peru, and Venezuela increased interest rates very dramatically in response to the terms-of-trade collapse and the Russian crisis.

The third stylized fact is that, most surprisingly, *interest rates moved least in countries with no exchange rate flexibility.* In Argentina and Panama there were very small movements in the domestic interest rate. In contrast, countries with formally floating systems such as Mexico and Peru saw very large interest rate movements. The same can be said of Chile, which started the period with a very wide exchange rate band.

To sum up, the evidence shows three things. In spite of large real and financial shocks, Latin American central banks use exchange rate flexibility very sparingly, even when they formally float or have wide bands. Interest rates are used much more aggressively in these latter countries. And contrary to conventional wisdom, exchange rate flexibility has seemed to go with higher not lower instability in interest rates.

This result is surprising and merits further exploration. Is something wrong with the conventional theory, and if so, what? Is this an anomaly or a predisposition? Is it a longstanding weakness or a recent phenomenon?

Exchange Rate Arrangements and Financial Systems

The choice of an exchange rate regime depends on the nature of the shocks faced by an economy—at least that is what the literature teaches. According to theory, countries that are subject to domestic monetary shocks benefit from a fixed exchange rate since the money supply automatically adjusts to accommodate changes in money demand (through variations in reserves) without affecting the real side of the economy. On the other hand, countries subject to external shocks or to domestic real shocks do better with flexible arrangements that allow the movement in relative prices needed to reallocate resources in response to these shocks. These prescriptions—fixed regimes for domestic monetary shocks, and floating for external and real shocks—have become deeply entrenched in the conventional wisdom.[2] Since Latin America is a region characterized by substantial terms-of-trade shocks, should countries in the region tend to adopt more-flexible arrangements?

---

[2] See, for example, the survey by Aghevli, Kahn, and Montiel (1991).

In answering this question, it is interesting to see whether countries have, in fact, followed the policy prescriptions of the literature in choosing their exchange rate regimes. Recent studies provide empirical evidence suggesting this is not the case. Lane (1995), using a sample of 110 countries during the 1982–1991 period, finds that, contrary to the conventional wisdom, the more variable the terms of trade are, the more likely a country will adopt a fixed exchange rate. The coefficient of his terms-of-trade volatility variable is highly significant and robust. Frieden, Ghezzi, and Stein (1998) have qualitatively similar findings using a panel of 26 Latin American countries for the period from 1960 to 1994. Again, countries subject to large terms-of-trade shocks tended to adopt less-flexible arrangements such as fixed exchange rates or forward-looking crawling pegs.

Both of these studies present this result as a puzzle. We will argue, however, that what seems puzzling at first glance may be explained by reexamining factors that were overlooked in the theory of optimal regime choice. More specifically, we will argue that fixed exchange rate regimes should result in deeper financial markets, which should be particularly important in economies facing important terms-of-trade shocks.

How does the argument go? First, remember that the exchange rate does not only affect the relative prices of goods or labor. It also affects the relative price of financial assets. Imagine that you are in a country that is subject to large terms-of-trade shocks. Suppose the government adopts a flexible exchange rate regime so that innovations (i.e., unexpected movements) in the terms of trade are transmitted to the exchange rate. In particular, when the terms of trade decline—because of a fall in the price of coffee or oil, for example—the currency would be expected to depreciate. Alternatively, the exchange rate would strengthen when export prices rise. Suppose the public is given the choice of saving in the domestic currency (call it pesos) or in dollars. What will people do?

In the case of a negative terms-of-trade shock, there will be a simultaneous decline in income and a currency depreciation. People holding domestic assets will be hit twice. Their income will drop; and on top of that, the depreciation will wipe out the real value of their peso deposits just when they need to dip into their stock of savings to compensate for their lower income. In the case of a positive terms-of-trade shock, both people's income and the value of their peso-denominated savings would increase at the same time. Said differently, letting the exchange rate fluctuate with innovations in the terms of trade will make the value of domestic financial assets have the wrong covariance with the income process, exacerbating rather than compensating losses. Consequently, the public will shy away from holding domestic assets and prefer to

Figure 6. Exchange Regime and Financial Depth

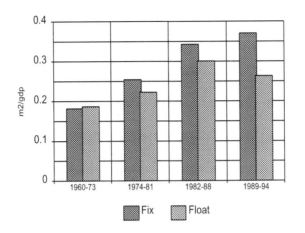

hold dollars instead. In order for people to hold domestic assets, they would demand a higher real interest rate.

This view has very important empirical implications. If it were right, one would expect fixed exchange rate countries to have deeper financial markets and lower real interest rates. In fact, such a benefit would explain why, contrary to the conventional wisdom, more-volatile terms of trade do not go hand in hand with more-flexible exchange rate arrangements.

Figure 6 looks at the financial depth (measured as the ratio of M2/GDP) of fixed vs. flexible exchange rate countries since 1960. We divided the sample time frame into four periods, corresponding to the Bretton Woods period (up to 1973), the period of oil crises (1974 through 1981), the period of the debt crisis (1982 through 1988), and the period when capital flows to the region resumed (1989 through 1994). While there is a tendency for financial depth to increase throughout the time frame in both regimes, it rose more rapidly for the fixed exchange rate countries. Since the vast majority of countries started with fixed exchange rate regimes, it can be said that financial depth rose faster in those countries that remained fixed. In fact, for the 1989–1994 period the average financial depth of countries under fixed exchange rates was 11 percentage points of GDP larger and 41 percent greater than that of countries under flexible arrangements.[3]

This graph, although highly consistent with our story, does not control for other factors that may influence the results (see Appendix A). In the appendix we ran a panel regression that controls for differences in inflation. It

---

[3] Other regimes, such as crawling pegs and bands, were excluded from this exercise, as were regimes that were formally fixed but subject to very frequent readjustments. The results are very similar, however, to our comparisons of financial depth in fixed regimes versus all other regimes.

also includes country dummies and time dummies to account for structural differences across countries or for international variables that have not been explicitly considered. After all these controls, the impact of the exchange rate regime on financial depth remains highly significant and accounts for 4 percentage points of GDP, or 15 percent of the financial depth of countries under flexible arrangements.[4]

This last result probably underestimates the effect of the regime on financial depth. The reason is that, by including country dummies, we capture the differences within countries, but disregard the differences across countries in measuring the effect of the regime. For this reason, we ran another set of regressions to capture the effects of differences across countries. The details of these regressions are also discussed in Appendix A. In this case, our results suggest that the average financial depth of countries under fixed arrangements for the entire sample period would have been 20 percentage points of GDP larger than that of countries under flexible arrangements.[5]

This last result likely overestimates the effect of the exchange rate regime on financial depth because it leaves out certain country characteristics that may explain both financial depth and the choice of regime, which in the previous regressions were captured by the country dummies. The true effect of the exchange rate regime on financial depth is probably somewhere in between the two sets. Notwithstanding the differences in the size of the effects, all of our evidence points in the same direction: Fixed exchange regimes are associated with deeper financial markets. The results are very large in economic terms and highly significant in statistical terms.

The Effect of Exchange Rate Regimes on Real Interest Rates

We have established that the statistical record for Latin America suggests that fixed exchange rate regimes generate deeper financial markets. We also conjectured that fixed regimes would lead to lower real interest rates. This result can be justified theoretically by the fact that since the fixed regime, as long as it is sustained, insures the exchange rate against movements in the terms of trade caused *inter alia* by terms of trade shocks, depositors will demand lower returns than those required under flexible regimes.

To assess this issue we developed a monthly database of monetary and exchange rate statistics for Argentina, Brazil, Chile, Colombia, Costa Rica,

---

[4] We also ran regressions controlling for GDP per capita, in addition to inflation. However this variable was excluded from the regressions shown in the appendix since it is subject to endogeneity problems. It should be noted, however, that the inclusion of this variable did not affect the results significantly.

[5] Since the regime variable in this case captures the time span that a country spent under fixed arrangements, the result can be stated in a different way: For each additional year spent under fixed arrangements, the average financial depth of a country would have increased by 0.2/35 years, i.e., by 0.57 percentage points of GDP.

Figure 7. Average Real Interest Rates under Alternative Exchange Regimes in Latin America

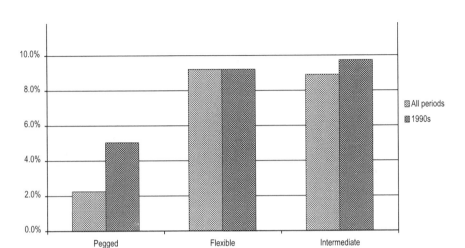

Ecuador, Mexico, Panama, Peru, Uruguay, and Venezuela for the period 1960–1998. As can be seen in Figure 7, fixed exchange rate regimes are associated with significantly lower real interest rates for deposits. For the 1990s, flexible regimes have averaged 9.2 percent real rates while fixed regimes have paid only 5.1 percent. In fact, the results shown compare periods in which annual inflation has been below 20 percent, in order not to skew the results in favor of fixed regimes. Moreover, the difference is statistically significant for the whole sample as well as for the low-inflation observation. The difference remains significant and similar in magnitude after the inclusion of country dummies (see Appendix B).

Hence, the proposition that fixed exchange rate regimes lead on average to lower real interest rates appears to have strong empirical support in Latin America. A lower real interest rate is not only good for borrowers; it is also good for the health of the financial system. If depositors demand high real rates, then bankers must look for higher-return borrowers, who also tend to be riskier. Hence, a lower real interest rate permits safer lending.

Do Fixed Exchange Regimes Lead to Less-Anticyclical Monetary Policy?

We have established that fixed exchange rate systems are not only associated with deeper financial markets but with lower average real interest rates. In this section we explore the cyclical properties of real interest rates to determine whether there has been a difference in the timing of real interest rate movements. Do flexible regimes allow for a more anticyclical policy? Does exchange rate flexibility allow for a more independent monetary policy?

To explore the cyclical properties of monetary policy, we looked at how real interest rates reacted to the output gap under alternative exchange rate regimes. The output gap is the difference between actual monthly industrial output and a fitted trend. Sample countries include Argentina, Brazil, Chile, Colombia, and Mexico. Data is monthly from 1960 to 1998, where available.

The results of our experiments are presented in Table 3. We find that there is a negative relationship between the output gap and real interest rates. This indicates that monetary outcomes have moved in a procyclical fashion: low real interest rates in expansions, high rates in contractions. To check whether this result is peculiar, we ran a similar regression for the United States. We found that while the U.S. regression coefficient is also negative (indicating procyclical outcomes), the estimated value of the coefficient was one-twentieth the size of the Latin American average when considering the whole sample but of similar value when excluding periods in which the annual inflation rate exceeded 20 percent. Said differently, Latin American monetary outcomes were very procyclical in periods of high inflation but normal (by U.S. standards) in periods of low inflation.

More interestingly, we included an interaction term between pegged exchange rates and the output gap to test whether fixed regimes were more or less procyclical than flexible regimes. Interestingly, while the results are not statistically significant, our estimates consistently indicate that fixed regimes

Table 3. Domestic Real Monthly Interest Rates and the Output Gap

Dependent variable: real ex-post monthly interest rates

	All Observations	Inflation <20%	Inflation <20% (with country dummies)
Pegged Exchange Rate	-0.0018	0.0014	.0101
	(-0.22)	(0.46)	(2.45)
Output Gap	-0.1577	-0.0050	-0.0130
	(-3.21)	(-0.40)	(-1.01)
Pegged Rate* Output Gap	0.1418	0.021	0.0316
	(1.21)	(1.07)	(1.59)
Number of Observations	867	388	388
R^2	0.07	0.58	0.60

Output gap is the difference between actual industrial output and a fitted trend. The t-stats are in parentheses.

are less procyclical than flexible regimes. Hence while we cannot say with confidence that fixed regimes are less procyclical than flexible regimes, we can say that they are definitely not more procyclical. This result contradicts the theoretical argument in favor of flexible regimes on the grounds that they have a stabilizing effect on output.

One interpretation for this result is the following. As argued previously, the revealed preference of Latin American central banks is to use exchange rate movements very sparingly, even after large real shocks such as those of 1998. We will rationalize this behavior below by making reference to wage indexation and dollarization. So, to a certain extent, flexible regimes are managed as if they were fixed but without the benefits of such precommitment. Hence when the market sees a bad shock and no depreciation, it anticipates that at any moment the authorities might change course and let devaluation occur. To correct for that possibility, real interest rates remain high, especially during bad times.

Hence the empirical record in Latin America does not argue in favor of a more stabilizing monetary policy under flexible regimes, even in periods of low inflation.

Another important empirical point is whether flexible regimes allow a certain degree of freedom to limit the domestic impact of movements in foreign interest rates. Are flexible regimes more insulating? Have they better sheltered the domestic economy from foreign interest rate shocks?

We have already established that, unlike Europe in 1992, exchange rate flexibility in Latin America leads to higher not lower interest rates. But are domestic interest rates less sensitive to movements in foreign rates under flexible regimes?

To find out we conducted two tests. First, we studied the relationship between daily movements in domestic 30-day interest rates (expressing internal monetary conditions) and foreign dollar rates on sovereign bonds of the same country (expressing the cost of access to world markets) for the period

Table 4. The Impact of the Foreign Cost of Borrowing on Domestic Interest Rates

	Yield*	Constant
Argentina	1.45	-7.19
9/12/97–2/18/99	(15.9)	(-7.2)
Mexico	5.93	-36.05
01/01/98–2/18/99	(27.4)	(-15.99)
Venezuela	2.77	-5.07
9/12/97–2/11/99	(21.6)	(-2.94)

* The yield on the 2026/2027 global bond for each of the three countries. The t-stats are in parentheses.

Figure 8. Monthly Correlation of Foreign and Domestic Interest Rates in Three Exchange Rate Regimes

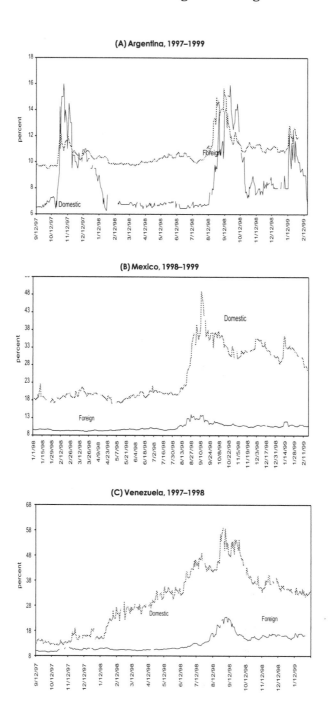

**Table 5. The Impact of Foreign Interest Rates
on Domestic Real Monthly Interest**

U.S. real interest rate	0.96
	(2.0)
Pegged exhange rate	-0.032
	(-1.02)
Peg* U.S. real interest rate	-0.25
	(-0.29)
Number of observations	2272
R^2	0.003

The t-stats are in parentheses.

between September 1997 and February 1999. We chose Argentina, Venezuela, and Mexico for our sample for reasons of data availability and because they represent three very distinct exchange rate systems. The results are presented in Table 4 and are illustrated graphically in Figure 8. As shown, a movement of 1 percent in the foreign interest rate in Argentina causes an increase of 1.45 percent in the domestic rate. The equivalent increase for Venezuela, a country with relatively narrow exchange rate bands, is 2.77 percent while for Mexico it is 5.93 percent. Said differently, movements in foreign interest rates have a maximum impact on domestic rates in Mexico (a country that floats), minimal impact in Argentina (a country with a strongly fixed regime), and intermediate effects in Venezuela (a country with limited flexibility). It is not the case that floating rates deliver monetary sovereignty, as customary logic would have it. In fact, floating seems to amplify the domestic effects of external movements.

This result holds for the very recent past, using daily data on three countries. Does it hold for the longer run, too? We ran a similar exercise using monthly data between 1960 and 1998 for the 11 countries mentioned in the previous section comparing exchange rate regimes and real interest rates. According to the results reported in Table 5, flexible regimes do not provide more insulation from movements in international interest rates. The estimated equation suggests that U.S. real interest rates affect domestic rates with an estimated coefficient very close to 1, as is assumed in most theories.[6] We find again that the average real annualized interest rate of fixed rates is 3.2 percent below that of floating rates in this equation. More importantly, when the U.S. real rate is interacted with the pegged exchange rate and included in the equa-

---

[6] This coefficient is different from the one estimated in the previous exercise because it measures a very different response. In this case, we are looking at the reaction of real domestic interest rates (i.e., nominal rates deflated by domestic inflation) to U.S. real rates (i.e., U.S. dollar rates deflated by U.S. inflation). In the previous exercise we looked at the response of nominal domestic rates to nominal dollar rates.

tion, we obtain a coefficient that is negative and large but statistically insignificant. The point estimate of the coefficient implies U.S. rates affect domestic rates by 25 percent less in countries that peg relative to other countries.

Hence this data set also provides no evidence to suggest that floating arrangements are better at insulating domestic interest rates from foreign rate movements. Instead the numbers, although not in a statistically significant manner, point mainly in the other direction.

Exchange Rate Flexibility and Competitiveness

In the previous section we found that, contrary to conventional wisdom, exchange rate flexibility in Latin America has neither allowed for a more accommodating monetary policy nor sheltered the domestic economy from movements in international interest rates. The conventional wisdom would also argue that by allowing depreciations to take place, the monetary authorities could achieve a more competitive real exchange rate, which will be good for output in the tradable sectors and for the sustainability of external accounts. By lowering wages, as measured in dollars, exchange rate depreciation improves competitiveness, thereby stimulating exports and reducing imports. Countries with flexible regimes can in principle use the exchange rate to affect dollar wages, while those with fixed regimes cannot.

One question is whether the real exchange rate has been more anticyclical in regimes that allow for more exchange rate flexibility. One would expect in boom times for domestic demand to be high, external resources abundant, and the real exchange rate relatively strong. By contrast, in bad times low domestic demand and the absence of real or financial external resources would lead to a weaker real exchange rate. To explore this question, we used our 11-country monthly database and ran the equation presented in Table 6. The regression suggests that real exchange rate movements have been anticyclical in the sense that the currency has been relatively strong when the output is high (the output gap is small) and relatively weak when there is a recession. The result is not statistically significant and the estimated effect is not large. A 10 percent drop in output would cause a 1.5 percent real depreciation in flexible exchange regimes. By contrast, in fixed regimes the effect is estimated to be about half as much, a difference that is not statistically significant. Hence the evidence suggests that real exchange rates have been very mildly anticyclical and more so under flexible regimes, although the difference is not statistically significant.

This result is interesting. One would have expected a clearer difference in the behavior of dollar wages and competitiveness. Don't flexible regimes allow better control over dollar wages and the real exchange rate than pegged systems? This proposition is based on the idea that wage-setting arrangements are not significantly affected by the choice of exchange rate regime.

**Table 6. The Co-Movement of Real Exchange
Rate Deviations and the Output Gap**

	Inflation <20%
Output gap	0.179
	(1.21)
Pegged exhange rate	.0832
	(6.91)
Peg* U.S. real interest rate	-0.079
	(-0.34)
Number of observations	460
R^2	0.098

Real exchange rate deviations are the difference between the real
exchange rate and a fitted trend.
The t-stats are in parentheses.

However we have reason to suspect that this is not so. Imagine two otherwise identical countries subject to relatively large real shocks. In one country the exchange rate is credibly fixed. In the other, it is freely floating so that real shocks are transmitted to the exchange rate. Consider the problem faced by a trade union representative of the widget industry that is negotiating a collective contract. He is asked to sign a contract that is implicitly denominated in dollars in the fixed exchange rate regime but is denominated in an erratic and unpredictable unit in a flexible regime. It is reasonable to assume that under the flexible regime the representative would bargain for a shorter life to the contract (to provide for more-rapid renegotiations), or for some form of indexation (to denominate the contract in a more stable unit). Under these conditions, nominal wages tend to react more swiftly to price shocks under flexible than under fixed regimes, leading to more de facto indexation.

To check for this intuition, we studied the dynamic properties of wages and prices under alternative exchange rate regimes for Argentina, Brazil, Chile, Peru, and Mexico, using monthly data. We inquired about the degree of response of nominal wages to jumps in the price level, after controlling for linear and quadratic trends intended to capture expected movements in inflation and unemployment. The results presented in Figure 9 tend to confirm the above-stated conjecture.

Let us start with Argentina. In the period between February 1986 and December 1988, in which average monthly inflation was 8.5 percent, the estimated elasticity of wage inflation to innovations in price inflation was 65 percent. This means that in the same month, wages recovered 65 percent of any unexpected change in inflation. But contrasted with the period after the convertibility plan had settled down (January 1993 to June 1998), the reaction of wages basically disappeared. A very similar pattern can be seen in Brazil.

Figure 9. Correlation of Wages to Prices in Flexible and Fixed Regimes

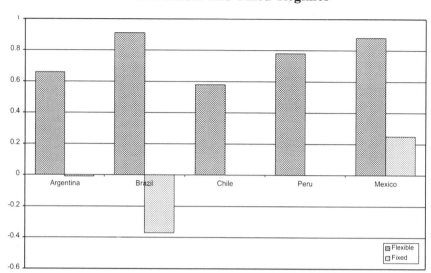

During the period prior to the Real Plan (June 1989 to June 1993) the elasticity of wage inflation was 91 percent, but this reaction disappeared once the Real Plan had stabilized.

These differences could be attributed to the substantial differences in average inflation rates across exchange rate regimes. Yet the evidence from Mexico, Peru, and Chile suggests that inflation is not the whole story. For example the Mexican case shows that indexation may be quite different at similar rates of inflation. In this country, we selected two periods in which the exchange rate regimes were different but average monthly inflation rates were about the same. While the wage inflation elasticity was 25 percent during the fixed exchange rate regime (February 1970 to January 1975), it increased to 88 percent during the crawling-band period in the early 1990s.

The case of Peru from 1992 to 1994 is another good example since it features a flexible exchange rate arrangement and low inflation. Despite the low levels of inflation, nominal wages responded substantially to changes in price inflation. Moreover, this response was much larger than the one featured in Argentina or Brazil during their fixed exchange rate periods.

The last case study focuses on Chile during the 1990s. Our results suggest that, despite low inflation, Chile's actual wage indexation is large but takes place over the course of a quarter. After three months the accumulated elasticity of wage inflation is 58 percent. Hence Chile's flexible exchange rate arrangement is accompanied by substantial de facto indexation, making real wages quite rigid.

Hence Chile and Peru have substantial de facto indexation in spite of low inflation. By contrast, Argentina and Brazil with more fixed arrangements were able to de-index wages in spite of previous histories of high indexation. This supports the idea that de facto indexation is not just the consequence of inflation. Instead it plays the role of an insurance device against the possibility of sudden price movements, which are more likely under flexible than fixed rates. Said differently, the possibility of lowering dollar wages through exchange rate depreciation is anticipated by employers and workers and incorporated in the wage negotiation process. This anticipation reduces the presumed ability of exchange rate flexibility to affect competitiveness.

De facto indexation also implies that the inflationary cost of any attempt to use the nominal exchange rate to achieve a relative price shift will be very high. This may explain the observed tendency of Latin American central banks to use depreciations very sparingly even after severe negative shocks. This logic may explain why Chile and Mexico in 1998 decided to prevent further movements in the exchange rate, opting instead for large increases in domestic interest rates. They argued that further depreciation would compromise their inflation targets even more.

Therefore, flexible regimes face heavy costs when they attempt to improve competitiveness through devaluation. Improvements come at the cost of substantial inflation and tend to be rather short-lived since de facto wage indexation (and the pass-through of imported inflation) nullifies the changes in competitiveness. This logic also explains why the economies in Mexico and in Venezuela returned to their precrisis real exchange rates within two years of massive devaluations in 1994 and 1996, respectively.

As noted, the evidence suggests that exchange rate flexibility leads to higher de facto wage indexation as employers and workers protect their agreements from unexpected changes in prices. Indexation caused by exchange rate flexibility will have important dynamic consequences since wages will then influence prices and fuel inflation. The response of wages will tend to limit the effect of nominal exchange rate movements on external competitiveness while amplifying the inflationary consequences. In this context, one would expect a central bank that is concerned about inflation to allow very little exchange rate flexibility, even under a formally floating exchange rate system.

De facto Dollarization

Latin America is heavily dollarized. In a few countries such as Argentina, Uruguay, Peru, and Bolivia, the formal domestic banking system has dollar deposits that are significantly higher than domestic currency deposits. In other countries the reality is similar but dollar deposits are held either in offshore institutions or abroad. In all countries, the governments, banks, and corporations have large liabilities denominated in dollars. Moreover, this dollarization is not just a temporary phenomenon promoted by high inflation. Although countries with highly dollarized banking systems have had reduced inflation for years, there has been no trend back toward local currency assets. On the contrary, the share of dollar deposits keeps increasing.

Dollarization has important implications for the conduct of macroeconomic policy. In particular, dollarization and foreign-denominated debt have quite unsavory effects on exchange rate movements. By suddenly increasing the value of dollar liabilities, it may bankrupt the banking system or raise the prospect of defaults on foreign debt, making capital flows more volatile.

In this context, devaluations can be highly disruptive and consequently may overshadow any expansionary effect from a more competitive exchange rate on output. Therefore central banks can reasonably be expected not to let the exchange rate move much, even in countries with flexible regimes such as Mexico and Peru and even after a serious real shock like the one in 1998.

Exchange Rates and Currency Crises

According to our results, fixed exchange rates deliver lower real interest rates, deeper financial markets, lower de facto wage indexation, less procyclical monetary policy, and lower domestic impact of foreign interest rate movements. With all these benefits, why the movement toward more flexible rates?

One major problem with fixed exchange rates is that they tend not to be fixed for very long. The history of Latin America and the world is full of fixed regimes that do not last. In fact, Obstfeld and Rogoff (1995) have shown that in the past 20 years fixed exchange rates have become a dying breed. For some time now, there have only been five countries where the exchange rate has been fixed for more than five years, even though the names of the countries keep changing.

One problem is that contracts in fixed exchange rate countries need to be flexible enough to respond swiftly to large negative shocks to avoid a long and protracted recession. This is well known. Yet it is interesting to note that the recovery after the Tequila crisis was as fast if not faster in Argentina, a country with quite rigid labor laws and a currency board, than in Mexico, which underwent a massive devaluation. The answer is very much related to the fact that real interest rates were much lower in Argentina than in Mexico and credit was much more abundant during the recovery. This difference is not only related to the properties of fixed exchange rate systems but also to the fact that Argentine banks were not weakened by devaluation. In this respect, the deeper financial markets associated with fixed exchange rate systems may allow for smoother intertemporal adjustments instead of devaluation-induced sudden relative price changes.

It is important to note that fixed exchange rate regimes may be more likely to suffer currency crises since a successful attack is often feasible.

Moreover, these crises may be more likely to put stress on the banking system under pegged regimes—since the collapse in deposit demand will cause a loss of liquidity—while only leading to a depreciation (and no loss of nominal liquidity) in a floating rate country. It is often argued that flexible regimes are immune to these inconveniences for two reasons: First, they cannot be successfully attacked; second, the central bank can act as lender of last resort.

These two considerations have received wide acceptance but have been shown to be formally wrong. First, as shown by Eichengreen (1998), it is not true empirically that fixed exchange rate systems are more prone to banking crises than flexible arrangements. Second, Chang and Velasco (1998) show that a flexible exchange rate system with foreign debt can be subject to self-fulfilling crises. The perverse dynamics can be characterized as follows: Fear that the currency might depreciate to the point where companies or the government are no longer able to pay will cause capital flight and a massive depreciation in anticipation of the meltdown. Such a scenario may well have happened in East Asia in 1997–1998.

In addition, it is not true that a central bank in a floating rate country can act as lender of last resort without fear of a serious currency crisis. If the market anticipates that the influx of last-resort lending to the banking system will rapidly expand the monetary base, it will expect the currency to lose value and a major destabilizing depreciation could occur. That is exactly what happened in Venezuela during the first half of 1994, when the Central Bank resorted to ample lending to quench the erupting banking crises. This action led to a 100 percent depreciation of the floating exchange rate until exchange controls were imposed. Last-resort lending will be destabilizing if it is based on the idea that money is easy to print. Argentina's new, innovative market-based arrangements are not only for countries that adopt currency boards. They are applicable to any economy, including those typical in Latin America, in which the market may react adversely to a lender of last resort based solely on fiat money.

The difficulties in providing last-resort lending under flexible arrangements, combined with their higher real interest rates and shallower financial markets, may explain Eichengreen's finding that floating rate countries are as likely to experience banking crises as fixed rate countries.

The "Peso Problem" as a Potential Source of Financial Vulnerability

It is easier for governments to prevent a sudden appreciation than a sudden depreciation. They also have a greater financial stake in a large depreciation since it will allow them to collect a hefty inflation tax. Consequently, market expectations about exchange rates tend to be skewed. There is always some probability of a large depreciation. To compensate for this eventuality, risk-neutral investors will demand a higher interest rate. This is known as the "peso problem." In fact, as argued previously, this problem is not exclusive to pegged systems since flexible exchange rate regimes also try to avoid exchange rate movements. In fact, our finding that real interest rates are higher in floating regimes may indicate that the problem is even more serious in those systems.

The point is that while ex-ante interest rates are reasonable, given the devaluation risk, ex-post rates are higher than expected if the devaluation does not take place. Investors will have received returns that are larger than expected; and borrowers, whether banks, corporations or the government, will have paid more than planned. Consequently borrowers' debts will be growing faster than expected. So as time passes, the borrower's ex-post position may consistently weaken solely because of the risk of an unrealized depreciation. In fact, a financial position that would have been sustainable in the absence of exchange rate risks may well become explosive due to the peso problem. It can be argued that the recent Russian and Brazilian crises have elements of this story: A large stock of debt denominated in local currency was issued at high interest rates to pay investors for the risk of devaluation. After enough time had elapsed with no depreciation, the debt had ballooned to unsustainable levels, prompting a crisis.

This problem need not take such spectacular proportions in order to pose a serious challenge. The higher domestic interest rates will cause the financial system to be smaller and riskier than it would otherwise be, and this may have important long-run effects on growth.

The Case for a Supranational Currency

We have argued that exchange rate flexibility has not been much of an asset for Latin America. It has not allowed for a more independent monetary policy. It has not permitted a more stabilizing monetary policy. It has produced higher real interest rates and smaller financial systems. It has prompted more indexed wage arrangements, making relative price movements more inflationary. De facto wage indexation and dollarization have inhibited the monetary authorities from using the exchange rate flexibility they formally have. And they have had to pay the price of that unused flexibility through higher interest rates.

If the benefits of exchange rate flexibility are limited and the costs are large, then fixing appears attractive. But if the currency is to remain fixed, what is the advantage of having your own currency? Imperfect credibility of the peg will make financial intermediation unnecessarily complex. This is expressed in the fact that not a single Latin American country today is able to place long-term debt denominated in its own currency. All long-term financial markets (e.g., those that fund infrastructure and housing needs) are denominated either in dollars or are indexed. In fact, even today the only country where a worker can get an unsubsidized 30-year mortgage loan at 9 percent interest that is denominated in the same currency as his wage is Panama!

The fact that long-term financial markets are either dollarized or indexed means that the balance sheets of corporations and individuals suffer from very serious exchange rate mismatches. This makes currency adjustments potentially devastating, as has been shown by recent crises in East Asia.

In this context, it is easy to understand the interest in a supranational currency. It is a way of seriously precommitting not to devalue, thus avoiding the nightmare scenario of wide-ranging defaults. It is a way to reduce the exchange rate mismatches caused by de facto dollarization and the lack of long-term financial markets denominated in the domestic currency. It is an idea that is prompted by the fact that the world is moving toward a situation in which there are two soft-drink corporations, two airplane manufacturers, three toothpaste producers, and 180 central banks printing their own currencies. Consequently, globalized companies, banks, and households have to manage serious problems of exchange rate risk in currencies that have no liquid derivative markets in which to hedge. In fact, even European companies have found these problems to be difficult and expensive, prompting their support for the Euro.

In Latin America the attraction of a supranational currency is understandable for the same reason that the Euro is more popular in Southern Europe than in Germany or France. Spain, Portugal, and Italy have seen much larger declines in inflation and interest rates and much larger financial benefits than have their neighbors to the north.

However, a supranational currency needs to address three issues: seigniorage, the need for a lender of last resort, and governance structure. Seigniorage, i.e., the revenue generated by printing fiat money, is a small but not unimportant source of income for most governments. For example, in Argentina it represents about US$750 million per year. As a principle of fairness among member countries, a supranational currency would need to have some acceptable mechanism to share the seigniorage proceeds.

Secondly, a lender-of-last-resort facility must be constructed. This is a tricky business because, up to now, last-resort lending has been done by national central banks to rescue domestic banks with the backing of domestic taxpayers. At the supranational level the problem presents new angles. Which tax payers will stand behind last-resort lending? Which banks are eligible, given their increasingly international character?

Finally, the question of governance is politically complex. Who will make what decisions? And what will the objectives be? And to whom will decision makers be accountable?

These three central questions need to be addressed in the context of concrete structures. In this respect, two models are in the air: mimicking the Euro or adopting the dollar. The European approach would surely provide a more negotiable governance structure and a more formalized lender of last resort. However, right now no Latin American currency is considered a reserve currency, and an amalgamation of many weak currencies may not create a particularly strong one. Countries may fear that instead of reducing risks by adopting a single currency, they may be importing significant volatility from their very unstable neighbors. In particular, the launching of the new supranational currency is unlikely to prompt asset holders to switch away from dollars or to generate long-term markets in the new denomination. Hence existing exchange rate risks and mismatches would survive.

Adopting the dollar would have clear advantages. It is the currency of choice for most international trade and for a large share of the region's financial assets and liabilities. Its adoption would eliminate most of the very large exchange rate risks that exist in the balance sheets of corporations, homeowners, and banks.

However, the sharing of seigniorage would constitute an issue that would have to be discussed in the context of a treaty with the U.S. government. Can the political case be made in the United States?

If this problem were resolved, the lender-of-last-resort problem could be more easily addressed. Even if the U.S. attempted to restrict access to the discount window of the Federal Reserve System, U.S. banks would line up to furnish the needed regulatory arbitrage provided they could be secured with adequate collateral. To meet that need, the future flow of seigniorage could be used as prime collateral to generate a "market-based" or privately arbitraged lender of last resort. Dollarization is also likely to increase the set of assets that are considered collateral. In a dollarized system, real estate could be considered collateral, unlike today when it is usually not used for international transactions because of the inherent exchange rate and convertibility risk. Moreover, the risks to U.S. taxpayers of lending to Latin banks is mitigated significantly by the fact that in most countries a majority of banks are already foreign owned. Hence they already receive consolidated home country supervision, a trend that will undoubtedly continue.

The difficult point with dollarization is the governance structure of the monetary authority. Given where Latin America is today—with dollar-denominated interest spreads that move by several hundred basis points on a monthly basis—it is hard to see how a 25 basis point move by the Federal Open Market Committee (FOMC) once in a blue moon would be much noticed. This is especially true since spreads are likely to decline significantly from their current levels. Moreover, as we have seen, the region already imports the decisions of the FOMC, especially in flexible exchange-rate regimes.

Politically, the Federal Reserve is likely to want to maintain total independence because it may fear that markets will think it might consider the economic conditions of Latin America when setting policy. But that fear is probably already a reality in today's world. Was it not the economic conditions of emerging markets and their impact on the U.S. financial system that prompted the interest rate cuts of October and November 1998?

For Latin America, the symbolic loss of its formal monetary institutions and national currencies is likely to be difficult. Globalization has caused the disappearance of many flagship airlines and the appearance of foreign artistic designs on the tails of British Airways' jumbo jets. Would a dollar bill with Columbus on it be a proper symbol for the currency of the Americas?

Ricardo Hausmann is Chief Economist of the Inter-American Development Bank; Michael Gavin is the Director of Financial Research for Latin America at Warburg Dillon Read; Carmen Pagés-Serra and Ernesto Stein are Research Economists in the Office of the Chief Economist, Inter-American Development Bank.

Appendix A. Exchange Rate Regimes and Financial Depth

In this appendix, we describe the data and present the evidence on the relationship between exchange rate regimes and financial depth. As a proxy for
financial depth, we used the ratio of M2/GDP.[7] In order to correct for the
effect of inflation, the value of the variable for a particular year was calculated
as the average of monthly M2 for the year, divided by that year's GDP. Had
we simply used M2 corresponding to the end of year, this variable would have
had an upward bias in years of high inflation.

To characterize exchange rate regimes, we used two different definitions: First, we defined as fixed (PEG) all regimes that were fixed to a single
currency or to a basket of currencies, according to the classification in the
Exchange Arrangements and Exchange Restrictions of the IMF. We excluded
from the definition those countries in which the value of the nominal exchange
rate lasted less than six months, in an attempt to separate the regimes that are
fixed for a reasonable length of time from those that are "fixed but adjustable."
Second, we use a more narrow definition (PEG1) in which the regime is
considered to be fixed if the nominal exchange rate is constant (or, more
precisely, did not change by more than 1 percent per year) during a period of
at least 24 months. This is an attempt to capture those cases in which the
exchange rate was "really fixed."[8]

Among other potential determinants of financial depth, we considered
inflation and per-capita GDP. Since the effect of inflation was not expected to
be linear, we used the log of inflation (or, more precisely, log 1 + inflation) as
a control variable. In order to capture nonlinear effects, we also added a
dummy for hyperinflation in addition to the log of inflation, but this variable
turned out to be insignificant and was excluded from the regressions shown
here. Similarly, the regressions using per-capita GDP are not shown. In this
case, our concern was the potential for endogeneity, particularly in the second
set of regressions discussed below. It should be noted, however, that the
inclusion of this variable did not change the effect of the regime on financial
depth in any significant way.[9]

---

[7] The source for M2 is the International Monetary Fund's *International Financial Statistics* (IFS). GDP was taken
from the Economic and Social Database (ESDB) of the IDB.

[8] We also used a third, broader definition, which groups the forward-looking regimes (such as the *tablitas*) together
with the fixed regimes. Perhaps due to the fact that there are few observations of forward-looking pegs and crawls
compared to the number of fixed regimes, the results varied little and are thus not reported here.

[9] The source for inflation is the IFS. Per-capita GDP was taken from the World Penn Tables.

Table A1 presents the results of our panel regressions, which include fixed effects for each country and each year. The country dummies capture the effect of omitted country characteristics, which are implicitly assumed to be invariant over time. The time dummies capture common shocks that could affect the degree of financial depth (such as the oil crises, the debt crisis, or common capital flows), as well as the effect of technological changes. As shown in the table, fixed exchange rate regimes increase financial depth between 4 and 5 percentage points of GDP, depending on the specification and the definition of regime chosen; and the coefficients are highly significant.

Table A1. Panel Regressions with (Country and Time) Fixed Effects*

	Using Peg		Using Peg1	
Fixed regime	0.047	0.0394	0.0487	0.455
	(4.564)	(3.655)	(5.203)	(4.604)
Log inflation		-0.0454		-0.0447
		(-5.89)		(-5.94)
Number of obs.	773	721	851	795
Adjusted R^2	0.654	0.665	0.651	0.658

*Dependent Variable: M2/GDP
Regressions include country dummies and time dummies, not shown in the table.
All t-stats are in parentheses.

Table A2. Between Regressions (Cross-Country Means of Each Variable for Each Country)

	Using Peg		Using Peg1	
Fixed regime	0.211	0.196	0.207	0.214
t-stat	(2.616)	(2.11)	(2.849)	(2.324)
Log inflation		-0.0337		-0.00867
		(-0.509)		(-0.11)
Number of obs.	773	721	851	795
Adjusted R^2	0.2219	0.2747	0.2527	0.2983

*Dependent Variable: M2/GDP
Regressions include country dummies and time dummies, not shown in the table.
All t-stats are in parentheses.

While the regressions discussed above account for country characteristics, they do not capture the differences across countries in measuring the effect of the regime. For this reason, we ran a second set of regressions (between regressions on panel data) to capture this cross-country variation. These regressions, presented in Table A2, are equivalent to a cross-section regression in which the dependent variable is the average financial depth over the sample period, and the independent variable of interest is the proportion of years in which the country has operated under fixed regimes. The measured effects are much larger in this case. Financial depth in countries that have had fixed regimes throughout the period is estimated to be around 20 percentage points of GDP larger than that in countries under flexible regimes. The coefficient is quite robust to changes in the specification of the equations and in the definition of the regime.

Appendix B. Nominal Wage Response to Changes in Inflation under Alternative Exchange Rate Regimes

To investigate nominal wage responses to inflationary surprises, we estimate the following regression using monthly data series for fixed and flexible exchange rate periods. In this equation,

$$d(\log w) = c + \beta_1{}^* \text{ trend} + \beta_2{}^*(\text{trend})^{\wedge}2 + \beta_3{}^*d(\log p)$$

where w is the nominal monthly industrial sector wage and p is the monthly consumer price index. Performing Dickey–Fuller tests on the monthly data, we did not reject the null hypothesis of unit root. For that reason, the specification was run in first differences. The linear and the quadratic terms reflect expected trends in inflation. Therefore, β_3 captures the contemporaneous response of wage inflation to unexpected surprises in price inflation.

Results for Chile indicate that the coefficient β_3 was almost zero, yet significant autocorrelation was present in the residuals. In order to test whether there were significant delays in responses, a second specification was run again for all countries including $d(\log P_{t-1})$ and $d(\log P_{t-2})$. These terms were highly significant for Chile. Therefore, in table B1 we report the quarterly cumulative response of wage inflation to a change in price inflation. This cumulative response is computed as the sum of the three coefficients on prices and lagged prices. In the rest of the cases, the inclusion of lags did not substantially affect the results. For instance, in Brazil, during the latter 1980s, the cumulative response resulted in 100 pecent versus the 91 percent same-

Table B1. Coefficient on d(log p)

	Flexible	Fixed
Argentina	86:02–88:12 [8.5%]	93:01–98:06 [0.2%]
β_3	0.66	-0.009
t-statistic	(2.72)	(-0.11)
Brazil	89:06–93:06 [19.3%]	94:12–96:12 [1.2%]
β_3	0.91	-0.37
t-statistic	(6.08)	(-0.24)
Chile[a]	90:02–94:01 [1.3%]	
β_3	0.58	NA
t-statistic	(2.95)	NA
Peru[b]	92:01–94:06 [2.9%]	
β_3	0.78	NA
t-statistic	(1.36)	NA
Mexico[c]	91:01–94:01 [0.99%]	70:02–75:01 [0.97%]
β_3	0.88	0.25
t-statistic	(1.03)	(0.43)

Note: The average inflation rate in the period is represented in the square brackets.
a. Results for Chile show the cumulative response of wages over a quarter.
b. Bimonthly Data.
c. The exchange regime during the period 91:01–94:01 was a backward-looking crawling peg.

month response reported in the previous table. In general the cumulative response was somewhat larger than the contemporaneous one under flexible regimes and smaller under more-fixed exchange regimes, reinforcing our results that wage responses are smaller under fixed than under flexible regimes.

References

Aghevli, B., M. Khan, and P. Montiel. 1991. *Exchange Rate Policy in Developing Countries: Some Analytical Issues*. Washington, D.C.: International Monetary Fund.

Chang, R., and A. Velasco. 1998. Financial Fragility and the Exchange Rate Regime. Inter-American Development Bank, Research Department, Washington, D.C. Mimeographed document.

Eichengreen, B. 1998. *Open Economies Review.* 9(S1): 569–607.

Freiden, J., P. Ghezzi, and E. Stein. 1998. The Political Economy of Exchange Rate Policy in Latin America. Working paper, Inter-American Development Bank, Washington, D.C.

Gavin, M., and R. Hausmann. 1999. Preventing Crisis and Contagion: Fiscal and Financial Dimensions. Paper presented at the Inter-American Development Bank seminar, New Initiatives to Tackle Financial Turmoil. Paris: France.

Lane, P. 1995. Determinants of Pegged Exchange Rates. Columbia University, New York, Mimeographed document.

McKinnon, R.I. 1962. "Optimum Currency Areas." *American Economic Review.* 53: 717–725.

Mundell, R.A. 1961. "A Theory of Optimum Currency Areas." *American Economic Review.* 51: 657–664.

Obstfeld, M., and K. Rogoff. 1995. The Mirage of Fixed Exchange Rates. *Journal of Economic Perspectives.* 9: 73–96.

Paris, March 1999

International Initiatives to Stabilize Financial Integration

Eduardo Fernández-Arias and Ricardo Hausmann

Financial liberalization and integration have generated disappointing results. They were supposed to set up a win–win situation: Capital would flow from capital-abundant, low-return, aging industrial countries to capital-scarce, high-return, young emerging countries. Growth in receiving countries would accelerate, and both giver and receiver would be happier since everyone's diversification opportunities would be improved. As a bonus, emerging-market policymakers would be disciplined by losing access to a captive local financial market.

But things have not worked out as advertised. Emerging markets have been rattled by financial turmoil, especially during the past 20 months. Depending on one's viewpoint as optimist or pessimist, financial integration and globalization have either generated excessive volatility or run amok. In either event, political support for liberalizing policies is harder to achieve, and the prospect of long-run growth has not compensated for these new headaches. While growth in Latin America has accelerated from 1 percent per year in the 1980s to some 4 percent in the 1990s, it has not reached the levels of the 1960s when capital flows were an order of magnitude smaller.[1] But it is the degree of financial volatility and the frequency of panics, crises, and contagion that have made the current state of affairs socially costly and politically disappointing. As a result, reform of the international financial architecture has become a booming industry.

Several reports have been, are being, and will be produced by multilateral organizations, think tanks, freethinkers, and G-*n* task forces, with *n* taking values between 7 and 30.[2] The question is whether any of the initiatives will be implemented before a temporary cease-fire on the financial battlefield is misinterpreted as the end of the war.

---

[1] Rodrik (1998) finds no relation between capital account liberalization and growth.

[2] Eichengreen (1999) provides an interesting survey of the main proposals on the table, and *The Economist* (1999) gives a very useful summary discussion on the topic. The following name some of the initiatives on the table: Bergsten (1998), Bergsten and Hennig (1996), Calomiris (1998), Camdessus (1998), Edwards (1998), Fischer (1999), Garten (1998), Government of France (1998), Government of the United States (1999), G7 (1998), G10 (1996), G22 (1998a,b,c), G30 (1997), Kaufman (1998a,b), Kenen (1998), Litan, et al. (1998), Meltzer (1998), Naciones Unidas (1999), Raffer (1990), Sachs (1998), Soros (1997, 1998), and Stiglitz (1998).

This paper provides an opinionated overview of many of the initiatives currently on the table. In effect, we will be discussing the different views about what is wrong with the world, or as an economist would say, the principal distortions that are present. The intent is to clarify the logic behind the proposals and provide a means of assessing them.

An overview suggests that these different views fall into two groups. The first identifies the main financial problem as an excess of capital flows due to moral hazard, which causes private returns to exceed social returns. This generates too much lending and distorts its allocation. Proposed remedies involve limiting moral hazard whenever possible and, as a fallback when this is not possible, discouraging capital flows through sand-in-the-wheels policies. One can think of this cluster of viewpoints as "Theories of Too Much."

The alternative cluster of views, which we label "Theories of Too Little," posits that the fundamental problem comes from distortions that cause capital flows to be too small and unstable relative to certain benchmarks. Theories under this heading would help explain a nagging puzzle in economic theory. The standard theory of international trade predicts that capital should move from capital-abundant to capital-scarce countries and tend to equalize capital–labor ratios. However, after decades of capital mobility, capital–labor ratio differentials remain enormous and there is scarcely any perceivable tendency toward equalization. The volume of flows observed, e.g., 5 percent of GDP in the recipient countries, appears small relative to what would be required to achieve equalization in a reasonable time period. This puzzle has also appeared in a different context. Feldstein and Horioka (1980) found that investment is financed fundamentally by domestic savings in a manner inconsistent with the notion of an integrated world capital market.

Several theories potentially can explain why so little capital is moving around. They can also explain some features of recent crises. We will explore theories, such as sovereign risk, that are based on willingness-to-pay problems; theories based on liquidity problems; and those that blame structurally weak national currencies. These theories have the virtue of explaining why certain countries in certain periods received massive flows without generating crises. Policies derived from them promise a future of more deeply integrated and stable global finance with much greater capital flows.

Theories of Too Much and Theories of Too Little are not mutually exclusive because they do not start from the same benchmarks. The former point out distortions that make the volume of capital flows larger *than they would otherwise be.* The latter point to distortions that make them smaller. Hence each theory takes all other distortions as given. The question is what would the world be like in the absence of most distortions. If that best of all worlds is one of smaller flows, restricting capital movements could be an effective shortcut. If, instead, it involves a radically larger flow of resources, then adopting policies that restrict the development of capital markets could be very inefficient. The ambitiousness of new architectural plans and the political importance they deserve depend critically on the characteristics of that first-best world. If the new architectural design does not address the structural problems and lay new foundations, it will be no more than interior decoration.

Table 1 summarizes the major distortions associated with the alternative theories and presents the policy initiatives associated with them. The table does not pass judgements. Our preferences are made more explicit in the text.

To unearth the causes of financial turmoil, it is important to review the salient features of recent crises. Starting with the Mexican crisis of 1994–1995, financial turmoil in emerging countries has puzzled analysts of all stripes. Surprise is perhaps the most striking feature of recent crises. A graphic way to view this is presented in "The New Features of Financial Crises in Emerging Markets," which appears in Part One of this book. There, the six crisis countries of 1997–1998 (Indonesia, Korea, Malaysia, Philippines, Russia, and Thailand) are compared with the six largest countries in our region (Argentina, Brazil, Colombia, Mexico, Peru, and Venezuela). If we classify these countries into low and high risk according to market risk spreads and ratings in mid-1997, right before the crises, we find that, except for Russia, crises occurred in the low-risk countries.

Some crisis narratives attribute this lack of predictability to the fact that crises have come in a variety of flavors, each triggered by yet-to-be-discovered factors. In fact, many of these "flavors" have been quite novel. The Mexican Tequila crisis of 1994–1995 came as a surprise because the key causal factor of the 1982 debt crisis—namely a high fiscal deficit—was not an issue. Eventually, many analysts came to blame a large current account deficit and low savings for Mexico's crisis, but neither of these would play a role in the Asian crises that followed several years later. Furthermore, the Asian crises would differ among themselves; for example, some involved banking problems, others did not. Then the Russian episode changed the pattern of the kaleidoscope again, returning to a traditional script for a public debt crisis. And most puzzling of all, and this is very important, the strong financial contagion associated with these crises infected countries enjoying strong fundamentals that had essentially no economic linkages with crisis countries. This was most notably so in Latin America during the Russian crisis.

We are more persuaded by the argument that lack of predictability is largely rooted in problems of multiple equilibria rather than in a misunderstanding of the workings of economies. This means that the existence of a potentially "bad" equilibrium may trigger a self-fulfilling financial panic, in which the collapse validates the state of panic that causes it. These problems resemble bank runs and are associated with liquidity problems.

Table 1. Initiatives for Reforming International Financial Architecture

Distortion	Policy Implementation		
	Emerging Markets Institutions	Current International Institutions	New International Institutions
Moral hazard due to implicit guarantees in domestic financial markets leads to excessive and misallocated international lending.	Improve regulation and supervision of capital adequacy requirements to align private and social returns. Impose capital controls to reduce excessive cross-border lending.	Eliminate/reduce international rescue packages in order to reduce the moral hazard faced by foreign lenders.	
Inadequate domestic bankruptcy law increases the costs of crisis and creates incentives for bailouts, aggravating moral hazard problems.	Improve bankruptcy legislation.		
Sovereign risk (i.e., the willingness-to-pay problem) makes cross-border lending too scarce, expensive, and unstable.		Limit sovereign risk by providing access to IFI and market finance only in situations when willingness to pay is not the issue.	
Strong contractual precommitments to address the willingness-to-pay problem may become too rigid when there is an inability to pay.	Incorporate loan and bond restructuring provisions in new debt contracts.		Create an international bankruptcy court to authorize nonpayment when the problem is inability to pay.

Table 1. Initiatives for Reforming International Financial Architecture (continued)

Illiquidity creates the risk of a self-fulfilling bank-run-like crisis that is costly, hard to predict, and avoidable		Provide the IMF with clearer lender-of-last-resort functions, following the similar principles as applied at the national level. Provide ex-ante contingent lending in order to mimic a lender-of-last resort function. Lending should be certain, fast, short-term, and expensive. Eligibility conditions should be met ex-ante, but no additional conditions should be applied at times of crisis. Increase resource availability by involving the private sector in such contingent arrangements. IFIs might provide enhancements.	Create regional structures
Weak national currencies in capital-importing countries cause very serious financial fragility through currency and term mismatches.	Adopt a supranational currency through a monetary union or association.		

We shall keep in mind some of these features when discussing different theories about "what is wrong in the world" and how to fix it.

Theories of Too Much

Theories of Too Much usually assume that moral hazard encourages excessive lending. Somebody is providing an implicit guarantee so that the parties to the transaction are not internalizing all the risks. Too much lending and too much risk-taking occur. Resources are also misallocated because they are apportioned to risky projects without internalizing the costs involved.[3] Eventually, the guarantee is called and a crisis emerges. The various scenarios differ in the source of the implicit guarantee.

Implicit Guarantees in the Domestic Banking System

The most traditional scenario involves government guarantees of the banking system. The same logic will apply to a corporation perceived as being "too big to fail," but banks remain the prime example because they play a critical role in the payments system. Governments cannot afford to let banks simply go broke because that would trigger a catastrophic sequence of defaults in which otherwise solvent firms go bust when their clients are unable to make payments from deposits frozen in problem banking institutions. Counting on the protection provided by an inevitable government bailout, bankers may assume too much risk.

The lower a bank's capital is, the more extreme its behavior. If a bank is very highly capitalized, it will pay its losses with its equity. When the bank has no more capital, it will be tempted to adopt a strategy known as "gambling for resurrection" in which depositors or the government will pay for any additional losses while the banker retains any upside potential for risky investments.

The standard solution to this problem is to impose, through regulation, a capital adequacy requirement and to check that it is being met. Since capital is the difference between many assets and many liabilities, proper valuation of each asset and liability is critical. Hence accounting standards are also central to this strategy.

The cautionary tale of moral hazard in a national banking system can become international when the domestic banks borrow abroad. Since financial liberalization may exacerbate the problem, some would argue for blanket restrictions on foreign borrowing by banks or for other forms of capital control until financial regulation and supervision is upgraded. We would argue that the principles of prudential regulation and supervision should be applied to

---

[3] Dooley (1997), Krugman (1998), and Corsetti, Pesenti, and Roubini (1998) provide formal models of this intuition.

international financial transactions, just as they apply to domestic intermediation. In particular, liquidity requirements may be imposed on the foreign borrowing of banks for the same reasons they are applied on domestic liabilities. This has become an increasingly common practice in the region.

Latin America has made very significant progress in improving banking supervision and regulation,[4] especially after the Tequila crisis in 1995. During the past two years, Latin American banks withstood quite well a very adverse external and natural environment given the Asian and Russian financial shocks, the decline in the terms of trade, and the effects of El Niño and of hurricanes Georges and Mitch. Domestic banks have been able to weather the storms without generating a banking crisis in any of the major economies of the region. Despite this performance, financial turmoil has been at a peak and access to world capital markets has been closed for long stretches. Hence, while nobody should question the importance of adequate regulation and supervision of the domestic financial system and of its international transactions, it is unlikely that failures in this area are at the root of the current financial turmoil or that further progress in supervision and regulation will alleviate the problem in any significant way.

Implicit International Guarantees

Another Theory of Too Much follows similar lines but blames the International Monetary Fund and multilateral development banks for providing rescue packages that shield either foreign investors or governments from the fallout of excessive risk-taking. This kind of moral hazard is thought to lead to excessive lending by foreign investors who expect to be repaid from resources provided through future rescue packages if real returns on investment do not materialize.

Advocates of this explanation propose eliminating rescue packages from the arsenal of international financial institutions. This theory has received much currency, especially among economists (see Sachs, 1998). Just as with nursery rhymes, its closure is reassuringly simplistic: The world would be a better place if not for these public sector interventions. However, given the massive losses stock- and bondholders have been subject to, and the enormous political costs paid by governments in crisis countries, it is hard to imagine that moral hazard alone could create such widespread financial havoc.

Theories of Too Little

For all the impressive growth in capital flows to emerging markets, they are surprisingly low relative to what one would expect given the dominant trade

---

[4] See IDB (1997) for a country-by-country assessment of how much progress has taken place and for an analysis of its contribution to growth in the region.

theories and the way open economies are usually modeled. In fact, current capital flows are low compared to those observed prior to World War I and, more recently, to those in some particularly telling countries. In this section, we will review crisis scenarios based on sovereign risk, on liquidity problems, and on weak national currencies.

Willingness to Pay

The first story is based on the willingness-to-pay problem. Loans are not self-enforcing contracts. They are often secured by collateral, and courts adjudicate problems that arise during the life of the contract. After receiving a loan, only coercion or the promise of future loans makes people want to fulfill their obligations. If the contract environment is not adequate and judicial enforcement is weak, borrowers may not want to repay, discouraging creditors from lending and leaving the credit market inefficiently small.[5]

Willingness-to-pay problems affect the size of the market through several channels. First, as lenders try to compensate for these risks with a higher spread, they increase the incentive for nonpayment. After all, borrowers are likely to feel overcharged when they are asked to compensate lenders for doing something that could have been done, but was not. As resentment builds, it may reach the point of eroding the incentive to repay. Secondly, the higher spread may affect the borrower's ability to repay, making loans riskier and profitable projects scarcer. Finally, the perception of excessive risk may prompt depositors to park their money in a foreign country where these problems are less severe, making the overall supply of funds smaller.

Willingness-to-pay problems can be addressed through the use of collateral. In the simplest example, Mary lends John money to buy a house worth 100 quarks. The loan is for 80 quarks and the house is the collateral. So long as the value of the house minus the judicial costs of repossession exceed 80 quarks, John will always be willing to repay. The availability of assets with liquid secondary markets that can act as collateral and the judicial costs of repossession are therefore important determinants of the ability of financial systems to address the willingness-to pay problem.[6]

When nonpayment occurs or is possible, bankruptcy procedures are set in motion. These allow ability-to-pay problems to be separated from the

---

[5] This problem is discussed in the domestic context in IDB (1998). Japelli and Pagano (1998) present evidence of how the behavior of institutions that affect willingness to pay has impacted credit markets for a selection of mainly Latin American and European countries.

[6] Notice that it is important for the collateral to have a liquid market. If it does not, the threat of repossession is unlikely to be credible. A banker will not want to repossess a widget-making machine from a borrower if not much can be redeemed for it. It's better to leave the asset with the borrower who can at least generate some cash flow out of it. We will study other effects of illiquid markets in the next section.

willingness-to-pay problems. They also provide a mechanism to secure the cooperation of the different creditors, to remove management if creditors find it necessary, and to transfer the ownership of assets to creditors.[7]

Absence of an adequate bankruptcy law and court system can have deleterious effects on the financial system. It makes coercion less credible, worsening the willingness-to-pay problem. It also increases the cost of crises because it precludes concerted action to provide additional financing needed for the company's survival. This increases the social costs associated with bankruptcies and makes too-big-to-fail arguments relevant even for relatively small firms. This may prompt governments into providing rescue packages to the corporate sector, which has traditionally been the case in Latin America's public enterprises and as just happened in East Asia.

Bankruptcy law and the court system are important areas of domestic financial policy in which the region is still far from where it could be.

Sovereign Risk

In cross-border finance, the willingness-to-pay problem is aggravated by the involvement of a sovereign government. Since sovereigns do not need to abide by the rulings of any foreign court, the problem may be serious and difficult to resolve. Sovereign risk may explain why cross-border lending is so small. In the standard model (Bulow and Rogoff, 1989) sovereigns will pay so long as it is in their interest to do so, given the "punishment" they may receive for nonpayment. However the incentive not to pay goes up with the volume of debt owed. This theory, originally developed for public debt, can be extended to apply to private sector borrowing under the "protection" of the sovereign, which may suspend convertibility, nationalize assets, or otherwise interfere in the payment process.

Sovereign risk will cause markets to impose a credit ceiling on countries so as to keep the volume of debt below the level that would create incentives for nonrepayment. The lighter the "punishment" the world can impose on the country, the lower the credit ceiling will be. Economies that are more integrated into the world are more easily "punished" and hence should get a higher credit ceiling.

The credit ceiling itself may be a source of crisis. First, the determinants of that credit ceiling might change, perhaps because of a deterioration in the country's terms of trade, causing the current debt level to exceed the ceiling and triggering a sudden stop in new lending. Second, even if the credit ceiling does not move, it may be destabilizing. As discussed in Fernández-Arias and Lombardo (1998a), an externality exists since the ceiling applies to the coun-

---

[7] La Porta and López-de-Silanes (1998) provide an empirical analysis of creditor and shareholder rights for a large set of countries and establish their importance as determinants of the level of development of financial systems.

try as a whole but borrowing is decentralized. Every borrower will have incentives to get his or her loan before a neighbor does, prompting temporary overborrowing followed by crisis.[8]

Sovereign risk helps explain the experience of some economies that are fortunate "outliers" in the history of international capital flows. A first example is Puerto Rico, where capital flows averaged about 15 percent of GDP between 1960 and 1994 and where payments to foreign capital account for 32 percent of GDP (see Hausmann, 1995). These numbers are striking since crises have been touched off elsewhere long before capital flows reached these magnitudes. For example, in 1982 and again in 1994, crisis erupted in Mexico when the current account reached 7 to 8 percent of GDP and when payments to foreign capital were less than 7 percent of GDP. Puerto Rico's peculiar political structure implies that it does not have a sovereign to restrict payments or suspend convertibility, thus eliminating sovereign risk. The other two exceptions are Australia and Ireland at the turn of the century.

Clearly, we are not proposing Puerto Rico as a political model. We are only using it to illustrate the magnitude of potential effects of sovereign risk on the volume of capital flows. These "outliers" in the history of capital flows all had peculiar political structures that significantly limited or eliminated sovereign risk. They also used the same currency of the country that constituted the principal source of capital, a point we shall return to below.

Notice that sovereign risk is a commitment problem. If the sovereign could somehow tie its hands and mandate future payments irrespective of change in ruling faction, the problem would disappear. Lending would be more ample and stable. Yet even when the sovereign might well be better off making such a commitment, the binding technology to make the pledge credible may be difficult to find.

From this point of view, the multilateral development banks such as the World Bank and the Inter-American Development Bank have something to offer. By charter, their policy requires them to suspend operations in countries that run into arrears. Since they are a cheap source of future credit and are committed to stop lending in case of arrears, sovereigns have always repaid, giving these multilateral institutions their preferred creditor status. In a world where such binding devices are scarce, questions have been raised about whether these institutions are making adequate use of their technology for proving commitment. In a later section we propose using this mechanism to

---

[8] George Soros's proposal for an international debt insurance scheme is a way to make explicit the debt ceiling and to administer it. One problem with this proposal is that it is not clear how the ceiling would be determined, changed, etc. In addition there is the issue of how to allocate it among different borrowers in a competitive market. If the ceiling is exceeded and/or if the guarantee is called, the financial support will be used in a solvency crisis, made more likely by the moral hazard that the sunk insurance would generate. It appears that this initiative would work only if the ceiling cannot be exceeded, which would amount to capital controls.

bail in the private sector for crisis prevention so that it won't have to be bailed out after a crisis hits.

Thus far, private markets have tried to insulate themselves from sovereign risk with relatively rigid contracts lacking clauses that could be exploited to justify nonpayment. Yet a solution tailored to a willingness-to-pay problem may make crises triggered by an ability-to-pay problem more difficult to manage and more costly. It usually makes debt workouts quite messy. Hence some authors have been proposing mechanisms to make such workouts more orderly without worsening the sovereign risk problem and without requiring the use of new public resources to take previously exposed creditors off the hook (see Eichengreen and Portes, 1995; Eichengreen, 1999).

Liquidity Crises

Markets did not predict either the Tequila or the East Asian crises. Russia and Brazil were less surprising given that market concerns were clearly expressed in high interest rates months before their crises erupted. Still, lack of predictability is one of the elements that make multiple-equilibria liquidity stories plausible. The second element is that the crisis often appears justified ex post. If a major economic collapse were about to happen, investors would, of course, have good reason to flee. Yet investor panic can also cause an unnecessary collapse.

The traditional example of liquidity crises is a bank run. Banks typically have a term mismatch: They receive short-term deposits, even sight deposits, and lend them at longer maturities. Assume all borrowers are doing just fine. If there is no attack, the bank will do just great. But if suddenly depositors all want their money at the same time, the bank will go bust. In fact, in the bank's attempts to collect loans too quickly, even borrowers may get into trouble due to the credit crunch. Hence expectations may be self-fulfilling: Both optimism and pessimism can be justified ex post.[9]

The standard solution to bank runs is a lender of last resort. If someone—e.g., the central bank—is willing to take out depositors and substitute itself temporarily as the source of funding for the bank's balance sheet, then pessimism is no longer justified and depositors have good cause to keep their money in the bank. Following Bagehot (1873), last-resort lending should be ample, automatic, collateralized, relatively short term, and expensive enough to reestablish confidence but not lead to abuse or to moral hazard problems by bankers.

---

[9] Currency devaluation may put in motion a similar mechanism, triggering either liquidity or solvency problems. See Fernández-Arias and Lombardo (1998b), Chang and Velasco (1998), and Krugman (1999).

Liquidity Crises in the International Arena

Capital account imbalances, especially in the presence of high levels of debt, raise the spectre of bank-run-like payments crises if market financing dries up. This market reaction may be based on a loss of confidence in a particular country or simply reflect global financial contagion. In an extreme case, creditors will seek to minimize their exposure in certain countries and refuse to refinance debts, provoking a grave short-term liquidity problem. The ensuing credit crunch can cause a serious contraction, high real interest rates, and payments problems in the corporate sector, thereby deteriorating the health of the financial system and justifying the attack.

In fact, a temporary disruption in financial flows, due for example to a prolonged bout of contagion, may cause enough real damage to generate a full-blown crisis. If the financial interruption is not justified—if, with adequate financing the economy would be perfectly capable of servicing its debts— then these types of crises must be considered unnecessary and a strong effort should be made to prevent them.

In some recent crises, fundamentals were consistent with the required capacity to service the debt load, but a sudden lack of liquidity severely damaged the economy, leading to an unexpected change in sentiment. The unnecessary nature of the run that provoked the liquidity crunch can account for the failure of the market to anticipate the crisis. More recently, and especially in the wake of the Russian crisis of August 1998, most emerging markets in the world have lost much of their access to external financing, even though their economies do not present any great inherent weaknesses.

Liquidity crises are different from solvency crises in two respects. First, they are not easily forecast because they arise from a movement to a bad equilibrium that is neither necessary nor inevitable. Second, they are preventable with sufficient financing. By contrast, additional funds injected into a solvency crisis would only postpone the moment of reckoning.

Finding the Source of Liquidity Problems

So far, we have simply stated that liquidity crises exist. Creating a last-resort lender or mimicking one through the use of existing institutions would constitute an improvement over the current situation, as we will argue later. Before prescribing a regimen of treatment, however, it would help to know where these liquidity problems ultimately come from so that we can focus on what can be done to prevent damage before it occurs.

A company or a country is solvent if the net present value of its future cash flow is positive. With complete markets there would never be a liquidity problem. One could always find someone willing to trade the future cash flow in exchange for cash today. Hence, illiquidity implies the lack of such markets.

One important example is the market for asset collateral. If such markets are liquid, then in times of crisis a firm should be able to find someone willing to provide a collateralized (i.e., practically risk-free) loan. However if the market for the asset is not liquid, then its use as collateral is severely limited.

What might cause market illiquidity for an asset? A market is liquid when there are many agents on both sides of the market, buying and selling. There are several potential explanations for why a market may not be liquid, including an inadequate business environment in terms of property rights and judicial enforcement. But one important factor is the presence of large aggregate shocks to the economy. Aggregate shocks imply that the market is likely to be unbalanced and hence illiquid. In good times, people are mainly on the buy side. In bad times, they move to the sell side. Since you need people on both sides to make a market, then very few transactions will take place and asset prices are likely to be very volatile, hence not very useful as collateral. In particular, falling asset prices during generalized downturns facilitate the occurrence of liquidity crises.

Problems Caused by Weak National Currencies

We will argue in this section that the presence of a weak national currency is likely to accentuate the problems of illiquidity and cause serious financial fragility in capital-importing countries. This illiquidity and fragility caused by weak domestic currencies make emerging markets riskier and smaller, thereby helping to explain their excessive volatility and the puzzle of why there is too little international lending.

But before tackling those questions, we must define what is meant by a weak domestic currency. A currency is weak when:
- Local money is not a reserve currency—e.g., there is very little demand by foreigners for assets denominated in pesos.
- There are no liquid long-term markets denominated in that currency.
- Residents hold significant financial assets denominated in foreign currency, whether domestically or abroad.

From the point of view of this definition, all Latin American currencies are weak. There isn't a single country in the region with a liquid market for long-term bonds denominated in the domestic currency. Most long-term markets are dollarized. A few (e.g., Colombia's and Chile's) are denominated in a price index. In most countries, currency substitution has led to high de facto dollarization of assets.

This has two important consequences. First, because countries in our region are net importers of capital and foreigners do not want to hold peso-denominated assets, the country in net terms will have an exchange rate exposure problem. Avoiding this problem by holding sufficient reserves means essentially foregoing the importation of capital (in net terms). This accounts for the puzzle of too-little financing. If instead the country decides to let capital in, then a currency mismatch will grow in tandem with the amount of imported foreign capital. Because of this aggregate mismatch, there will not be a sufficiently large derivative market in which to hedge all this exchange risk. This means that a significant devaluation in such a country is bound to generate great internal dislocation.

Second, the fact that all long-term lending is available only in dollars creates a mismatch problem.[10] On the one hand, the absence of long-term markets in the domestic currency forces borrowers who need long-term financing to choose either to accept the currency risk involved in dollar loans or to accept a maturity mismatch by repeated short-term borrowing in the domestic currency. Either alternative will generate financial fragility through term or exchange-rate mismatches.

Third, since much of the financial intermediation in the economy is dollarized, much of the supply of short-term loans is also in dollars, thus aggravating the currency mismatch problem.

Given this structure, exchange rate flexibility is unlikely to deliver any of the benefits usually assumed. Hausmann, et al. (1999) find that more-flexible exchange rate arrangements in Latin America have not delivered a more anticyclical or stabilizing monetary policy than have fixed regimes. The more flexible regimes have amplified the effects of, rather than sheltering the domestic economy from, movements in foreign interest rates. They have generated smaller financial systems and higher real interest rates. Central banks have tended to shy away from allowing the exchange rate to fluctuate much, even in formally floating regimes, because of concerns about generalized currency mismatches.

It is important in this context to ask what would happen to financial turmoil if countries were to abandon their weak domestic currencies in favor of a strong supranational currency. One would expect the sudden elimination of significant exchange rate and maturity mismatches throughout the balance sheets of households and firms in the economy to facilitate financial integration and lead to safer, deeper markets.

Evidence supporting this hypothesis comes from the fact that capital flows were proportionally much higher prior to World War I than any time afterward. One explanation for this was the existence of a global currency system: the gold standard. Panama, which uses the U.S. dollar, is better rated in bond markets today than other Latin American countries with stronger fundamentals. It is the only Latin American country with a highly liquid and competitive market of 30-year mortgages at about 9 percent interest rates. Its domestic interest rates are the least rattled by international contagion.

---

[10] Indexed instruments are also sometimes used.

Major Debates about the New Financial Architecture

The theories or "stories" discussed above provide justification for some of the initiatives that are on the table in the current debate about financial architecture. In this section, we review some of the debates that we consider central. These include the choice of monetary arrangements, alternatives for a lender of last resort, and a comparison of rescue packages versus workouts. We omit many other initiatives, not because they are without use or importance but because they are either uncontroversial or propose changes that are more decorative than foundational, i.e., they take too many walls and windows for granted.

Monetary Arrangements

A major issue of the global architecture is the nature of the monetary arrangements that countries will adopt. Views vary, depending on whether there are reasons to suspect that weak national currencies (as defined above) are important actors in the narrative of financial turmoil. Five alternatives are on the table. The first option would maintain the status quo, with a system of weak national currencies. The second would adopt currency boards linked to the dollar. The third would adopt unilateral dollarization. The fourth would be to join a monetary association with the United States. The final option would create a regional currency, à la the Euro, as a substitute for the current set of weak national currencies.

Obviously, the willingness to abandon current monetary arrangements will be related to the degree of frustration they generate. Hausmann, et al. (1999) provide evidence that the costs associated with current policies may be quite large. However the four other alternatives have different attributes whose relative value is not easy to establish (see Table 2). A currency board linked to a strong currency fortifies a weak currency, but does not completely eliminate the risk of devaluation. Unilateral dollarization implies substituting the weak currency with a strong currency that is already widely used both in trade and finance, thus eliminating the risk of devaluation (perhaps aggravating the risk of default). But this alternative, in contrast to a currency board, implies losing the seigniorage revenue that is generated by printing fiat money. This makes the proposition quite expensive, especially at the beginning when the domestic currency needs to be exchanged for the strong currency. In addition, it does not provide for a last-resort mechanism. Finally, it does not permit political participation in the determination of monetary policy.

By contrast, a monetary association with the United States would presumably include some understanding over the distribution of seigniorage revenue. If this can be done, seigniorage revenue and other assets can be used as prime collateral to secure last-resort lending. Even if the U.S. Federal Reserve

Table 2. Alternative Monetary Arrangements

	Weak Domestic Currency	Regional (weak) Currency	Currency Board	Unilateral Dollarization	Monetary Association
Seigniorage	Yes	Yes	Yes	No	Maybe
Lender of last resort	Yes, but insufficient	Yes	No	No	Maybe
Participation in policy	Yes	Yes	No	No	No

refuses to play a lender-of-last-resort role, the market could provide the regulatory arbitrage through collateralized contingent lending.

Finally, a regional currency that is issued to substitute for a set of weak currencies could permit sharing the seigniorage, providing a lender of last resort and securing political participation in decision making. However, it probably would not reduce existing dollarization nor would it be easy to develop long-term markets denominated in the regional currency. Hence, there is the risk that the new currency would also be weak, replicating rather than eliminating the problems associated with existing currency arrangements.

Right now, neither a regional currency nor monetary association is on the table for active consideration. However, as debate rages about the international financial architecture, discussion about whether they should be is likely to grow.

Lenders of Last Resort

We have argued that liquidity crises may be behind financial turmoil. This is consistent with such characteristics of recent crises as their unpredictability and their ex-post justification. Moreover, liquidity crises are usually addressed through the provision of last-resort lending. In fact, simply the existence of such a lender may be sufficient to prevent destructive runs and panics.

From this point of view, a central problem in the world may be that the globalization of financial flows has overwhelmed the capacity of national central banks in emerging countries to credibly provide enough last-resort lending to prevent liquidity crises. The challenge then is to recreate that function at an international level.

Not everyone agrees. Critics who argue that the recent financial turmoil is not associated with liquidity crises think that the provision of last-resort lending would only exacerbate moral hazard problems, thereby aggravating rather than resolving the situation.

If our diagnosis is correct, the provision of last-resort lending at the international level could proceed in three different ways. First, it could involve the creation of a global lender of last resort or, more specifically, the reform of the IMF so that it could better play this role. Second, the lending function could be created within the bounds of a monetary association. The final alternative would be to mimic last-resort lending by using extant institutions and bailing in the private sector.

• *A Global Lender of Last Resort.* Making the IMF a global lender of last resort is an idea that was discussed at the time of the Bretton Woods conference in 1944. In spite of the eloquence of John Maynard Keynes, the American representatives were not willing to provide the institution with the ability to print money. After all, the world was adopting a dollar standard and the United States was not about to renounce sovereignty over the management of its own currency.

Since then the political-economy problems of providing a global lender of last resort have been insurmountable, but for other reasons. First, there is reticence to create a powerful global institution that may not be fully accountable. Second, there is the fear that taxpayers in industrial countries would be asked to pay for bailouts in emerging countries. These fears could probably be addressed through the right governance structure and the use of collateral to protect taxpayers from undue risk. The idea has gained the support of Stanley Fischer (1999), the second in command at the IMF. However, as *The Economist* (1999) concluded in its recent review of global architectural initiatives, there is very little support for anything this ambitious at the global level.

• *Last-Resort Lending in a Monetary Association.* Last-resort lending may be more easily provided at the regional level through a monetary association, in which the political interests of the parties are less diluted and some technical aspects are easier to address. First, a monetary association with the United States would imply the disappearance of exchange risk, which together with the increasing internationalization of the domestic banking system would probably be less susceptible to liquidity crises. More importantly, and as previously noted, if the monetary association shares the seigniorage revenues with member countries, that revenue could be used as prime collateral to assure access to liquidity in times of crises. In fact, even if there is no formal access to the rediscount window of the Federal Reserve System, banks with access to that facility would be willing to provide the regulatory arbitrage, provided their lending is adequately collateralized. Said differently, within a monetary area it is not possible to provide last-resort lending to one part of the market without having a major stabilizing influence over the other.

• *Mimicking Last Resort Lending with Existing Institutions.* In the absence of a global or regional lender of last resort, the IMF and the other International Financial Institutions (IFIs) face a daunting task in dealing with potential liquidity crises. Current rescue packages may not be adequate because, unlike last-resort lending, they are not committed ex ante but are nego-tiated after a crisis has occurred.

Once a financial crisis erupts, experience shows that it quickly develops into a meltdown with enormous output losses. Reasons for this may reside in the incomplete financial markets and hard-to-enforce contracts in developing countries. For example, as argued above, inadequate bankruptcy laws can lead to socially costly disruptions when activity is suspended until property rights are reestablished. These distortions are intensified by the breakdown of "implicit" contracts across firms (inter-firm credit and supply/demand rela-tions) and between employers and employees at times of crises.

Interestingly, this diagnosis implies that a financial crisis sets off a chain of destructive events that would not be undone if financing returned to its original level. Although such a development would be beneficial, it would not restore the unbroken network of relations that the market requires.

This pessimistic outlook may help explain the relative failure of the res-cue packages for most of the crisis countries in recent years. Although these packages generally were very large, coming close to offsetting in size the initial negative financial shocks, they did not come close to erasing the devas-tating real impacts.

This calls into question the traditional rescue package strategy. Typi-cally, once a crisis occurs in a country, the IMF and other official entities examine the situation and provide support in line with circumstances of the moment. Experience with recent crises—from Mexico to Russia—suggests that this strategy is insufficient to avoid enormous damage to the well-being of the countries involved or to prevent the contagion from spreading internation-ally, even if there is ample financial support.

The principal limitations of this traditional ex-post strategy of crisis man-agement have been noted in "Preventing Crisis and Contagion: The Role of International Financial Institutions," which appears in the first paper presented in Part Three of this book. First, prevention is better than cure because a financial crisis quickly leads to deterioration of the economic fundamentals that is not easy to reverse or repair. Second, current procedural requirements for IFI emergency support create uncertainties and delays that make it nearly impossible to stem market panic in a liquidity crisis before serious damage occurs. Third, conditionality is likely to be hastily conceived and ineffectively applied. And finally, private investors would benefit without shouldering any of the burdens. Unless the rules of the game change, the private sector is unlikely in the short term to cooperate in defraying the costs of an emergency package. And over the long term, the implicit guarantee that such a rescue package represents may further undermine market discipline, and by inducing less caution in lending lead to new crises.

"Preventing Crisis and Contagion" also notes principles that would apply in formulating an alternative strategy that uses existing institutions to mimic an international lender of last resort. The first and governing principle is to strengthen mechanisms designed to prevent a liquidity crisis or lack of financing. To work, these programs must be applied only when the economic fundamentals are sufficiently sound for there to be reasonable expectation that market confidence and access can be restored and held. This will also require that financial support be of sufficient critical mass to dampen or forestall a liquidity crunch capable of triggering a crisis.

Second, there must be certainty that the support provided—whether a guarantee, a loan, or a line of credit—will be available immediately when funds are needed. Consequently the conditionality applied in such operations must not impede timely disbursements, and disbursement conditions must be replaced by conditions of approval.

Third, these "conditions of approval" mean that support should be offered selectively to countries able to meet a series of preconditions. Their economic fundamentals and their economic policy commitments must be compatible with warding off a crisis and conform to prudential standards and efforts to reduce financial vulnerability. Regular review by the IMF will be needed to ensure compliance over time. If conditions are not met, a delayed exit mechanism must be implemented to ensure that exit does not trigger crisis.

Fourth, IFI support will be more effective if it is supplementary to market mechanisms and can be leveraged through the private sector. In other words, this initiative is designed to *bail in* the private sector. To do so, official international cooperation is essential for achieving the necessary critical mass.

Finally, disbursed loans, including guarantees that have been called, should be relatively short-term and repayable early without penalty. They should carry sufficiently high interest rates to ensure they will be drawn upon only when there is a financing shortfall. On the other hand, the loans' commitment fee, whether a guarantee or a line of credit, should be priced to reflect the financial cost of such commitment since low fees would provide further incentives to draw down the loan only if the need is clear. These facilities should be designed as prudential planning tools: Abstention from disbursement would be normal and should not be discouraged with artificially high predisbursement fees.

The main risk in this lender-of-last-resort strategy is that the financial support will be misapplied to a potential solvency crisis. Such financial support would hasten and deepen the inevitable crisis, diluting the market discipline that would otherwise be exerted when fundamentals turn riskier and, in extreme cases, postponing needed policy reforms in lieu of a major bailout. Anticipation that liquidity support will be available in insolvency cases would cause moral hazard in investment. According to Fernández-Arias (1996), the program might even turn counterproductive, depending on the frequency with which it is misapplied; "constructive ambiguity" would also have a deleterious effect.

The need to screen out insolvency cases underlines the previously noted point that these programs must be available only for those countries with sufficiently sound economic fundamentals and policies to strengthen rather than undermine market confidence. Private participation in the program would add a critical element of assurance that these conditions will be fulfilled. In particular, keeping official pricing in line with private sector pricing will expose beneficiary countries to market discipline while protecting the financial sustainability of the programs.

While this lender-of-last-resort role may be risky for IFIs, responding to crises with rescue packages is a costly and ineffective alternative. The merits of preventive operations are best judged when weighed against this benchmark.

Workouts vs. Rescue Packages

The final area of major debate about financial architecture concerns the relative merits of workouts and rescue packages. Workouts permit a country unable to service its debts to suspend payment while terms are adjusted. They are an attractive tool in the context of solvency crises because their application does not generate moral hazard. Indeed, investors are asked to share the burden of crisis. If the determination of inability to pay is abused, however, this scheme increases sovereign risk and leads to less financial integration. Moreover, workouts may be highly counterproductive in the context of liquidity crises. Despite the fact that a suspension of payments in the context of an orderly workout restores solvency, anticipation of the suspension can be expected to contribute to the likelihood of panic.

One initiative to prevent that is crisis burden sharing. In extremes, forced burden sharing is an openly nonvoluntary way of bailing in the private sector. Clearly there is a positive role to be played by IFIs in coordinating the process. The question is to what extent the application of pressure is appropriate. Obviously, in a crisis any financial room for maneuver is very valuable. Yet if forced burden sharing becomes part of the "implicit contract," future lending will become more costly. This need not be a bad trade-off if the conditions for burden sharing are clear and not subject to abuse; in that case, they would define a standard of "excusable default" that would ensure flexibility when needed. However the case-by-case, secretive approach usually followed makes this proposition doubtful. It also aggravates the distortions associated with sovereign risk since investors view nonpayment as just one more acceptable decision that a sovereign can make.

Another proposal is to create an *international bankruptcy court*, which would be modeled on the equivalent domestic institution. This court would authorize sovereigns not to repay or to prevent domestic borrowers from repaying when the country is deemed unable, rather than simply unwilling, to pay. By transferring the power to authorize nonrepayment to an independent court that does not have a willingness-to-pay problem, this arrangement provides more flexibility while keeping sovereign risk under control. Obviously the sovereign could still decide to violate the decisions of the international court, but presumably it would have little incentive to do so.

One question about this initiative is whether it is possible to gather sufficient political support from sovereigns to effectively empower the court. Indeed, unlike a domestic bankruptcy court, the international version would not be able to replace management. It has also been argued that since, realistically speaking, this court would at most be able to impose a stay on payments, it would add nothing to what sovereigns can already do unilaterally. Others answer that a distinction will be made about trustworthiness in future dealings since an independent body will have declared the default to be "excusable" on the merits rather than a unilateral decision by a sovereign.

This proposal in fact duplicates some of the functions the International Monetary Fund already performs. When a country gets in trouble, the IMF determines the amount of adjustment that is feasible or reasonable, calculates a financing gap, and coordinates with official creditors and commercial banks a financial plan to make the program consistent. By deciding how much the country can pay, it differentiates between ability and willingness to pay, thus solving the problem in a way similar to a bankruptcy court.

An alternative arrangement would use *loan-restructuring provisions* to give additional flexibility to workouts without aggravating sovereign risk. The trend toward "securitization" makes it increasingly difficult to restructure debt because of collective action problems. This issue applies with particular force to sovereign bonds. As a result, the options become extreme: either default or full payment. Whether this is good or bad is not entirely clear: Ex post, it is better to have flexibility; but lack of flexibility may provide better terms ex ante, especially if you do not plan to default.

It is interesting how conventional wisdom is changing in this regard. It was once widely believed that too much flexibility to renegotiate bank debt during the 1980s debt crisis had spawned endless renegotiations. Now, in the face of a different kind of crisis, many analysts favor the reintroduction of flexibility. Specifically, there is a proposal to modify the standard debt contract to include provisions to facilitate renegotiations, including majority rather than unanimous voting, sharing clauses, and collective representation.

Each emerging country could redesign its contracts along these lines. However, just as a prenuptial agreement would, a unilateral change might be interpreted negatively as a signal of lack of commitment. A more collective approach would provide governments and fiancées alike with cover about their honorable intentions. This would call for an international agreement on loan restructuring provisions.

Rescue packages heighten the risk of moral hazard that may be present in preventive contingent packages because it may be difficult to deny assistance during a crisis if noneligibility has not been clarified beforehand. Relative to rescue packages, workout initiatives require fewer public resources and imply less moral hazard since investors must internalize the prospect of nonpayment. However, they may increase default risk, thus reducing financial integration, and would disrupt many private contracts, thus increasing the economic costs of crises.

Too Much or Too Little?

Debate about the new financial architecture is spurred by dissatisfaction with the world as we find it. Financial turmoil is exacting enormous social costs in all emerging market countries. Contagion has made the problem more difficult and costly to address through the exercise of national virtue. It has transformed localized infections into an international disease that needs an international cure. But it is critical to reach fundamental agreement on what the problem is. Paraphrasing Robert Kennedy, theorists of "too much" see all these capital flows and ask, why? Theorists of "too little" imagine a world in which each household and firm would have access to the same financial opportunities and ask, why not? How much of current social suffering is attributable to an inadequate financial architecture is an open question. But it is clear that the costs of this inadequacy are borne mostly by emerging countries, while any decisions on how to change international institutions inevitably involve the industrial countries. One is reminded of Ortega y Gasset's remark that the pain of others is so much easier to bear than one's own.

Eduardo Fernández-Arias is Lead Research Economist at the Inter-American Development Bank; Ricardo Hausmann is Chief Economist at the Inter-American Development Bank.

References

Bagehot, W. 1873. *Lombard Street: A Description of the Money Market.* London: William Clowes and Sons.

Bergsten, C. F. 1998. "How to Target Exchange Rates." *Financial Times* (20 November).

Bergsten, C. F., and C. R. Henning. 1996. *Global Economic Leadership and the Group of Seven.* Washington, D.C.: Institute for International Economics.

Bulow, J., and K. Rogoff. 1989. "Sovereign Debt: Is to Forgive to Forget?" *American Economic Review.* 79: 43–50.

Calomiris, C. 1998. "Blueprints for a New Global Financial Architecture." Columbia University, New York, Mimeographed document.

Camdessus, M. 1998. "Toward an Agenda for International Monetary and Financial Reform." Address to the World Affairs Council, Philadelphia: United States.

Chang, R., and A. Velasco. 1998. *The Asian Liquidity Crisis.* Working Paper No. 6796. Cambridge, MA: National Bureau of Economic Research (November).

Corsetti, G., P. Pesenti, and N. Roubini. 1998. Paper Tigers? A Preliminary Assesment of the Asian Crisis. Mimeograph. Yale University, Princeton University, and New York University.

Dooley, M. 1997. "A Model of Crisis in Emerging Markets." Working Paper No. 6300. Cambridge, MA: National Bureau for Economic Research.

The Economist. 1999. "A Survey of Global Finance" (January 30).

Edwards, S. 1998. "Abolish the IMF." *Financial Times* (13 November): A1.

Eichengreen B. 1999. *Toward a New International Financial Architecture.* Washington, D.C.: Institute for International Economics.

Eichengreen, B., and R. Portes, with Francesco Cornelli, Leonardo Felli, Julian Franks, Christopher Greenwood, Hugh Mercer, and Giovanni Vitale. 1995. *Crisis? What Crisis? Orderly Workouts for Sovereign Debtors.* London: Centre for Economic Policy Research.

Feldstein, M., and C. Horioka. 1980. "Domestic Savings and International Capital Flows." *Economic Journal.* 90 (June): 314–29.

Fernández-Arias, E. 1996. "Balance of Payments Rescue Packages: Can They Work?" Working Paper 333. Washington, D.C.: Inter-American Development Bank.

Fernández-Arias, E., and D. Lombardo. 1998a. "Private Overborrowing in Undistorted Markets." Working Paper 369. Washington, D.C.: Inter-American Development Bank.

———. 1998b. "Market Discipline and Exuberant Foreign Borrowing." Paper presented at symposium, Banking, Financial Integration, and Macroeconomic Stability. Second Annual Conference of the Central Bank of Chile, September 1998.

Fischer, S. 1999. "On the Need for an International Lender of Last Report." International Monetary Fund, Washington, D.C. Mimeographed document.

Garten, J. 1998. "In This Economic Chaos, a Global Bank Can Help." *International Herald Tribune* (25 September): 8.

Government of France. 1998. *Facing International Instability: Twelve Proposals for a European Initiative.* Paris: Government of France.

Government of the United States. 1999. *Economic Report of the President.* Washington, D.C.: Government of the United States.

Group of Seven (G7). 1998. *Declaration of G7 Finance Ministers and Central Bank Governors.* Washington, D.C.: G7.

Group of 10 (G10). 1996. *Resolving Sovereign Liquidity Crises.* Washington, D.C.: G10.

Group of 22 (G22). 1998a. *Report of the Working Group on Transparency and Accountability.* Washington, D.C.: G22.

————. 1998b. *Report of the Working Group on Strengthening Financial Systems*. Washington, D.C.: G22.

————. 1998c. *Report of the Working Group on International Financial Crises*. Washington, D.C.: G22.

Group of 30 (G30). 1997. *Global Institutions, National Supervision, and Systemic Risk*. Washington, D.C.: G30.

Hausmann, R. 1995. On the Road to Deeper Integration with the North. *Crecimiento Economico*: 221–254.

Hausmann, R., M. Gavin, C. Pages-Serra, and E. Stein. 1999. "Financial Turmoil and the Choice of Exchange Rate Regime." Paper delivered at the Inter-American Development Bank seminar, New Initiatives to Tackle Financial Turmoil. Paris: France.

Inter-American Development Bank (IDB). 1996. *Economic and Social Progress 1996. Part II*. Washington, D.C.: IDB.

————. 1997. *Economic and Social Progress 1997. Part II*. Washington, D.C.: IDB.

————. 1998. In *Economic and Social Progress 1998*. Chapter 7. Washington, D.C.: IDB.

Jappelli, T., and M. Pagano. 1998. "Information Sharing in Credit Markets: International Evidence." Mimeographed document.

Kaufman, H. 1998a. "Preventing the Next Global Financial Crisis." *Washington Post* (28 January): A17.

————. 1998b. "Proposal for Improving the Structure of Financial Supervision and Regulation." Outline of remarks to Brookings Institution symposium, Limiting Moral Hazard in Financial Rescues, June 4, Washington, D.C.: United States.

Kenen, P. B., ed. 1998. *Should the IMF Pursue Capital Account Convertibility?* Essays in International Finance No. 207 (January). Princeton, N.J.: International Finance Section, Department of Economics, Princeton University.

Krugman, P. 1998. "What Happened in Asia." MIT, Cambridge, MA, Mimeographed document.

———. 1999. "Balance Sheet, the Transfer Problem, and Financial Crises." Paper presented at the IMF Conference in Celebration of the Contribution of Robert Flood, January 1999, Washington, D.C.

La Porta, R., and F. López-de-Silanes. 1998. "Creditor Rights." Harvard University, Cambridge, MA, Mimeographed document.

Litan, R., et al. 1998. "Statement of the Shadow Financial Regulatory Committee on International Monetary Fund Assistance and International Crises." Statement No. 145, Shadow Financial Regulatory Committee.

McKinnon, R., and H. Pill. 1996. "Credible Liberalizations and International Capital Flows: The Overborrowing Syndrome." In I. Ito and A.O. Krueger, editors. *Financial Deregulation and Integration in East Asia.* Chicago: Chicago University Press.

Meltzer, A. 1998. "Asian Problems and the IMF." Testimony prepared for the Joint Economic Committee, U.S. Congress, 24 February, Washington, D.C.

Naciones Unidas. 1999. *Hacia una Nueva Arquitectura Financiera Internacional.* Washington, D.C.: Naciones Unidas.

Raffer, K. 1990. "Applying Chapter 9 Insolvency to International Debts: An Economically Efficient Solution with a Human Face." *World Development.* 18: 301–11.

Rodrik, D. 1998. "Who Needs Capital Account Liberalization?" In Peter B. Kenen, editor. *Should the IMF Pursue Capital Account Convertibility?* Essays in International Finance No. 207 (January). Princeton, NJ: International Finance Section, Department of Economics, Princeton University.

Sachs, J. 1998. "Global Capitalism: Making it Work." *The Economist* (12–18 September): 23–26.

Soros, G. 1997. "Avoiding a Breakdown: Asia's Crisis Demands a Rethink of International Regulation." *Financial Times* (31 December): 12.

————. 1998. *The Crisis of Global Capitalism.* New York: Public Affairs Press.

Stiglitz, J. 1998. "The Role of International Financial Institutions in the Current Global Economy." World Bank, Washington, D.C., Mimeographed document.

Comment

Jean Lemierre

France is honored to host the annual meeting of the Inter-American Development Bank. It is especially fitting since our debates will revolve around two important considerations for us here in France specifically, and in Europe generally. First, we are delighted to be in a position to contribute to the search for solutions to the difficulties Latin America is facing today. Second, Europe has recently constructed a new currency: the Euro. We believe this is a useful and important element to be considered in the debate, and are anxious to know what contribution you think we Europeans might make to enhance world financial stability.

The difficulties facing us today are enormous: financial instability, investors' aversion to risk, budgetary tension, the threat of an economic slowdown, and deeply held perceptions of the links between different Latin American economies and the world economy. We have to analyze the situation more closely. I should like very much to see our discussion here framed in a wider context. A great deal of work has been carried out at the International Monetary Fund, the World Bank, the regional development banks, the G7, as well as other institutions such as the G22 and this week's G33. In short, there has been much reflection. During this past year, the perception, analysis, and even the orientations have become considerably clearer.

I believe this seminar, given the quality of its participants, will undoubtedly contribute to this clarification. The first session will look at the lessons to be drawn from the crisis and the reforms that appear today to be absolutely vital. At a second roundtable, we will see what initiatives can be taken, more generally, to adapt the international monetary system to the new situation and help it confront the various crises it may face in the future.

France has proposed several initiatives on this subject. It has expressed in other fora a number of ideas with many of the participants who have gathered here today. We will view, therefore, with great interest how these and other ideas are debated by representatives from Latin America and Larry Summers of the U.S. Treasury. What is learned here should be reflected in the future discussions of concerned decision-making bodies.

Today's meeting will help clarify the thinking that needs to be done. And it will also enable the world and investors to see that there is a pilot in the cockpit, that there are indeed people calling for reforms.

Additional Comments by Jean Lemierre

I would now like to make a few comments in response to the arguments presented today. I think we all share the idea that international stability is first and foremost the result of good national macroeconomic policies. And yet, this is not sufficient. Even if we all agree on this point, we need to go beyond it.

This leads into my second remark, which concerns the enormous importance of multilateral institutions: the International Monetary Fund; the World Bank; and the regional development banks, led of course by the Inter-American Development Bank. The multilateral institutions have an essential role to play, not only in the handling of crises, but also in attempts to prevent crises. In this regard, I would like to pay homage to the imagination of the IMF, the World Bank, and the Inter-American Development Bank in creating instruments, particularly for financing structural reforms, urgent or otherwise. This is exactly the sort of initiative we should be developing because it is absolutely essential. I also would like to stress the importance of mechanisms that allow early lines of credit to be negotiated, principally with the International Monetary Fund but with the regional development banks as well. Negotiating these instruments during calm periods gives emerging market countries a solid and durable macroeconomic policy barrier against external shocks. Of course, this implies the need to reinforce the legitimacy and the cohesion of the actions carried out by the Bretton Woods institutions.

A third and final remark concerns exchange rate policies and systems. Personally, I am always cautious when I hear extreme positions being expressed, when people say we have to go from a pure floating system to an extremely rigid system. I believe, as many of you do, that the reality is certainly less black and white than that, and that each case must be considered individually. I can only insist that any consideration of a new exchange rate system be examined carefully.

This leads me to make two simple remarks on exchange rate systems. The first concerns the importance of a regional approach, particularly in those economic and commercial matters that affect exchange rates. I understand that the situations we face today do not encourage us to think this way, but one of the interesting paths open to us is to consider both an anchor system and what the regional framework for such a system might be. This is a debate that is probably as important in certain countries of Central Europe and Asia as it is in Latin America.

My second remark concerns the capacity that exchange rate systems have for evolving, especially in the case of extremely rigid systems. History teaches us that what is most difficult to deal with are the breakdowns. For reasons that are probably more political than economic, these breakdowns are difficult to come to terms with. It would be desirable for us and the International Monetary Fund and the Inter-American Development Bank to think more closely about the technical and, undoubtedly, the political preparations needed for changing exchange rate systems. All of us, particularly Europeans during the past 50 years, know that it is difficult to make the transition between different approaches and that these approaches generally are very expensive. This suggests another area for reflection: to try to anticipate the breakdowns, which are extraordinarily difficult in economic terms.

I offer one final comment. I was struck by the fact our discussion did not even touch on the social repercussions of economic crises. These social costs cannot be ignored because structural reforms exact a heavy toll. Many countries around the world are undergoing adjustments, and it is vital that institutions such as the World Bank and the Inter-American Development Bank take into account during the preparation stage, but more particularly during an adjustment, the social consequences of macroeconomic changes. Without social cohesion and advancement, I fear that many developmental steps will prove difficult to make, and that we will fail to construct sounder structures.

Jean Lemierre is the Director of Treasury of France.

Comment

José Antonio Ocampo

This panel deals with national policies for managing international financial volatility. Ricardo Hausmann raises some important points. He did not dwell on the first two policy areas, pointing out that there tended to be a consensus on fiscal and financial policies. He gave us a long account of exchange rate issues, demonstrating that flexibility was viewed with some reluctance by the authorities, then mentioned what is perhaps a fourth policy area: management of international capital flows, which has been important in some countries.

Fiscal policies provoke at least two kinds of important questions. First, how procyclical do these policies need to be in times of turmoil? I will illustrate this with the Asian case. The Asian policies agreed to by the International Monetary Fund were always very restrictive in their early stages. But following the strong criticism received in the first months of the adjustments, the Fund has tended to allow much larger fiscal deficits, which indicates that they were indeed excessively recessive. Second, the subject of fiscal institutions obviously has very important implications because of their necessarily political nature. As political institutions they must involve the participation of parliaments. Any institutional design in the fiscal area has to take this feature of democracy into account, which is a laudable objective in any social order.

In the financial area, I believe Hausmann is correct when he says there is much more consensus. Still, there are questions about the type of regulations needed beyond the basic Basle criteria. For example, should the move be toward more active management with liquidity requirements, which has proven to be a good instrument in Argentina in recent years. Or should much stronger regulations be established to make financial systems more prudent and less vulnerable in crisis situations? I leave these questions open to discussion.

On exchange policy, a comment can be added that in practice not a single Latin American country has really had a strictly clean float. All the flexible systems—not only in Latin America but throughout the world—have some degree of dirty float. Even the systems of intra-band intervention used in several countries have elements of a dirty float inside the exchange bands. The question that market observers would ask is whether a different rule of intervention by the authorities is being proposed in relation to the existing flotation rules. It could also be asked whether the reluctance of authorities to allow a greater devaluation in 1998 is a reflection of the rules of flotation, or of not having permitted more flotation. And when the authorities adopt a freer flotation system are they simply floating earlier and for longer rather than waiting until the process has advanced or market pressures intensify?

Lastly, I again leave open the issue of whether—apart from fiscal, monetary, financial, and exchange rules—the authorities should also participate more in regulating capital flows. This could have elements of the Chilean or Colombian system of reserves, or systems that are more market-oriented than based upon traditional controls.

José Antonio Ocampo is the Executive Secretary of the Economic Commission for Latin America and the Caribbean (ECLAC) .

Comment

Pablo Guidotti

In the past two years, instability in capital markets has forced us to concentrate our energies on finding ways to manage this volatile situation. Often, we have forgotten other policies that are tremendously important. In Argentina's case, in the debate on exchange rate policy, the currency board is one of the policies recommended as an alternative to floating exchange rates. Yet we often forget that in Argentina the board is much more than a simple fixed exchange rate. It is, in fact, a system embedded in very important reforms in many areas. This is why the Argentine system is successful. A lot of work would be needed before it could be successfully applied in other countries.

Since 1989, Argentina has totally deregulated its economic system, opened its capital account to international markets, substantially liberalized its trade, transformed its social security system from "pay as you go" to a capitalization system, consolidated its fiscal accounts in relation to its deficit and spending, and improved the transparency of the information available to the public. The monetary system has undergone drastic changes, one of which is the Convertibility Law. Another is the transformation of the Central Bank's statutes, which have given the bank independence and defined its relations with the Treasury. The Central Bank itself has radically overhauled banking regulations, enormously strengthened its supervision of the banking system, and introduced policies such as liquidity requirements, which have given the banking system the capacity to resist shocks. In my opinion, without these changes, convertibility—that is, strictly the exchange or conversion board aspect—would not be sufficient. All these reforms, as well as the massive privatization program that Argentina has put through in this period, are important.

This process has obviously generated an improvement in the country's economic performance and in growth, which is what really matters. Growth has gone from negative in the so-called lost decade to above 15 percent today. Estimates of Argentina's potential growth based on its structural reforms put sustainable rates at around 6 percent annually for the next decade. This is reflected in the enormous change in the attitude of investors, and in a stronger export sector.

However, in the past two years, the world has moved on. While in the 1970s and 1980s we were concerned about the flow variables, the 1990s—especially the second half—is a story of stocks. The international financial system is not well equipped to deal with this change, which is why the discussion on international financial architecture is important. The points that Ricardo Hausmann raised in his presentation should be discussed without ideological biases.

Clearly, this new trend has greatly affected growth, which is the variable that interests us. In Argentina's case, there is a close relationship between the growth of the economy and the flow of capital to the private sector. We could almost say that the principal determinants of the fluctuations and volatility of our real economy are directly related to the changes occurring in financing for the private sector.

Finance for the private sector is obviously closely linked to the perception of country risk. In the last two years, while Argentina was pushing through all the transformations we have just mentioned, the perception of country risk was changing, first with the Tequila crisis, then the Asian crisis, more recently the Russian crisis, and now, regional problems.

Interestingly, one of the components of this volatility in capital markets is associated with the composition of capital flows, which have changed considerably in this decade. While in the 1980s the greater part of the flow of capital was in the form of bank loans, in the 1990s the boom has been in the bond markets. Looking at the composition of capital flows to the private sector, broken down into financial and nonfinancial, we find an interesting characteristic: The financial sector was more stable in these years and operated countercyclically during the crises, increasing its share of financing to the economy, whereas the bond market fell. This trend in the bond markets has made movements of capital more volatile; today, the most urgent problem for economic policymakers is how to manage this volatility.

In this respect, I think Hausmann's paper focuses on the important points. The markets are looking for two things: fiscal solvency and liquidity. Fiscal solvency is achieved by doing everything possible to reduce the deficit and improve the primary surplus, which is what we have done in Argentina. On the liquidity side, there are two fundamental aspects: the banking system and debt maturity.

The banking system has typically been the weak link in the chain. It is not enough to require banks to have a higher capital reserve than the 8 percent suggested by Basle, and to reinforce bank supervision by improving reserve systems and giving ample information to the public in an effort to increase market discipline in the financial system. In emerging countries, where public securities are prone to market volatility, the financial system must also be liquid in terms of international reserve units.

Our policy has been to require the financial system to comply with liquidity requirements defined as a proportion of its deposits and short-term liabilities. This has now been increased by a contingent credit line of over $6 billion with international commercial banks. The sum of the liquidity requirements in international reserves plus the contingent credit line now represents 30 percent of the liabilities in the financial system, deposits in this case. These requirements were fundamental during the Tequila crisis when we allowed the system to use that liquidity to offset a fall in deposits.

The second aspect is debt maturity. We have made a considerable effort to extend the maturity of our debt. This has not meant that Argentina has had less access to the capital market; on the contrary, access has increased. Today our public sector debt has an average maturity of about nine years. These are all domestic policies aimed at reducing volatility.

Looking ahead, what more can we do? First, as we are interested in the growth of the real economy, we must continue to make structural reforms in the labor market, advance toward more-efficient tax systems in Argentina's case, attack tax subsidies for company borrowing, strengthen finance through the capital market, and reduce labor costs.

In this consolidation process, there has been a deliberate policy of reducing payroll taxes, resulting in a drop of over 25 percent in labor costs since 1995, in comparison with wage levels in the United States, after taking into account the tax burden. We clearly have to continue working on the productive side of the economy.

Second, on the financial side, we have to bring down financial costs for companies and analyze how to reduce the volatility of the capital account. These points will be dealt with more fully in discussions of how to improve the operation of the international system.

Here I want to make two points that underlie the discussion of dollarization and single currencies, which have been proposed in Argentina. First, in emerging countries, we would like to continue to benefit from globalized markets as reflected in the phenomenal increase in trade flows between industrial countries and our own. We would also like to enjoy the advantages of increased foreign direct investment, which quintupled in the Western Hemisphere in the 1990s. But these benefits have to be accompanied by larger capital flows and greater participation by the private sector, fundamentally the private sector in international debt and equity markets.

This participation in international markets will have to be in reserve currencies because they give access to markets in which companies can generate hedges, manage their liquidity risk better, and make long-term issues. Domestic markets, as Hausmann's paper pointed out, do not permit long-term debt or they make it very costly. Economic policy has to adapt to this situation.

Second, to improve the capacity of the International Monetary Fund and the official community to manage volatility without phenomenal aid packages that generate the process of moral hazard, countries have to put more emphasis on managing their domestic debt and extending the maturities of both external and domestic debt. I believe the debate is poorly focused because it concentrates only on external debt when we know that Brazil and Russia are cases where the domestic debt played a very important role.

In this respect, emerging countries need longer-term debt, and the only way this can happen is through issues in reserve currencies. Economic policy has to adapt to these facts. Argentina firmly believes that the IMF should create a contingent credit line, which can be effective if it is limited in access and amount to avoid problems of moral hazard.

As to what countries can do, we have to put more emphasis on managing the reduction of liquidity risk. What implication does this have for exchange systems? The obvious implication is that although each country will have to evaluate the costs and benefits for itself, it will be very costly for countries to use nonreserve currencies that fluctuate independently of reserve currencies. They add one more uncertainty, one more cost that generates higher risk premiums, higher interest rates, and lower growth.

Both the design of the role of the IMF and market trends will eventually require fewer currencies. We do not know at this time what an efficient number of currencies would be. This is the dilemma that Hausmann mentioned. There is no clear reason for 180 different currencies, particularly considering the specialization that exists in many activities.

If we compare Mexico and Argentina during the crisis period, the volatility in Mexico was exactly equal to that in Argentina, even though Mexico had a floating rate and Argentina a fixed rate. The international financial system requires mechanisms to reduce the risk and uncertainty that the market injects into the systems, which basically means that nonreserve currencies should be disassociated from the provision of low-cost, stable finance for growth and investment.

Pablo Guidotti is the Secretary of Finance of Argentina.

Comment

Manuel Hinds

The subject of international financial turmoil is very important, and the presentation by the Office of the Chief Economist is an excellent piece of work that I would personally like to call, "The emperor has no clothes."

For years at the university or at symposiums where a professor is invited to present an academic paper, we have heard the same story: Country X refuses to devalue and its interest rate is extremely high. The country is not growing and is very unstable. Everyone says, "What a foolish country!" In the end, the country will have no alternative but to devalue so that interest rates will fall and the country will begin to grow again and stabilize. Sure enough, tomorrow's newspaper reads: "Country X devalues." And everyone is happy, at first.

The country has announced it will devalue by 5 percent; then it appears that it was not 5 percent but 15 percent. The next day, the 15 percent changes to 25 percent. Then the question becomes, What happened to the interest rate? It has gone sky high. Before it was 12 percent, which was extremely high, and today 80 percent! And what happened to the inflation rate? It shot up again. What happened to growth? Don't ask. The country has to negotiate an agreement with the International Monetary Fund to stabilize its currency, which is out of control again. The IMF insists on raising interest rates and on tight fiscal and financial policies.

What happened? How is it possible to insist year after year that interest rates will fall if you devalue, when in fact the opposite is true. Taking a long-term view, Latin America has differed from Europe in this respect, and I believe the difference mentioned in the IDB study is very important. Latin American countries have had many opportunities to devalue and to exercise independent monetary policies, which always end in tragedy.

For example, an analysis of wage series in different countries in Latin America shows exponential curves in most countries in nominal terms. We have to use a measure that makes sense, such as dollars. In many countries, prices or wages in dollars begin to climb steadily and then suddenly fall. Later, they begin to rise again and the cycle is repeated. In dollar terms, Latin American countries have cycles of about 10 years. Every 10 years they regress to where they were 10 years earlier, and the cycle starts again.

Businessmen and bankers usually adopt a hands-off attitude to investing in Latin America. They mention continuous instability, the ever-present possibility of devaluation, and out-of-control monetary policies, etc. These factors make it very difficult to invest in our countries for both foreigners and local people. Generally, business in Latin American countries is very short term compared to other areas in the world. This makes a lot of sense. If there is always a possibility that relative prices are going to change because devaluation is imminent, the best strategy is to invest for the shortest possible period at the highest return.

The study makes a very thorough analysis of several of the subjects under discussion. Many of the predictions of the theory—the need for independent monetary policies, flexible exchange rates, and the possibility of devaluation—are exactly the opposite of what really happens in our countries. Hausmann has covered all these points very well, particularly the fact that we are living in a world in which theory contradicts reality.

However, there is a point that has not really been mentioned that I believe is very important, and I have had to deal with it several times. In El Salvador we tried dollarization four years ago but were unable to do so for purely internal reasons. We had the reserves to buy the monetary base, but internal political circumstances, which are now changing, prevented it. During the debate on the change in El Salvador it was argued that the possibility of devaluation was necessary because of destabilizing capital flows. At that time, the Mexican crisis was fresh in our minds, and later there were other examples of destabilizing flows. The argument was that if a country suffers one of these capital flights, devaluation has to be an option or reserves could be lost.

Now that we are looking at ways to manage these flows, the obvious questions are: How and why do these destabilizing flows occur? And why are they much less destabilizing in some countries than in others? The truth is that money flows because of large interest rate differentials, which are normally determined by monetary policy. This has happened very often in Latin America. A country moves into a domestic boom, which attracts a lot of short-term capital. The country has an independent monetary policy, and the money supply has nothing to do with its reserves. Suddenly, people are alarmed when the relationship between monetary strength and reserves becomes destabilizing, and they withdraw their money. Once a very violent outflow of capital begins, the only solution is devaluation.

But why do investors start to move their money out? It is not because the country risk is higher, nor is it a reaction to a small change in the interest rate, it is simply that people fear a devaluation. It is that simple. A few days after these violent outflows of capital and the subsequent devaluation, people calm down and see that the currency has found its level. Funds start to return and the currency begins to appreciate again. The problem has been solved but the solution is the start of the next round of devaluation. A flexible exchange system and an independent monetary policy create a vicious circle through which Latin America has passed time and again.

About five years ago I read that Latin America is the region with the greatest number of macroeconomists per square meter because a devaluation or revaluation is always about to occur somewhere in some country—and the economies never improve. The time has come when the need for stability is obvious.

What would happen if we did not have an independent monetary policy? In El Salvador, we decided for political reasons against dollarization, although we did recommend it. In the long run it is better not to have independent monetary policies as a protection against populism.

All of us know that countercyclical monetary policies are very difficult to manage. They are very difficult for large countries, even very sophisticated countries; but for Latin American countries, monetary policy always ends up being procyclical. The IDB study shows that the countries that have not had independent monetary policies are the ones that have had more countercyclical macroeconomic reactions.

Another important point is that we are always being told to maintain competitiveness. It is contradictory to say that competitiveness is linked to the possibility of devaluing. If a country has to devalue, it is because it is not competitive. If I can sell something at 100, why would I want to sell it at 50? Simply because I am not competitive, because I do not offer good quality or good service, or other such reasons. To develop a country based on constant devaluation is simply to play *Alice in Wonderland*, where one has to run faster and faster to stay in the same place. This is not development

But then how does a country increase its exports? How does it increase competitiveness? The answer is by working, reducing costs, increasing efficiency, slashing bureaucracy, and improving the customs service and the ports. This is what really increases a country's competitiveness—not devaluation.

In El Salvador, we have not devalued for six years, and in that time we have practically tripled our net international reserves. Not only that, the financial system has grown substantially. M2 is presently 50 percent of GDP, whereas seven years ago it was around 15 percent. Exports have grown at a compound annual rate of 19 percent, almost tripling in the last four years despite falling coffee prices. We left traditional exports and moved into nontraditional exports, which are not affected by commodity cycles and which have grown at a compound annual rate of 24 percent, with the exchange rate at exactly the same level as six years ago but in a much more transparent economy. People no longer expect the government to devalue to gain an advantage of two months, in the belief that devaluation is more profitable, until the trade unions, the bankers, and the depositors realize they have the same real exchange rate as before but with higher inflation.

To conclude, our experience with a fixed exchange rate has been very positive. Exports have not been adversely affected; on the contrary we believe productivity has increased, although interest rates in El Salvador are still too high. Our country risk is now a little over 1 percent. We calculate the exchange risk at something like 3 percent, which is less than half what it was six years ago, but still too high.

We believe it is better to move toward a system of currency areas. We would prefer to go directly to the dollar. Rather than saying we are going to be linked to the dollar, it is better to say we are going to the dollar.

Manuel Hinds is the Minister of Finance of El Salvador

Comment

Eduardo Aninat

Chile is a small, open country that has made many structural reforms that are similar to and even go beyond what has been described here this morning. Therefore, for me it is a little surprising or paradoxical that a very academic debate dating back many decades, perhaps even hundreds of years, has returned with such strength in the throes of the most serious international financial crisis the world has experienced since the 1930s. I mean, of course, the dichotomy between fixed and flexible exchange rates, which is taking place during the most extended crisis ever, if measured according to affected countries and time. This world turmoil has already lasted since June or July 1997 and has provoked great instability in two or three Asian countries, as well as in Russia and, more recently, Brazil.

I am surprised because, on the one hand, the debate reflects a renewal of interest by professional economists in bringing new elements on the scene to tackle this crisis and look to the future, which is positive. On the other hand, it has the flavor of a search for *deus ex machina* solutions to a serious and extreme situation, which is actually deeper and more complex and involves all our institutions.

In my opinion, the data this process provides about a financial crisis that is still unfolding, and which unfortunately has more chapters to go, does not clearly resolve the long debate on the advantages of one system over the other. Rather, we are seeing a kaleidoscope of symptoms in a many-faceted puzzle.

Before going on, let us look at some evidence. First, if we take a longer view over 25 or 30 years, the ranking of the sample changes. The number of countries that have joined the bandwagon of flexible exchange rates around the world has multiplied by a factor of almost three in relation to countries that have retained a fixed system. Thus, we are looking at only a snapshot of the economic cycle and not viewing it from a longer perspective with all its ups and downs, the boom and bust and the convergence that has still not happened in this particular economic cycle.

Second, the analyses that have been done are very respectable but too focused on the financial variable. I agree with [Pablo] Guidotti that the emerging countries of Latin America require a large amount of imported capital to maximize their growth rates. Likewise, international financial markets need countries that function with institutions that have political backing, combined with balanced social and domestic policies. Both need each other, and we cannot look at the need for future changes only from the point of view of a particular financial bank variable. Some paradoxes come to mind. For instance, the conversion board in Argentina has been a fascinating experience that has endured and withstood the most pessimistic predictions and now forms part of the modern economic history of Argentina. We also have to recognize that the same situation in Hong Kong has been under strong pressure in the financial and banking area for the past two years and has needed the support of China to continue functioning. A third example of a conversion board in one of the small independent republics of the ex-Soviet Union is a very special experience quite different from the others.

To recommend this type of system or the larger step of full dollarization for an entire region has not been academically proven or endorsed by the experience of the countries that would be affected by the change. I say this after careful consideration because I have great admiration and friendship for the Argentine economic team. But it is a risky step that requires careful thought, given where the world economy is in the international financial cycle at this time. In today's world, there are growth paradoxes. Capital flees from one country to another; and growth is basically driven by the United States, which has been growing for over eight years in a special cycle, but not by the Europe of the Euro.

Timing and sequencing is an extremely important subject that I have not seen considered here at all. One does not have to return to Rostow or to so many others to realize that stages or thresholds make a difference from the institutional point of view of economic policy. On sequencing, it is good that so many countries have now completely opened their capital accounts. This is praiseworthy and positive and helps globalization, which we all favor.

But there are other aspects of the economy in which deregulation is blocked and the opening has not been complete—for example, trade policy. In Chile, the tariff opening was much greater than in the other cases described here because of a pragmatic and conscious decision based on the design of our integration into the world economy, which we do not recommend for others but which has not worked badly for us. Three years from now, we will have a general tariff rate for the world of no more than 6 percent, which will in fact average only 3 or 4 percent when the bilateral agreements we have signed are taken into account. Other countries have chosen a complete financial opening but have maintained a higher external tariff, double that of Chile, with many exceptions and even controls.

Why is this trade variable ignored? Why is no analysis made of its impact on global exchange policy, which is influenced by more than just financial factors? We have to go back and make an economic analysis with more finesse and take into account other policy variables. In this respect, Hausmann was right to note that we need to examine fiscal policy very carefully.

What is the background of exchange policy? Under Mexico's flexible exchange system, which is very flexible but within certain limits, when the peso–dollar devaluation in Mexico reaches about 10 pesos, interventions and other things occur. At the other extreme of the fixed exchange rate, we know it is backed by a regulatory and privatization policy, by each country's fiscal stance and the composition of public spending. In this respect, I was pleased to hear Hausmann say that, in these cycles, the successful countries are going to be the ones that have a relatively conservative or prudent policy reflecting a fiscal stance that is adjusted to the point of the cycle. In Chile, we have had 10 years of fiscal surplus, but there has been some debate in public opinion about our net fiscal savings position, which has fallen 1 percent of gross domestic product to a level of 0.4 percent. With a downturn in the economic cycle and a very low copper price, there is an obvious need for comparisons based on a more structural definition of the cycle of fiscal adjustment and position.

Given the global uncertainty and volatility, and the recently initiated discussion at the highest levels of the G22, G30, and G7 in Washington and Europe on the seeds of a new international financial architecture, I am not sure that our small, open countries—many of which have made substantial reforms—should rush into a major change in their exchange policy. They should wait until the IMF, World Bank, United Nations, or World Trade Organization (WTO) provide us with the global ground rules to play by. The new Bretton Woods has not yet evolved or matured. We are rushing to conclusions that are too extreme and dangerous at this point in the economic cycle.

I would like to conclude, and it is my obligation to do so as a minister, by stimulating the debate and adding a new element to the sample Hausmann gave us and correcting one or two of his figures without detracting from his magnificent work.

The comparison given us was polar. Such comparisons—either totally flexible or totally fixed exchange rates—almost always arouse suspicion a priori, at least to Chileans who have been through so many polarized political experiences.

Chile has followed a pragmatic intermediate policy adapted to its situation. We have used a cone for a flotation band that now has a width of more or less 10 percent, varying from day to day, based on a basket of currencies: Euro, Japanese yen, U.S. dollar. The band has been appropriately flexible, which has provoked a real devaluation in the last 12 months. I am more optimistic than Manuel Hinds on this because from 4 to 6 real percent with a controlled inflation does not give results. Annualized inflation in Chile has fallen not risen, to 3.8 percent for the 12 months through February.

We have the lowest interest rates in Latin America, after a period of very high rates. Last week, the Central Bank lowered rates to only 7 real percentage points, half the rate in Argentina where rates have also been falling. We are now about to begin a cycle of reactivation after an inevitable slowdown in the rate of growth of GDP; even so, growth in 1998 was 3.3 percent. Moreover, it is said there is no room for domestic currencies and that capital markets are operating noisily. In the Chilean case, there is a very broad mortgage market. Every day, instruments at 20 or 25 years are traded at reasonable interest rates in the real estate and securities sectors. Then there are the pension funds and the reforms that have been put through in all of Latin America, which have resulted in a capital deepening.

I believe we have steered the economy well. There have been no polarized correlations between inflation, flexibility, and the volatility of interest rates except for a few weeks or months when not only our countries—but everyone, including the major international financial centers—were affected by a liquidity squeeze of unprecedented proportions.

The intermediate experiences need to be analyzed more calmly. They respond to something that is much needed in the proposed changes, something that economists cannot ignore, which is the political support for these changes. What will our people say about them? There are elements of institutionality, social support, stability, and general comprehension accompanying economic policy that cannot be written on a blackboard or in a vacuum. Our countries are entering an election cycle in which the results in employment, joblessness, and social policy are fundamental ingredients, at least for democratic governments. All of us here are professional economists, and I have enjoyed the debate here, but we have to recognize that we are all part of governments elected by the ballot box. This means that all our theoretical constructions and policies have to pass the test of real long-term viability.

In brief, I am skeptical about extreme movements in the existing exchange systems. I believe the debate has gone a little beyond the reasonable. In the future, we are going to see more pragmatism, more adaptability, improvements in monetary policy, and especially a more effective fiscal policy. In practice, we are probably not going to see too many changes in the short term in exchange systems in Latin America.

Eduardo Aninat is the Minister of Finance of Chile.

Comment

Arminio Fraga

This is a long historical debate, and there is much to say, but I will spend most of my time talking about Brazil. First, on exchange rate regimes, my view both as an economist and as a practitioner is that the systems that work in the long run are those closest to the extremes, that is, closer to either a very fixed exchange rate or to a freely floating one. Some of you may look at me and immediately ask, what about Chile? In my view, Chile has done so many things so well that it is the exception that proves the rule. So let's leave Chile out of the picture because it is in a class all by itself.

Let's look at most other countries. We have decades of experience with gold standards, fixed exchange rates, floating exchange rates; and to me the answer is not very obvious. There is no evidence that Latin America is any different than any other region. Thailand had a fixed exchange rate and ran into trouble. The gold standard is a wonderful example. Latin America did very well when it abandoned the gold standard, so I am a bit concerned that we have short memories. I can only say that looking at a broader sample may lead to different questions.

How do we intend to make a floating exchange rate system work in Brazil? Brazil, as you know, has just gone through a fairly dramatic devaluation. As Manuel Hinds commented, it was not one of choice. It was not a conscious decision. Brazil fought to defend the prior regime but circumstances made that impossible. The question is, why? Why did that happen? Where was Brazil? And where is Brazil heading now?

About two years ago, Brazil successfully launched the Real Plan and suffered through a number of structural reforms. Brazil was going through a second round of adjustments that were being implemented gradually on the fiscal and balance-of-payments fronts. Thus, there was a gradual improvement in the fiscal accounts and a gradual adjustment of the exchange rate in the balance of payments. These gradual policies were supported or supplemented by very tight money. Monetary policy was extremely tight, which in turn was possible because Brazil addressed its banking problems early on with the PROER program aimed at private sector banks and the PROES program aimed at state banks. A strong monetary policy, and this very strong and broad privatization program, helped with many economic problems, including balance-of-payments and deficit financing.

More recently, however, particularly in the past year and a half or so, it became clear that the fiscal policy of Brazil had slipped and that it was no longer on a fiscal adjustment path, but rather, moving in the opposite direction. At the same time, as is often the case, the international financial environment became quite hostile. As always happens, a country in a vulnerable position was caught in a global liquidity squeeze, and that combination always leads to trouble. Now, in the case of Brazil this combined lack of fiscal adjustment and a balance-of-payments fragility led to the perception that the country had a debt dynamics problem, or a debt trap, and a real balance-of-payments problem. These problems were first addressed in September and November 1998 with fiscal announcements, but they were insufficient and there were slippages in the domestic congressional calendar. Eventually, the situation became such that Brazil floated its currency. This is the background to my assessment.

Given this background, what has been the policy response in Brazil and where are we headed? The policy response can be broken down into three large blocks. Again, I will leave out the structural reforms that I consider a very important part of the permanent task but not necessarily crucial elements of where we are now. On the policy front, the first response was the announcement late last year of fiscal goals that were set by President Cardoso and Mr. Malan to yield a primary surplus this year of 3.1 percent of GDP. This is a slow year in Brazil. We expect a decline in our GDP, and to go from 0 or a deficit in the primary the year before to a surplus of this magnitude represents quite an effort. The effort itself is possible because much has been done in recent years, including the first round of social security reform, the administrative reform, and so on. But I won't belabor that. The first major policy response was to produce a fiscal surplus. Without that we'd still be classified—and correctly so—as a country with a seriously flawed fiscal future.

In addition, we have planned privatization sales for this year that will reduce debt by more than 2 percent of GDP. The sales include the state bank of São Paulo (Banespa), the power companies, water companies, some remaining shares in Petrobras, CVRD (the mining company), and so on. It is a very substantial program that could represent up to 2.5 or 2.7 percent of GDP. So that is the first element.

The second one has to do with the main theme of this panel, and it is the issue closest to my own backyard at the moment: that is, the exchange rate regime. The decision we have taken is to go for a floating exchange regime. Our main concern is to make sure that Brazilian society, and markets in general, understand that we are not abandoning anchorage but switching anchors. To make that clear, we have decided to go for an inflation-targeting framework such as the ones effectively being used in many countries, including the U.K., Mexico, Canada, Chile, Australia, and others. In the inflation-targeting scheme, we will be announcing a target for inflation and developing a policy response transparent enough to make it credible. One could argue that the United States has that in place already, and the European Central Bank will be moving in that direction as well.

The third element in our adjustment program is of course the balance of payments. In this area, the devaluation itself will help. With a weaker exchange rate, this year we expect to have a current account deficit that will be closer to or lower than foreign direct investment (FDI), even factoring in lower FDI this year than last year. We have negotiated a program with the IMF that is being supported by the bilaterals. The program brings in ample bridge financing for this transition period from one regime to the other. The numbers have been made public. We have $8 billion for the next four months. That is more than enough to cover our projected gap in the period and should help us deal with the initial overshooting features of our floating regime. Beyond that we basically intend to float and see no reason why it cannot work. The private sector has joined in support of our program. Minister Malan and I have just come from a tour of the main financial capitals of the world. We still have teams going to a few more capitals, and the response of the private sector has been very good. They have demonstrated their intention to increase the trade and inter-bank financing available to Brazil, and to maintain their exposure. With that, we have a balance-of-payments situation that looks quite stable and is definitely an important change from recent months. These, then, are the three blocks.

A fourth element is the regulation and supervision of the banking sector. Our view is that if the exchange rate regime is well-defined and clean and if your banks are well-supervised with prudent regulations, there is no need for capital controls and that is the path we intend to follow in Brazil.

What are the implications of our policy response to the crisis we are going through, and why do I think this is going to work? First, I see the primary surplus, the floating exchange rate, and healthy banks, and then I remind you that the banking sector in Brazil is well-capitalized, well-provisioned, and underleveraged. I expect real interest rates to decline from the very high levels of recent years in Brazil, and the reason is clear: The credit risk has gone down. The exchange rate risk is not there. If you recall, Brazil was in the unfortunate position of having its exchange rate seen as a one-way bet by markets. It is not in that situation anymore, and lower interest rates are definitely going to be a byproduct of these policies in a healthy financial sector.

With lower real interest rates, the debt-to-GDP ratio is clearly going to be declining. The impact of the devaluation has taken our debt-to-GDP ratio to slightly above 50 percent. Projecting ahead with simple simulations, we have the primary surplus, the privatization plans, and lower real interest rates. The declining path should be very clear. Moreover, there is a lot of room in Brazil for good, old-fashioned, open-market operations and debt management. Last week's auctions were proof of that; for the first time in a while, we sold quite a bit more than was maturing in the two auctions. And I am also happy to report that we now have in Brazil, for the first time I can remember, an inverted yield curve. Overnight rates are around 45 percent and one-year rates were 40 or 41 percent. I have great faith that this trend will be maintained and probably deepened in the near future. With this in mind and with the Central Bank looking cleanly at inflation, I expect to see a price increase in the short term, but not the follow-up inflation. The economy now has virtually no indexation, and with the pillars I mentioned—fiscal, monetary, and balance of payments—there is no reason why this price jump should lead to an inflationary spiral. The virtuous circle of lower inflation and lower interest rates should lie just a few months ahead, and I anticipate a good second half of 1999.

That, in my opinion, is the right path for Brazil. And there is a clear understanding in Brazil, from President Cardoso on down, that the path we were on before was not sustainable. It is being openly admitted at all levels that the policies had to change. The commitment is there, the understanding is there, and now it takes time. Credibility cannot be recovered instantly, but I assure you that we are ready to pursue the right path and the right policies. I hope I can come back in a year's time to an IDB forum and discuss the fascinating theoretical issues we address here, but for the time-being we must focus on the task at hand.

Arminio Fraga is President of the Central Bank of Brazil.

Comment

Pedro Pou

Let me thank the Office of the Chief Economist of the Inter-American Development Bank for inviting me to make these remarks on this extremely important topic and in the company of such a distinguished panel. I would like to congratulate Ricardo Hausmann and his coauthors for writing such an interesting paper on exchange rate arrangements. This paper sets out very clearly the current range of views on exchange rate management and gives one of the best real accounts, backed by evidence rather than just by theory, of the costs and benefits of fixed and floating rates. I think this paper may become a milestone in the current debate. This morning's debate and Ricardo and his colleagues' paper have helped put into context the choices faced in developing a new financial architecture.

In my brief presentation I will outline these choices, and argue that the world cannot shy away from them. To be able to deal with such an important and complex issue as the new financial architecture, I will focus my presentation on a few topics. It may first be convenient to identify the issues about which we believe there is general consensus. To save time, I will not dwell on these consensus points. Three such important issues are (a) capital controls, (b) domestic economic policy, and (c) the strength of the financial system.

Capital Controls

My first assumption is that international capital flows are beneficial and that we wish to keep the capital account open. Clearly, without this assumption it would cost countries little to close their capital accounts, and then issues of international financial architecture would not be particularly important. However, I firmly believe, and the experience of Argentina shows this very clearly, that international capital can be an extremely important positive force, not just because it provides financing but also because of the other elements it brings. These include technical expertise, management systems and capabilities, and last but not least a monitoring role that helps to keep domestic vested interests in check. At the same time, international global capital flows also bring risks. The increase in flows to emerging countries has led to large stocks of foreign financial liabilities in those countries. The risk, which clearly depends on the nature and maturity of each type of investment, is that foreign as well as domestic investors may wish to withdraw their capital. This should not be thought of as a reversal of flows, but rather as a rapid exit of a very large stock. Any country subject to a sudden withdrawal of a large part of its financial liabilities will then suffer a crisis, whatever the fundamentals of that country. It is therefore absolutely essential to ensure that there is no reason for this to occur.

Domestic Economic Policy

The second important assumption is with respect to the role of domestic economic policies. It goes without saying that whatever the design of the so-called international architecture, it is vital that national authorities do their job, maintain good fundamentals, and ensure that macroeconomic policies—especially fiscal, monetary, and exchange rate policy—are consistent. There is no substitute for good economic policy. If this is true for industrialized nations, it is even more so for emerging markets. Given the lack of depth of financial markets in emerging countries and the lack of such a loyal investor base compared to super-investment-grade-rated industrialized countries, poor economic policy is likely to be punished even more quickly by the markets in an emerging country context, exacerbating any weak fundamentals.

Strengthening the Financial System

Last but not least, I will assume that we all believe now that a strong financial system is an absolute necessity for an emerging country. Indeed, given the higher volatility in the emerging world, it is my view that the Basle capital rules, developed with industrialized countries in mind, should be stress-tested and modified accordingly. Furthermore, I hope that we can all agree that the recommendations of the G22's excellent report on *Strengthening Financial Systems* provide a good blueprint for the issues that need to be addressed. In particular, apart from the implementation of standard Basle-style rules, this report stresses the importance of liquidity for emerging countries. We consider this to be a crucial issue given the fact that emerging countries, virtually by definition, cannot always count on access to international capital. I hope we can also agree that the other concerns of the G22 working parties on transparency, appropriate methods for crisis resolution, and other financial sector "infrastructure" are also vital components for strengthening emerging-country economies. In particular, transparency and the related issues of good accounting standards and disclosure for the public and private sector alike are very important components of a safe and sound financial system.

Choices Faced by Small, Open Economies

Having stated our assumptions, let me turn to my main points. Recent events have shown that excellent fundamentals and a very strong liquidity policy are not enough. For example, Argentina has both of these virtues but has still suffered significantly as a result of the international financial crisis. Although markets have now discriminated significantly and, for example, Argentina has regained access to international credit, growth has suffered considerably simply because Argentina is labeled an "emerging market." I am not suggesting that the markets are irrational. Quite the reverse, if I believe other investors are going to flee a country labeled an emerging market, despite excellent fundamentals, then it would be perfectly rational for me to flee as well. This behavior may be nondiscriminatory but it is certainly rational. We believe that the real alternatives facing small open economies, if they wish to keep their capital account open, are quite limited. In particular, we see two main alternatives. The first would be to work with the international financial community to create a credible international lender of last resort [LOLR]; the second is to consider joining currency areas. This choice may seem extreme, but studying extreme cases is often very useful because they make the choices more clear. That does not mean that the world is always black or white, but at least the true menu of options becomes more clear.

The Nature of Monetary Policy (and the Role of Fiat Money)

Let me talk briefly about the role of money to explain the limited choices available more clearly. To have an independent monetary policy, an independent fiat money is needed. No matter how close to our sentiment this institution is, the fact is that only very recently (perhaps in the last 30 years or so) has the world decided that each country should develop its own fiat money. In previous centuries, gold or other valuable metals served as currency, either directly or indirectly, and this was essentially the idea behind Bretton Woods as well. The well-understood problem is that a fiat money, in the hands of politicians and policymakers, creates too great an incentive for misuse. Let me remind you what David Ricardo said in 1817 in his *Principles of Political Economy and Taxation:*

> There is no point more important than to be fully impressed with the effects that follow from the principle of limitation of quantity. It is not necessary that paper should be payable in specie (i.e., gold or silver) to preserve its value, it is only necessary that its quantity should be regulated. Experience, however, shows that neither the State nor a bank ever has had the unrestricted power of issuing paper money without abusing that power. In all states, therefore, the issue of paper money ought to be under some check and control; and none seems so proper for that purpose as that of subjecting the issuers of paper money to the obligation of paying their notes either in gold or in bullion.

However, some countries (in fact very few) have developed very strong institutions to control these incentives to debase their currency, and so have created very successful fiat moneys. I must congratulate the next panelist [Larry Summers] as being part of the process of creating one of the great currencies in today's world.

Floating Exchange Rates and the Lender of Last Resort

However, if we maintain this very recent view that each and every country should have its own fiat money, then for currencies to gain the necessary credibility to stop a flight at the first sign of trouble we need an effective international LOLR. Without such an independent institution to give a seal of approval to macroeconomic policies and to back this up with adequate resources, I predict that there will be very few truly successful fiat moneys in the future and that countries that seek to maintain their own fiat money without the necessary strong institutions will encounter trouble sooner or later. However, many have objected to this policy of a lender of last resort on the basis of the moral hazard that might be created by its very existence. Many of these objections may be exaggerated, and with imagination there may be ways to construct a meaningful international LOLR. The recent initiative by President Clinton, the proposal that the IMF establish a contingent credit line, and the support by Stanley Fischer for some role by the IMF as LOLR, make me moderately optimistic that we are advancing in that direction. If that were the case,—i.e., if there existed an effective LOLR with ex-ante conditionality rather than ex-post lines of credit to help in crisis resolution—then we may be optimistic that even small countries may hope to have a fiat money of their own, that is a floating exchange rate vis-á-vis all the currencies of the world, together with an open capital account. This is certainly not an easy task, but we should not exaggerate the difficulties either.

Currency Unions

The second alternative is a 180-degree turnaround from this very recent view that every country should maintain its own currency. As John Stuart Mill said in his *Principles of Political Economy* in 1894, just 70 years after David Ricardo: "So much of barbarism however still remains in the transactions of most civilized Nations, that almost all independent countries choose to assert their nationality by having, to their own inconvenience and that of their neighbors, a peculiar currency of their own."

Why keep that barbarian world? After all, the growth of trade in goods and capital that characterized the gold standard period was as large as it is today during the Bretton Woods period. I am not proposing a move to just one currency, basically because I think that it is too early for this idea. But I would not be surprised if in the next 10 to 20 years we see a significant reduction in the number of currencies. This may take some time since every country feels obliged to produce the services of money without thinking whether or not it has any competitive advantage in doing so. We are very clear that it may not be in the interest of every country to produce cars or TV sets, and that it may be more convenient to import these goods from more-efficient producers. Why should we not then import money from the most-efficient producer? Why take a different approach with money?

The Costs of Currency Unions

One of the issues that complicates the discussion is the issue of sovereignty, and the thinking that money is an expression of sovereignty. However, I believe that sovereignty consists of a country using as effectively as possible its available instruments of policy to achieve its national objectives. Not having its own currency, and therefore not having the possibility of using monetary policy as an anticyclical instrument, is then only a loss of sovereignty if it is believed that monetary policy could act anticyclically. However, the Argentine experience has shown that monetary policy is pro- rather than anticyclical. The Hausmann et al. paper shows that this same conclusion can be drawn for all of Latin America. Even if we recognize that these costs may be more important for some countries that have been better able to develop credibility in their own currencies, it is not clear at all that they outweigh the benefits that arise from having a credible monetary policy.

The Argentine Experience

In my view, if an emerging country adopted a highly credible reserve currency as its own unit of account and transaction vehicle, then I think it would have a tremendous effect on the country concerned. It is useful at this point to refer specifically to the experience of Argentina during the so-called Convertibility period, i.e., since inception of the currency board policy in 1991. This policy fixed the Argentine currency to that of the U.S. dollar by law, and the policy was backed by a currency board system, which implies that monetary policy is completely subordinate to the exchange rate target. In effect, we have imported wholesale U.S. monetary policy.

Our experience has been that this system has benefited Argentina tremendously. Even though it is clear that Argentina and the United States do not form an optimal currency area and that large asymmetric shocks have hit Argentina from different sources, and despite a recession of 4 percent in 1995, Argentina has grown at an average annual rate of 6.1 percent in the last eight years. Moreover, this policy has much more political support today than when it was introduced in March 1991. This is because it has brought financial stability and low inflation and has created an environment for profitable investment and hence growth. For a country such as Argentina, creating such an environment is much more important than any fine-tuning that one might be able to do through anticyclical monetary policy. Indeed, I have long suspected (and the results presented by Hausmann earlier today confirm that suspicion) that monetary policy has been largely pro- rather than countercyclical in the region.

However, you may ask, if convertibility has been so successful, why might one want to move further to a full currency union? The answer is that although Argentina has gained from convertibility, market spreads indicate that the regime has not gained total credibility.

As Larry Summers has said, the exchange rate can be seen either as a price or as a promise. The difference is very important since a price may change without hurting anyone's feelings. The same thing is not true for a promise. This distinction is crucial for the debate, and Argentina thinks about exchange rates and their regimes in terms of a promise.

Presumably, however, as the convertibility system was implemented unilaterally there remains a doubt that it could also be changed unilaterally. In contrast, a currency union or other type of international monetary agreement, including obviously the full monetary union represented by an arrangement such as the EMU, is more difficult to change unilaterally. To enter into such an arrangement would mean that, at a stroke of a pen, devaluation risk would be eliminated. And it is our experience that this in turn would reduce the risk of default considerably. Indeed our analysis is that currency risk and default risk are very highly correlated, and this is logical. It is impossible to think of Argentina devaluing, but if someone thought the possibility existed, then they would presumably also think that—given the structure of claims in both the government and the financial sector—devaluation would severely increase the probability of default. For this reason, a reduction in the perceived risk of devaluation would also reduce the perceived default probabilities significantly. The gain from a currency union over convertibility for Argentina would then be a very sharp drop in perceived country risk with a corresponding decline in interest rates.

We recognize that monetary policy may be different from other fields of economic policy since it is a field where history certainly does matter. This is because monetary policy depends on expectations and these, in turn, depend on experience. However, I think Argentina's experience with the currency board system could also be useful for other countries considering how to deal with such enormous capital mobility. Our experience shows that the fact that two or more countries do not form today an optimal currency area does not mean that there cannot be very significant advantages in fixing exchange rates irreversibly. First, we firmly believe that there is a significant amount of endogeneity in many of the optimal currency area conditions, and we have seen how Argentina has been able to cope with large shocks, both real and financial, without having a significant impact on the growth rate. Second, the benefit of eliminating the risk of devaluation may more than compensate all other costs. Indeed, it might be argued that an emerging country that has eliminated exchange rate risk, may have more flexibility to respond to a negative shock than one that purports to maintain an independent monetary policy.

Conclusions

Let me conclude these brief comments by giving a realistic view of the future. Suppose we have no real progress on establishing an international lender of last resort (and many see the problems as insurmountable). Then, I see countries facing a difficult choice: They must either join a currency union, or introduce controls on capital flows. Countries that are in a position to join a currency union will probably find it economically beneficial to do so, and if politics does not get in the way, then the future may include very few currencies in the world.

However, countries that cannot join a currency union may find it is just too dangerous to keep the capital account open. As I have stressed, even with the best fundamentals in the world, markets may rationally initiate a huge capital flight that, even if it lasts only a limited period—until markets differentiate "correctly"—can be very costly. The price of keeping the capital account open in such countries may then simply be too great, and sooner or later, many may decide to close significantly to foreign capital. I think we must, as soon as possible, face up to this uncomfortable reality of volatility, contagion and high swings in capital movements, and not shy away from some very tough decisions that must be made. Significant progress is being made. But if we want the world to be a truly global economy and reap the benefits of global trade in capital as well as goods, then we need to make real progress on the critical issue of strengthening financial institutions and establishing an effective lender of last resort.

Pedro Pou is President of the Central Bank of Argentina.

Comment

Lawrence H. Summers

Before I say anything else, I want to compliment Ricardo Hausmann for framing issues of profound importance that stimulate our thinking in important ways. From the vantage point of one who briefly occupied such a position, I think that this is exactly the contribution that the Chief Economist of any multilateral development bank should be making.

I will focus my brief remarks on five aspects of the global financial architecture, in ascending order of the controversy they stir. First, there is no substitute for, nor anything else as important as, national policy in shaping national outcomes. Time and again we have seen in recent months and years that countries shape their own destinies. Those that respond strongly to crisis do much better than those that choose to drift. And those with strong fundamentals are much less likely to be caught-up in problems than those with weaker fundamentals. The truest observation about this aspect, and the single best rule that I have heard for thinking about it, was made by President Zedillo in answer to a question from President Clinton. Asked about the lessons of Mexico's very difficult experience in 1995, President Zedillo said, "Markets do overreact, and that is why policy must overreact if confidence is to be restored."

I think that is a very important lesson, and one that is being learned increasingly in this region. But as important as the lesson is, it is not sufficient. It's a little like telling someone concerned about avoiding an auto accident to drive his or her car well. Just as there are many other things that can affect the risk of automobile accidents, there is a great deal else that can be done to have an impact on the risk of financial accidents.

My second observation moves in that direction. A crucial priority for greater stability is the development of what I like to call "the intangible infrastructure of a financial system." This includes everything from laws that make it possible to actually take security in lending and borrowing to those that regularize risks through formal bankruptcy procedures. Of particular importance, from my perspective, are measures that promote transparency and accurate reporting. If you look at the history of the capital market in the United States, nothing was as important an innovation during the last century as generally accepted accounting principles. Accurate and reliable information permits more-rapid responses to problems. And it offers something else. As someone once remarked, "Conscience is the knowledge that someone is watching." Transparency makes it impossible to avoid being watched, preventing a variety of untoward practices that would otherwise take place. Generally accepted accounting principles are not an institution, and they are not codified in one law. They are ongoing collaborative efforts between the public and private sectors that strengthen the systems over time. That is the very thing we need, in my view, in the global capital market.

The third critical architectural aspect for reducing the risk of crises, and containing one should it occur, is the avoidance of excessive and destabilizing capital flows. Here a number of steps are crucial. The private sector has learned a great deal about risk management in the past two years, but there is a tendency for these kinds of lessons to be forgotten quickly. Hopefully that will not be the case this time. But to help jog memories, we are taking steps to improve the quality of financial regulation in both the developed and the developing countries. The agreement at the recent G7 meeting to establish a financial stability forum will at last do what probably should have been done long ago. By bringing together the regulators from the Basle Committee, the BIS, the IMF, the World Bank, and the major countries into a common institution, it will forge common approaches to these problems. But when the subject is excessive and destabilizing capital flows, I would suggest that this is still an area where national responsibility is paramount. Rather than be overwhelmed by capital flows that they couldn't control, many countries have actively pursued short-term capital flows, only to find that they were very destabilizing and led to financial crises. I think of Mexico's issuance of $30 billion in *tesobonos* in 1994; I think of the Bangkok Offshore Banking Facility; I think of Russian treasury bills (GKOs) tailored to meet hedge fund preferences. Clearly there are concerns about excessive capital flows, but we should not let size obscure the question of how these flows are structured. Before we worry about discouraging capital per se, it seems to me appropriate to downshift into neutral, and look very hard at practices to create an active policy bias to limit the danger from excessive short-term capital flows.

The fourth area involves crisis resolution. I think we can all agree that national policy is the single most important element involved. Looking at the history of recent experiences, we see that crises can take on a feature that economists call multiple equilibrium, the public calls a bank run, and philosophers call a self-fulfilling prophecy. When investors stop looking at overall market conditions, stop looking to fundamentals, and start looking at the behavior of other investors, conditions are ripe for doubt to spread that no amount of fundamental improvement will be sufficient to stem. This is a generally recognized aspect of the problem, and responding to it requires the provision of appropriate conditional liquidity. I believe the international financial institutions have taken an important step in the past 15 months to gear up and provide substantial liquidity at premium interest rates. These are substantial premium interest rates, on which I suspect they will earn significant profits over time and on shorter than normal terms.

That is a constructive step forward, but we also need to look at ways of building on experiences in a number of countries to increase the private sector's capacity to provide crisis liquidity. This is a central issue that the international community will be grappling with in the next year or two involving the role of private creditors. Certainly, when the issue is insolvency rather than liquidity, new money is not the answer, creditor involvement is. And even when the issue is liquidity, creditors who recognize their mutual interest in staying the course can make a large difference. This is something that needs to be promoted as it was in Korea, and the assurances that the banks have given Brazil recently are certainly an encouraging development.

But this is an issue that will have to be considered with great care. Borrowers must be aware that debt contracts will be entered into under the presumption that they will be honored, or they will not be entered into. Lenders, meanwhile, must be aware that actions taken in one country can have important impacts on the availability of finance to other countries, and that changes in the rules of the game may have material effects in an anticipatory sense or alter the supply of capital. We will do well to remember the irony that financial crises caused by excessive lending may have to be solved by more lending. If the problem of several years ago was the issuance of too many bad loans, one suspects that the problem for the next several years will be the failure to provide enough good loans. This is a very difficult issue and we are still looking for the answers. There is no question that the private sector has a crucial role to play.

Finally I come to the question of exchange rate regimes. Some valid statements in this area are, I think, relatively easy to make. There is no one-size-fits-all solution. Countries will have to make appropriate choices. One of the great debates among economists cuts across normal ideological lines: Should one think of exchange rates as a price to be determined flexibly through a float, or as a promise, in which case they are fixed? This debate has raged among economists for many, many years. We can perhaps agree that where exchange rates are a promise, that promise should not be broken since the consequences of doing so are often very serious.

I am intrigued by recent discussions, including in the papers presented here, about the possibilities of currency unions in which one or more countries use the currency of another country as their own. Certainly we have been following very closely what is being said about dollarization. It might be useful and appropriate to offer here our thinking about these general discussions.

The choice by a country to dollarize its monetary system, to adopt the U.S.'s or some other country's currency for its own use, is not to be made casually. The country making the decision must do so on the basis of careful and extended analysis. Dollarization offers the attractive promise of enhanced stability in the dollarizing country by adding to the credibility and discipline of its national economic and financial policies and by advancing its integration with the world economy. However, a country considering this course also must be prepared to embrace the discipline and inflexibility that it brings—along with the potentially significant consequences of doing without monetary independence externally, the exchange rate adjustment; and internally, the direction of interest rates. It would not be appropriate for U.S. authorities to adjust their bank supervisory responsibilities, access to the Federal Reserve discount window, or the procedures or orientation of U.S. monetary policy in light of another country's decision to dollarize or make other changes in its monetary system. So any country contemplating dollarization will have to weigh carefully the implications of making the change. These considerations and many others make it appropriate for representatives from the government agencies involved to seek technical consultation with U.S. authorities so that we can jointly think through the implications for both our economies.

Lawrence H. Summers is Secretary of the U.S. Department of Treasury.

Comment

José Angel Gurria

Before turning to the focus of this particular panel, I would like to express very serious disagreement regarding the whole approach of the paper on exchange rate regimes, including both the methodology and the conclusions.

Pedro [Pou] was telling me that in his view we would have some important differences of opinion here, given the fact that—not surprisingly—he was going to support fixed exchange rate regimes. I replied that there would be no disagreement at all, because I agree that such a regime is the right one for Argentina while the floating exchange rate we currently have in Mexico is the right one for our country. Therefore, there is no cause for controversy.

But before going on to the subject at hand, let me first take issue with a notion put forward in Ricardo Hausmann's paper, according to which "financial turmoil is becoming a fact of life in Argentina." It would seem that we have no memory of the past or that we were born yesterday or, at most, the day before that. If one looks at the history of Latin America, it would be impossible to find a period in which, notwithstanding the problems we have endured lately, there has been such progress in terms of the solidity and depth of the policies in force. We have made substantial progress, and yet we carry on as though nothing had been accomplished.

Yesterday I attended a Deutsche Bank seminar entitled "Economic and Financial Stability: the Impossible Dream for Latin America." The assumptions underlying that title make one think of the situation that prevailed some 20 years ago. Such a view is completely out of phase with the current situation. We cannot ignore the progress made in key economic areas such as fiscal and monetary policies, debt management, domestic savings, and trade liberalization. In its final section, the seminar considered the question, "Would the image of Columbus be an appropriate symbol for a currency of the Americas?" To put it briefly, the answer is "no."

A preliminary but nonetheless crucial issue is that we all have to agree on what exactly we mean by exchange rate regimes. In Mexico this is a newsworthy topic, but there is an obvious lack of clarity in many people's minds about it. Some refer to currency boards, while others prefer to talk about dollarization. The president of the IDB recently talked about a currency for the Americas, and I have also come across proposals for the launching of a single currency for Latin America. Yet people talk about these various options as if they were one and the same thing, as though they were simply interchangeable.

Thus, the first thing is to be much more rigorous with ourselves and much more strict in our approach. We must not attempt to draw general conclusions from situations that are clearly specific to a country, or to extrapolate policy guidelines from one nation to another. Among its many drawbacks, the lack of rigor causes great confusion in public opinion, as it neither informs nor prepares the public for such discussions. It also contributes to the apparently irresistible temptation to conduct this debate in the papers, which frankly creates a lot of confusion and disorientation. Here I end my remarks on the issue of the exchange rate regime. I will now turn to the subject of this particular panel: Why do crises happen and what are we supposed to do about them at the international level?

The first point that needs to be made is that each country must do its homework. This simple truth is the key to success, particularly in the case of emerging economies. It involves dealing with a number of issues, which, once they have been addressed, make it less relevant whether you have one currency regime or another. To put it in a nutshell, the fiscal situation must be sound, monetary policy must be consistent, and a watchful eye must be kept on the interaction between the two.

One of the reasons why we are so hot under the collar about exchange rate regimes today is that we have not given the regimes that we now have in place enough time to come to fruition. We are living with the consequences of mistakes that were made years ago and, in the case of some of the larger countries in the region, the consequences of actions taken only a few days ago. Those mistakes have not yet been corrected because we have not given the floating exchange rate regime enough time to come to fruition.

We have to consider that the exchange regime has implications for the whole approach to economic policy. Thus, it is true that we had heavy external imbalances, but that was partly the result of having fallen into debt in order to support a fixed exchange rate regime. In some instances, we even borrowed in order to try to sustain a rate of exchange that in the end proved to be unsustainable. We also had fiscal problems that we failed to correct in time and became exacerbated as a result. At the same time we had a fiscal imbalance that caused, as was to be expected, an overflow in aggregate demand. Thus, the coexistence of a fixed or semifixed exchange rate regime with a less than virtuous fiscal and monetary policy was at the root of our troubles.

And we are still living with those troubles. It is not so much that we need a new exchange rate regime in order to solve them. The problem is that even if we are now practicing virtuous policies, we have to live with the consequences of our past sins. The imbalances are still there, and we have only had a few years in the so-called first derivative, and now the second derivative, approaches to virtuous policies. We've been at it for a short time, and the new policies have not yet worked their way through. And now we are talking about changing gears yet again. This would be inappropriate, it would be inefficient, and it is ill-advised.

There are many other matters that we should be looking into, such as fiscal policy, the fostering of domestic savings, export diversification, trade liberalization, responsible debt management, and the strengthening of the banking sector, particularly through the regulatory and the supervisory system. Other questions include labor market flexibility, structural change issues, deregulation, and privatization. These are the kinds of things we should be spending time on, rather than debating endlessly about exchange rate regimes.

And then there are issues such as those suggested in the paper, namely bankruptcy laws, suspension-of-payments laws, and so on. These will give economic agents confidence about contract compliance and about the rightful and expeditious enforcement of law. We have to make sure that parties in litigation are able to arrive at a satisfactory solution under law in two to three months, rather than two to three years.

At the same time, a question that has arisen recently is whether there is a reward for virtuous economic policy other than the satisfaction of doing what is right. In other words, if we believe in the need for open financial flows and are in fact open to them, we must face volatility in our own markets caused by events in other parts of the world. For example, during the second half of 1998, everything that happened in Russia was critical to the exchange rate regime and the interest rates in Mexico. More recently, we were affected, although to a lesser extent, by the financial crisis in Brazil. The fact that we do less than 1 percent of our trade with that country and that it is as far away from Mexico as Libya or Liverpool was of no consequence whatever. By the look of the repercussions of the Brazilian crisis in Mexico, it seemed as if it was a neighboring country. Everything that was happening there during January had a severe effect on Mexico.

The problem is that we have not yet organized ourselves to do the second derivative of the virtuous circle. That is, many countries practice good policies but there is no barrier, there is no defense, against the onslaught that is brought about by inadequate policies or unforeseen problems in other countries. This is another consequence of the globalization process. It also results from the fact that there is as yet very little discrimination among emerging markets, although there is some evidence that this is starting to happen. Nevertheless, for the 15 months during which we had financial volatility, there was no discrimination. We were all emerging markets and we were all placed in one single basket, all dealt with in the same way. So we all suffered as a result of the volatile environment, regardless of how good our policies were.

We have been talking since then about the new architecture of the international financial system. The question is basically whether a country that is practicing virtuous policies will be eligible to receive timely support so that it can continue to carry on with those policies. This would be crucial in order to protect hard-earned results, as well as to avoid problems in the markets because of a sudden inability to refinance debt maturities.

I would like to give an example in that respect. We were discussing with the World Bank the possibility of receiving an enhancement to the National Bank of Foreign Trade of Mexico, our Export–Import Bank equivalent. The objective of the operation was to facilitate the access of Bancomex to international capital markets in order to obtain a substantial amount of money and use it to support our exports. After three or four months, the deal fell through and we were told it was not on tap anymore.

On the other hand, we have been talking to the IDB about a guarantee to a Federal Government bond issue that would also have a multiplier effect. This could be achieved through the A/B type of technique and could provide access to about half a billion dollars worth of IDB exposure, and then maybe a billion and a half or two billion dollars worth of market exposure.

On the issue of bailing out or crowding in market participants, we are having very serious and now increasingly complex and difficult discussions. The people in the IDB are considering granting the status of preferred creditors to those countries that would need to come under that particular facility. This approach will not work if it does not first create that particular quality, otherwise the attraction of the operation is not there. If nothing is given in addition, then the IDB can give it to us in any fashion they want. We do not have to leverage; we do not have to mount a complex operation of financial engineering in order to put it together. Because then it is just one more dollar, it is just one more operation. The idea here is that one dollar can bring in three or four from the markets.

Discussions about private sector involvement in generating a more stable financial environment are welcome. We can also talk about contingent lines of credit. Mexico negotiated one in the good times—which is the only time you can negotiate one—amounting to US$2.7 billion. It was provided by 30 banks, US$80 million each. Yet it was very tough to draw it. You have to have an unexpected drop in your fiscal revenues, in your foreign exchange, and you have to have an impact in your accounts. Unfortunately, they all actually materialized.

In view of the substantial decline in Mexico's oil revenues during 1998, we decided to actually draw the line. In fact, we had been paying a commitment fee in order for the line to be there. We drew it and everyone was furious. Everybody called us to say we were irreparably damaging the credit prestige of Mexico. It seemed as if every chairman in the world called us. We drew it about a week before the IMF meeting in September in Washington. You cannot imagine how reticent we were to even attend the meeting, because we knew we were going to meet there all the chairmen who had been calling to say how bad all this was.

The logic of the line of credit for bad times was completely distorted. At the time we drew it, it was cheap relative to the market, and people did not want us to use it anymore. I wished they had been willing to extend it during the good times, when they knew we had no immediate need to use it. Obviously, there is a problem with the design of this facility because if you are going to use it only when you are facing bad times, then clearly people will not want to extend the loan at all.

At the IMF somebody is calling that credit line the anti-crisis window. However, I think this is an unfortunate expression, because the idea is precisely that countries that practice good policies could have access to contingent support in case they are affected by events that take place in other latitudes. When you call it anti-crisis, you immediately bring to mind the notion that *you* are indeed having a crisis. This is hardly a wise move. I suppose we need, first of all, to find a proper name for such a facility. But there is also an ongoing discussion as to whether it should exist at all. Several European countries are questioning the need for a similar facility. This view seems to be a step backwards, forcing countries to undertake crisis resolution once there is a crisis in place already. What is required is to prevent similar crises and to support enlightened policies.

So, again, it is not very elegant, it is not very sophisticated to say, "Show me the money." We are told that the facility is not going to be available through the window of the IMF. It is not going to be available through the guarantees of the World Bank. It is not going to be available through the guarantees of the IMF or, of course, the banks in the IDB. The banks are reticent to provide it when there is a problem. They are already in. The only question is to make sure that they cannot get out. Restructured in-bond issues, again, may not be a very good idea if the IDB, the World Bank, and the European Development Bank and the triple-A borrowers of the world do not take the initiative. The reason is simply that if you only do it for developing countries you will turn them into financial pariahs, and it will cost one or two additional points to have a restructuring clause for bond issues. Whether there should be an international court to sanction the circumstances and terms under which a country can default or not is a tough issue that I will not address at this point. On the one hand, extension of credit causes problems but, on the other hand, if you suddenly stop it, there is bound to be even more trouble. In short, extending more credit can solve some of the problems; but if you do not have adequate facilities in place, you will also face problems.

To conclude, I want to reiterate that domestic policies—fiscal policies in particular—have the most important role in ensuring stability and are the key to success. As we have seen, they are not enough because nowadays, as a result of globalization, you can suffer shocks from the most unexpected sources. Therefore, transparency as well as adequate regulation and supervision in the financial system will be extremely important. This is something we all have to upgrade. We never focused on this in the past, but now it has become critical. A mistake in that area can cost you up to 12 points of GDP, as we have all found out.

One may undertake lengthy discussions with the IMF about whether to have a deficit level of 0.5 or 1 percent. However if you neglect your banking system, it can suddenly come to a crisis. It has happened in France, Mexico, and Japan. It also happened in the United States and in many of the emerging countries. It just seems as if we have not been able to get a handle on that. Above all, we are not doing a good job, in my view, of setting up a system that rewards virtue or, as I suggested yesterday, a system that ensures virtue stays in place once it is there.

José Angel Gurria is the Secretary of Finance and Public Credit of Mexico.

Comment

Michael Gavin

For financial and fiscal policy, the three objectives—solvency, liquidity, and confidence—have pretty much hung together. They have been complementary. More solvency is more confidence. But in the case of exchange rate regimes, we would argue that there is a trade-off between the solvency, or in this case the sustainability, of a regime and the confidence that the regime needs to generate.

Exchange rate flexibility, or the explicit option to devalue that policymakers retain when they either have a managed float or a peg that everybody knows could be devalued under circumstances future policymakers define as appropriate, has the virtue of being sustainable as a regime. But that sustainability is cold comfort during uncertain economic and financial times. What the world is crying out for is not sustainability or confidence in the regime, but confidence in the value of the domestic money, pure and simple. And that is what flexible exchange rates do not provide.

It isn't just holders of domestic money or potential speculators against domestic money who need to be concerned about whether or not instability or stability is expected for future valuations. It is also all providers of finance to the local corporate sector, whether the financing is in the form of equity or foreign currency debt or local currency debt. Because after all, everybody knows that, in the event of a real bout of monetary instability, loans to those guys are quite likely to go bad. So when times do get unstable and uncertainty swells, the option to devalue becomes potentially very valuable to the policymaker but very costly to the private sector, which is on the other side of this option. The result is a flight that leads almost inevitably—as it has in Mexico, Colombia, and Ecuador—to the requirement to raise interest rates and that forecloses the latitude to reduce them. So to us, if there is any causality in conventional wisdom about exchange rate management, it is that flexible exchange rates provide latitude to lower interest rates during periods of crisis because they reduce the need to defend the exchange rate. If one compares Mexico to Argentina, the country where domestic interest rates are the lowest on the continent, the point comes across pretty clearly.

Michael Gavin is Director of Economic Research for Latin America at Warburg Dillon Read.

Comment

Shahid Javed Burki

It is a great honor to provide some closing comments in this important debate. I read with great interest the papers prepared for the Paris meeting. I listened with equal interest to the discussion among the two sets of panelists. The papers and the comments underscored a number of important points, all of them of great relevance for the situation we face today. If I were to pick some of the more critical themes that emerged, I would highlight the following five.

First, in a highly interdependent world in which large volumes of capital move across borders, even minor policy infractions can cause severe disturbances. These disturbances are usually caused by a sudden loss of confidence on the part of international financial markets in one, two, or several developing economies.

Second—and here I must differ with José Angel Gurria—while markets can react quickly, moving large amounts of capital back and forth, they have learned to be more discriminating. This was not always so. The debt crisis of the early 1980s engulfed the entire developing world. Even the crisis that was caused by the devaluation of the Mexican peso in December 1994 produced waves that reached many shores. The markets now have more knowledge about the Third World; they are able to differentiate among developing economies of the Third World. For this reason, we did not see a contagion spreading in Latin America. The markets punished only those countries they perceived as having weak fundamentals.

Third, the markets dislike disequilibria. They have reacted vigorously and punished heavily the countries that ran large fiscal/external imbalances while attempting to constrain exchange rate movements. Once the markets decided to move, no amount of reserves, even when augmented by relatively large international support packages, were able to turn the tide. This was the experience of Brazil, and it will happen again to those countries that stray out of line in a palpable way.

Fourth, these crises—and they seem to be coming more frequently and leaving a deeper impact on the affected economies—take a very heavy economic and social toll. Years of progress, especially in reducing the incidence of poverty, can be wiped out in a few weeks or months. Some people now argue that it is not certain whether the net benefit from the easy access to foreign savings, when calculated over a number of years, is positive or negative for the countries that have lived through these crises. Implicit in this argument is the thought that the economic opening of the last dozen or so years may not have been entirely beneficial for the countries that opted for such an approach.

Fifth, and finally, international financial turmoil can not be allowed to persist. The cost of inaction is great, and governments around the globe must act in concert to erect a new financial architecture on more solid and durable foundations.

These, then, were some of the more important arguments I picked up from reading the papers and listening to the views of the panelists. In response to them, I would like to offer five points of my own.

First, I believe there is little point in fretting that the new global economic system has created an environment in which emerging markets have become subject to crises that arrive at ever-increasing frequency. What the organizers of this seminar have termed "international financial turmoil" is now a fact of life. It will persist for as long as the policies pursued by some countries—especially such large economies as Brazil—run counter to those the markets perceive as rational and prudent. A new financial architecture can not be erected on weak policy foundations; it cannot overcome the financial markets' aversion to risk.

Second, I would like to suggest that no amount of thinking by governments done by whichever group of countries—G7, G8, G10, G22, or G-whatever—would be able to build a new architecture. The new structure will evolve more or less spontaneously in response to the challenges posed by the rapid evolution of a highly integrated global economy.

The belief that the solution for the current turbulence in the global economic order must come from active deliberations among governments has, of course, many powerful antecedents. Those who advocate it are no doubt thinking of the days of the conference at Bretton Woods, when a few clever individuals, working overtime, were able to devise a new financial order for the postwar world. The Bretton Woods system worked well in bringing stability and growth. If it could be done then, goes the argument, why cannot it be done now? The same belief in the ability of governments to fashion a new global economic order prompted a number of Third World countries to agitate in the 1960s and 1970s for the establishment of a new international economic order (NIEO). Industrial countries were drawn into the NIEO dialogue largely because of the imperatives dictated by the Cold War. Eventually, nothing came of it—even the commitment by the industrial world to transfer 0.7 percent of their collective GNP as official development assistance did not stop a precipitous decline in those flows in recent years.

My third observation builds on the second one. Those of us who were active participants in the NIEO debate of a quarter century ago should look around and notice that a new international economic order has in fact emerged. However, it was not produced by the political will of governments but by the needs and perceptions of the marketplace. If I were to pick three groups of actors who have contributed more to the emergence of the new global order than any other, it would be central bankers, financial regulators, and credit agencies. They have already laid the foundation of a new financial architecture and will continue to build upon it, brick by brick, to meet market demands. If governments want to act, they should prompt and facilitate the work of these agents of change.

The fourth point I would like to underscore is the need to recognize that markets form judgments not only on economic fundamentals, but also on the political environment in which policymakers operate. A very good illustration of this comes from recent developments in Brazil. It had been recognized, for a while, that Brazil was running fiscal deficits at a level at which they could not be sustained. However, President Fernando Henrique Cardoso's decisive victory persuaded the markets that the Brazilian authorities had the political resolve to begin to address the structural problems that had kept deficits so high for such a long period of time. That confidence was suddenly eroded when a governor from a large state declared his inability to service his debt to the central government. The market's reaction to this unexpected development was swift and unforgiving.

I now come to the fifth, final, and more speculative point of my presentation. The debate about the most viable exchange rate regime in the emerging markets is now intense. Earlier today, Ricardo Hausmann summarized very well the main points of this debate. The recent Brazilian move to abandon a tightly controlled rate for its currency has provided some more evidence for those who believe that, in today's global financial environment, maintenance of fixed rates is no longer an acceptable option. While the policymakers in the developing world are agonizing over the question of efficiency of various types of regimes, there is another development taking place that needs to be factored into this debate. I refer here to the move toward the formulation of large currency blocs. The success of the Euro has demonstrated that it is possible for reasonably well-integrated and converging economies to adopt a common currency. Might not similar developments take place in the Western Hemisphere with the possible dollarization of Argentina, Ecuador, and Central America? If the countries of the Western Hemisphere succeed in meeting their goal of forming a free trade zone in the next few years, wouldn't that be the first move toward the adoption of the dollar as the common currency by the entire region? If Europe and the Western Hemisphere move toward the adoption of common currencies, would it not induce East Asia, including Japan, to adopt one as well? If the Asians move in that direction, would they favor the yen as the currency of choice, opt for the Chinese renminbi, or introduce an entirely new currency?

My guess at this point is that in the next couple of decades we will see a move toward fewer currencies and a move toward the formation of large currency blocs. By the year 2025 we might see much of the industrial and semi-industrial worlds organized in just three currency blocs—the dollar, the Euro, and the yen/renminbi.

The best way to wrap up this discussion is to highlight some thoughts from the presentations made by the members of the first panel. The only practical and pragmatic way of dealing with the profound changes taking place in the structure of the global economy is not to impose on it a new architecture. Instead, what is required is to balance the profound changes that have already occurred in the global economic and financial system with an equally profound restructuring of domestic economies. Examples of the successful adoption of this approach are to be found in Argentina and Chile. The policy reforms now being contemplated by Brazil will also build on the impressive structural changes that have already been put in place. The main point I wish to highlight here is that incremental changes will suffice to deal with rapid changes in global markets. A good illustration of this approach is the one underscored by Pablo Guidotti in his presentation. This approach saved Argentina from being buffeted by the turmoil in international financial markets. There is always the temptation to contemplate revolution in response to revolutionary change. The need of the moment instead, I believe, is to devise a careful incremental policy response aimed at maintaining domestic solvency and ensuring liquidity.

Shahid Javed Burki is the Regional Vice President for Latin America and the Caribbean, the World Bank.